Sponsoring Nature

Sponsoring Nature

Environmental Philanthropy for Conservation

Maano Ramutsindela, Marja Spierenburg and Harry Wels

First published 2011
by Earthscan

2 Park Square, Milton Park, Abingdon, Oxfordshire OX14 4RN
711 Third Avenue, New York, NY 10017

Routledge is an imprint of the Taylor & Francis Group, an informa business

First issued in paperback 2017

© 2011 Maano Ramutsindela, Marja Spierenburg and Harry Wels

The right of Maano Ramutsindela, Marja Spierenburg and Harry Wels to be identified as author[s] of this work has been asserted by him/her/them in accordance with sections 77 and 78 of the Copyright, Designs and Patents Act 1988.

All rights reserved. No part of this book may be reprinted or reproduced or utilised in any form or by any electronic, mechanical, or other means, now known or hereafter invented, including photocopying and recording, or in any information storage or retrieval system, without permission in writing from the publishers.

The content of this book has been subject to independent peer review.

Trademark notice: Product or corporate names may be trademarks or registered trademarks, and are used only for identification and explanation without intent to infringe.

British Library Cataloguing in Publication Data
A catalogue record for this book is available from the British Library

Library of Congress Cataloging in Publication Data
Ramutsindela, Maano.
  Sponsoring nature : environmental philanthropy for conservation / Maano Ramutsindela, Marja Spierenburg, and Harry Wels. – 1st ed.
      p. cm.
  Includes bibliographical references and index.
  ISBN 978-1-84407-904-9 (hardback)
 1. Nature conservation–Economic aspects. 2. Nature conservation–Management. 3. Philanthropists--Charitable contributions. 4. Non-governmental organizations–Management. 5. Community-based conservation. 6. Charitable uses, trusts, and foundations. 7. Environmental policy. I. Spierenburg, Marja. II. Wels, Harry, 1961- III. Title.
  QH75.R36 2011
  333.72–dc22
                                        2010050904

ISBN: 978-1-84407-904-9 (hbk)
ISBN: 978-0-8153-5743-8 (pbk)

Typeset in Garamond by JS Typesetting Ltd, Porthcawl, Mid Glamorgan

Contents

List of tables	*vi*
Preface	*vii*
Acknowledgements	*viii*
List of acronyms and abbreviations	*ix*
1 Shades of Philanthropy	1
2 Environmental Philanthropy	25
3 The South–North Connections	45
4 Philanthropists, Capitalists and Environmental NGOs	67
5 Framing Environmental Threats: Implications for Funding	89
6 The Global Environment Facility: Financing Conservation in the Global South	105
7 Mapping Environmental Philanthropy in Africa	121
8 Rising to Local Challenges: Grassroots Conservation Initiatives	143
9 State-Sponsored Community Conservation	161
10 Power Relations, Priorities and the Future of Environmental Philanthropy	177
Selected further reading	*189*
Index	*199*

List of Tables

2.1	Approximate areas and frequency of support by the 50 most generous philanthropists, 2009	38
2.2	Philanthropic donations in the US, 2009	38
6.1	GEF focal areas and project funds committed until 2005	110
6.2	Comparison of focal areas in five GEF-SGP regions	113
6.3	Number of GEF-SGP projects in Africa, January 1990–June 2010	114
6.4	Number of GEF-SGP projects in Arab states, January 1990–June 2010	115
6.5	Number of GEF-SGP projects in Asia and the Pacific, January 1990–June 2010	116
6.6	Number of GEF-SGP projects in Europe and the CIS, January 1990–June 2010	117
6.7	Number of GEF-SGP projects in Latin America and the Caribbean, January 1990–June 2010	117
8.1	Africa region finalists for the Equator Prize, 2002–2010	146
8.2	Asia and Pacific region finalists for the Equator Prize, 2002–2010	147
8.3	Latin America and the Caribbean region finalists for the Equator Prize, 2002–2010	148
9.1	NHT government revenues, 1997–2007	171

Preface

The ideas and perspectives we present in this book originate from our session on 'Transfrontier Conservation Areas in Southern Africa and Western Business Philanthropy', which we organized at the conference of the European Society for Environmental History held in Amsterdam in June 2007. We would like to thank the participants on that panel for their helpful comments and feedback, in particular Malcolm Draper, Bernhard Gissibl, Anna-Katharina Wöbse and Jane Carruthers. We developed our ideas further at the Symposium on Conservation and Capitalism that was organized by Dan Brockington and Rosaleen Duffy at the University of Manchester in September 2008. The useful comments we received from this symposium and our reflections on the themes at hand convinced us of the need to put together a book of this kind. The main thoughts that occupied our minds were the resurgence of a robust critique on conservation networks at the time when, in the alarming context of 'global climate change', the need for more conservation is being proposed and supported by philanthropists all around the world. Our thinking was also stimulated and challenged by work on environmental non-governmental organizations and how these are connected to the market and the elites or become flagship organizations or 'nationals'. We feel that such work appears insulated from research on philanthropy that could shed light on various dimensions, faces and phases of philanthropy as both an ideology and a practice in the environmental domain. This book forges new ground in conversations between conservation and philanthropy through the analytic of environmental philanthropy.

Acknowledgements

We are thankful to Tim Hardwick who was receptive to the book prospectus and to all anonymous reviewers who commented on this book at various stages. Our thanks go to George Holmes at the University of Leeds, UK, who provided expert commentary on all the chapters in this book. Desmond Tutu Professor Stephen Ellis at VU University of Amsterdam proved to be an inspiring sparring partner while we were finalizing the book. The various chapters of the book draw on our research supported by the South Africa–Netherlands research Programme on Alternatives in Development (SANPAD) and the National Research Foundation (NRF) in South Africa, for which we are thankful. Last but not least it is worth mentioning that it was a great pleasure to work together on this book as a team!

List of Acronyms and Abbreviations

ACF	Australian Conservation Foundation
ADMADE	Administrative Management Design for Game Management Areas
ANC	African National Congress
ASEAN	Association of South East Asia Nations
AWF	African Wildlife Foundation
BRIC	Brazil, Russia, India and China
CAMPFIRE	Communal Areas Management Programme for Indigenous Resources
CBC	community-based conservation
CBD	Convention on Biological Diversity
CBNRM	community-based natural resource management
CBO	community-based organization
CCLI	Conserving California Landscape Initiative
CIA	Central Intelligence Agency
CIS	Commonwealth of Independent States
CITES	Convention on International Trade in Endangered Species of Wild Fauna and Flora
COP	Conference of the Parties
CPR	Committee for People's Rights
CSR	corporate social responsibility
DNPWLM	Department of National Parks and Wildlife Management
EFL	Environmental Foundation Ltd
EI	Equator Initiative
ENGO	environmental non-governmental organization
FRELIMO	Front for the Liberation of Mozambique
GEF	Global Environment Facility
GEF-SGP	Global Environment Facility Small Grants Programme
GONGO	government-organized non-governmental organization
GRA	Game Rangers Association

IAC	Industries Assistance Commission
ICFP	International Conservation Financing Programme
IFF	International Freedom Foundation
IFP	Inkatha Freedom Party
IMF	International Monetary Fund
IUCN	International Union for Conservation of Nature
IUPN	International Union for the Protection of Nature
LIFE	Living in a Finite Environment
MPLA	Popular Movement for the Liberation of Angola
NATO	North Atlantic Treaty Organization
NFF	National Farmers Federation
NGO	non-governmental organization
NHT	Natural Heritage Trust
NLP	National Landcare Programme
NPB	National Parks Board
NRF	National Research Foundation
OP	operational programme
POP	persistent organic pollutant
PPF	Peace Parks Foundation
PR	public relations
PRIA	Public Relations Institute of Australia
REDD	reducing emissions from deforestation and forest degradation
RESG	Rhino and Elephant Security Group
RMG	Rhino Management Group
SACP	South African Communist Party
SADC	Southern African Development Community
SADF	South African Defence Force
SAFF	Southern African Freedom Foundation
SANPAD	South Africa–Netherlands research Programme on Alternatives in Development
SAP	South African Police
SGP	Small Grants Programme
SPU	self-protection unit
SWAPO	South West Africa People's Organization
TFCA	Transfrontier Conservation Area
TRC	Truth and Reconciliation Commission
UNDP	United Nations Development Programme
UNEP	United Nations Environment Programme
UNESCO	United Nations Educational, Scientific, and Cultural Organization
UNFCCC	United Nations Framework Convention on Climate Change
UNITA	National Union for the Total Independence of Angola
USAID	United States Agency for International Development
WCED	World Commission on Environment and Development

WILDCON	Wilderness Conservancy
WWF	World Wide Fund for Nature (formerly, World Wildlife Fund)
ZAPU	Zimbabwe African Peoples Union
ZANU	Zimbabwe African National Union

1

Shades of Philanthropy

INTRODUCTION

Philanthropy is generally understood as reflecting the best part of human nature and 'philanthropic gifts have filled the world with knowledge, art, healing, and enduring cultural institutions dedicated to the betterment of society' (Damon, 2006, p1). Indeed, the love of humankind drives philanthropy in various cultural contexts and has led to different kinds of interventions for the good of humanity. Philanthropists have, through the generosity of spirit, used their time and savings to advance a human cause, and have expanded their ethical concerns to non-humans. The claim that philanthropists are motivated by the ideology of liberation that seeks to free both humans and non-humans is clear from one of the principal founders of the Wilderness Society, Bob Marshall, who considered philanthropists supporting nature conservation as people who fought for the freedom of the wilderness (Aplet, 1999). Nevertheless, questions regarding philanthropic practices have also arisen in part as the public faith in the non-profit sector, which acts as a conduit for philanthropy, was shaken when the lines between non-profit, for-profit and public institutions became blurred (Clotfelter and Ehrlich, 1999). These lines were constitutive of the 'old covenant' between philanthropy, the non-profit sector and society.

According to this covenant, the non-profit philanthropic sector was expected to demonstrate that its activities were a work of altruism and that such activities were not linked to commercial or political interests. For example, non-profit organizations were not supposed to engage in efforts to influence either legislation or the outcomes of elections (Clotfelter and Ehrlich, 1999). In other words, foundations promoting charity were not to involve themselves in public affairs as to do so would be construed as using charity for ulterior motives – thereby forsaking the sacred principles of altruism. Trust as a necessary condition for philanthropy was compromised when some philanthropic activities failed to stay clear from business and partisan politics. Berman (1983) suggests that major US foundations such as Ford, Rockefeller and Carnegie played a significant role in promoting American foreign policy interests in Africa in the post-war era. Governments have also collaborated with organized philanthropy to carry out their policies and to create constituencies in the international arena:

> It seem[ed] paradoxical that, at the same time that public policy issues, as one category of controversial matters, were generally understood to be off-limits to organized philanthropy, [the US] government was collaborating increasingly with organized philanthropy and using it to carry out its policies. (Clotfelter and Ehrlich 1999, p506)

This paradox of philanthropy as a geopolitical tool has been complicated by the links between philanthropy and the expansion of markets under global capitalism (see Chapter 4). Indeed, a common theme in studies in corporate social responsibility is the intersection between philanthropy and capitalism (see Schramm, 2006; Newell, 2008), or 'philanthrocapitalism' as journalist Matthew Bishop nicknamed it (Bishop, 2007).

Our message in this chapter, and this book as a whole, is that, like all other interventions, philanthropy requires serious introspection if it is to uphold its positive public image. We support this line of thinking by drawing on the works of scholars of philanthropy and by using examples from nature conservation. In his book, the *Moral Advantage*, William Damon (2004) draws on the findings from the Good Work Project to demonstrate that philanthropy can in some instances lead to the following types of harms: direct harms to life; weakening valuable non-profit organizations; disrupting real social improvement; destabilizing communities; creating unhealthy dependencies; creating an underclass of non-profits; subverting democratic principles; and harm to philanthropic endeavour. Philanthropy becomes harmful when gifts are made with impure motives, distributed carelessly – as with the distribution of smallpox-ridden blankets to the Sioux in the 19th century – and when it perpetuates the very ills it is meant to mitigate (Damon, 2006).

The potential for philanthropy to do harm was recognized by pioneers of philanthropy such as Andrew Carnegie who warned that indiscriminate giving is a drawback to philanthropy and that the purpose for which wealth is spent should not have a degrading, pauperizing tendency upon its recipients (Carnegie, 2006). Edwards vividly captures this sentiment about today's breed of philanthrocapitalists, when he argues that '(p)hilanthrocapitalism is a symptom of a disordered and profoundly unequal world. It hasn't yet demonstrated that it provides the cure [for inequality]' (Edwards, 2008, p8). Carnegie maintained that, 'as a rule, the sins of millionaires in [philanthropy] are not those of omission, but commission, because it is much easier to give than to refuse' (Carnegie, 2006, p17), an observation that is broadly recognized in academic literature and debates on reciprocity in general and the phenomenon of the gift in particular (cf. Mauss, 1924; Sahlins, 1972; Schrift, 1997). In what became known as 'the Gospel of Wealth', Carnegie argued that the wealthy are trustees and that their surplus wealth should be considered a sacred trust for the best good of the community from which it was acquired

(Carnegie, 2006). That is to say, Carnegie's philanthropy was founded on the belief that wealth should be returned to the larger community where it rightfully belongs. By this he answers the universal and age old reciprocal obligation to repay gifts received (cf. Mauss, 1924). As trustees, the wealthy have a duty to administer the wealth for the public good during their lifetime instead of leaving bequeaths that Carnegie regarded as an improper mode of disposing wealth. According to Carnegie, bequeaths become a burden to those charged to carry out the duties that the wealthy failed to achieve during their lifetime. They are not necessarily a gift because the wealthy could not take them with them when they died even if they had wanted to. Bequeaths are torn from the giver rather than given from him/her, adding to conceptual debates on what is exactly to be considered a 'pure' gift, what people consider to be gifts and what people will never give away as a gift (resp. cf. Derrida, 1992; Godelier, 1999).

The link between philanthropy and liberty has also been questioned. For example, Bob Reich (2006) suggests that philanthropy encompasses principles of liberty such as freedom of association but nevertheless masks the rocky relationship it has with equality to which it can be indifferent, running parallel to descriptions and analysis of a particular example of gift giving and unequal reciprocal relations, the so-called 'potlatch' of the Indians of the northwest coast of North America (see Reich, 2005). Furthermore, Reich also draws the distinction between institutional and individual harms associated with philanthropy. Whereas institutional harms refer to those harms that are a product of public policies, individual harms are a result of the actions of a philanthropist – there are of course interactions between the two (Reich, 2006). This is not to say that these 'harmful consequences' are always or even ever intentional. The harms can be a matter of 'unintended consequences' (cf. Elias, 1971). Though they might be 'unintended', they seem at the same time predictable, as Edwards (2008) makes clear when he asks the question about the evidence of 'doing good' (or harm) by philanthrocapitalists: 'few of these efforts have any substantial, long-term, broad-based impact on social transformation, with the possible exception of micro-credit. The reason is pretty obvious: systemic change involves social movements, politics and the state, *which these experiments generally ignore*' (Edwards, 2008, p37; emphasis added).

Philanthropists and the foundations/organizations through which they channel their resources are most likely to dismiss harms done by philanthropy as a result of misguided efforts or the work of a tiny minority. The Philanthropy Roundtable participants, for instance, think that there is no need to suspect or even police philanthropy as it exemplifies the American ideal of private action in the public interest and the commitment to the well-being of the neighbours (Philanthropy Roundtable, 2006). It dismisses attempts to regulate philanthropy in the following words:

> *We deplore the transgressions of a tiny minority within our community and urge that the laws they have violated be conscientiously and vigorously enforced. Yet we also insist that government's most important*

> *role vis-à-vis the philanthropic sector is to vouchsafe its millions of honourable members the freedom and encouragement they need to do their best. This vital and diverse element of civil society should be honoured as one of America's finest achievements and as evidence of people's capacity for individual initiative and self-governance, not burdened with costly and potentially crippling constraints on its important work.* (Philanthropy Roundtable, 2006)

Thinking about 'the good' and 'the harm' that philanthropy can do is not only useful to the field of philanthropy but is also important for all areas of human endeavours and interventions, particularly the protection of the environment. Our main goal in this book is to bring these two sides of philanthropy to bear on the environmental domain. We argue that the properties of philanthropy – good and bad – also play out in the sponsorship for nature conservation. We endorse William Damon's view that 'philanthropy can turn out badly if not done in the right way ... It is even possible to do more harm than good with the wrong kinds of philanthropy – a bitter irony indeed for those who give generously of their time and money only to see their efforts wreak havoc among those they intended to help' (Damon, 2004, p129). The message of our book is that environmental philanthropy has yielded positive results that should be appreciated and celebrated. These include the creation of city parks and gardens, the establishment of national parks and nature reserves, the protection of wetlands, support for community conservation, and so on. These good things are often ignored by scholarship that emphasizes the negative impact of philanthropy. The same one-sidedness is true for philanthropists who present their work as an act of altruism only, as if they cannot be harmful. The Janus face of philanthropy calls for a careful assessment of both sides of philanthropy and this book is intended to open lines of communication between the field of philanthropy and environmentalism.

Much of the work on philanthropy and related themes is polarized along the lines of the good and the harm that are associated with philanthropy. We think that these two sides of philanthropy can best be understood by studying philanthropy in its various forms and contexts; its time–space dimensions; its relationships with socio-political changes and economic landscapes; and how it connects to a range of activities and individuals and organizations. In our view, a useful approach to philanthropic practice is to understand it as a concept, a philosophy and a set of practices, and to appreciate its multiple dimensions. This chapter seeks to understand these various dimensions of philanthropy in the environmental domain. To this end the chapter proceeds as follows: it first paints a general picture of the debates about philanthropy and its meanings. This is followed by discussion on the relevance of contexts for understanding different variants of philanthropy. The last part of the chapter guides the reader to the content of the book as a whole.

PHILANTHROPY AND ITS DIMENSIONS

In the absence of a unified theoretical concept of philanthropy analysts have often deployed terms such as philanthropy, charity, benevolence, giving, donation, voluntary sector, third sector, independent sector, non-profit organization and non-governmental organization (NGO) interchangeably (Adam, 2004). The use of these terminologies is complicated by the fact that their meanings have not only changed over time but their interpretations are also steeped in different disciplinary and cultural backgrounds and ideological orientations (Marinetto, 1999; Adam, 2004; Sawaya, 2008; Muukkonen, 2009; Sulek, 2010). In this book we use philanthropy as a broad term that should be understood as, in the words of Robert Payton, 'voluntary action for the public good' (Payton, cited in Ilchman et al, 1998, px). We are aware that the term is vague when placed under a microscope but think that it offers a useful lens through which we can understand and evaluate sets of activities associated with the love of humankind and activities flowing there from. Our objective is therefore neither to work towards a particular definition nor to address the vagaries of the terms per se. Rather, the intention is to tease out dimensions of philanthropy that we see as necessary for understanding philanthropic practices in different contexts around the world. Our view is that adopting a single version of philanthropy in the context of environmental philanthropy potentially narrows down the scope of engaging with philanthropic practices from various angles. For example, adopting Bourdievian and Weberian interpretations of philanthropy with their focus on philanthropy as a bourgeois phenomenon 'which has nothing to do with a disinterested love of humankind and everything to do with elite, interclass struggles over status and cultural capital' would mean that we should overlook other equally important types of philanthropy that are rooted in different cultural settings but useful for understanding peoples' 'love of the environment' (Sawaya, 2008, p204).

Since philanthropy has to do with 'giving', most definitions of the term seem to be influenced by economics, hence income is regarded as an important determinant of charitable contribution. It has been suggested that giving is proportional to income and that it is affected by external factors such as tax regimes. Also, the propensity to bequeath is mainly dependent on wealth. Against this backdrop, Brown has estimated that philanthropists will bequeath not less than US$7 trillion to the US between 1996 and 2020 (Brown, 1999). The use of econometric measures is understandable given that the research on who gives relies heavily on statistical data on tax files. It is not surprising that people qualify as 'leading philanthropists' on the basis of how much money they give as evident in various issues of the US-based *BusinessWeek* magazine. This philanthropic orthodoxy sees philanthropy as a vertical transfer of resources from the rich to the poor. By using personal income as a measure of charity this type of philanthropy excludes low-income households and individuals who do not file the necessary tax returns. This way, the contribution of the low-income group to philanthropy is seldom captured in the analysis of philanthropy.

The vertical nature of orthodox philanthropy and its overemphasis on Wall Street titans has a number of implications for philanthropy as a concept and as a practice. First, by using income as a determinant of charity, orthodox philanthropy overlooks the universality of the charitable impulse that is not the preserve of the rich. The poor, like all other human beings, have a charitable impulse and they have their own ways of giving that are encapsulated in the notion of horizontal philanthropy. In contrast to the assistance that follows a vertical route from the rich to the poor, horizontal philanthropy entails assistance that flows from the poor to the poor. Horizontal philanthropy is guided by principles of reciprocity and cooperation, is not random or disorganized but 'is part and parcel of the social fabric [and] follows proven, unwritten, acculturated rules with associated sanctions for non-compliance' (Wilkinson-Maposa et al, 2005).

Second, orthodox philanthropy and its vertical character suggest that philanthropy is a preserve of rich countries and their cultures, and that its geography follows the North–South alignment as a 'natural' direction. A telling example of the territorialization of philanthropy is the often cited idea that philanthropy is largely an American tradition (Butler et al, 2010). Clotfelter and Ehrlich have, for instance, suggested that the US stands out among nations of the world in the number, strength and diversity of philanthropic and non-profit institutions (Clotfelter and Ehrlich, 1999). This conception of philanthropy in geographical, economic and cultural terms overlooks both the existence of philanthropy in other parts of the world and the forms it takes in different contexts (see Alterman and Hunter, 2004). Leona Anderson summarized the universality of philanthropy as follows: 'each tradition or culture has its own unique characteristics and each its own manner of setting the parameters for the occasion for giving, for what is to be given, who is to give, and who is to receive' (Anderson, 1998, p57). Research has shown that institutionalized private philanthropy is a growing and increasing significant reality in Africa, Asia and Latin America – areas that are not often thought of as constituting 'sources of philanthropy' (see Dulany and Winder, 2001). In this book we adopt a multidimensional view of philanthropy that encompasses various conceptions of philanthropy. In the context of the environment, various dimensions of philanthropy help us understand the ways in which ordinary people get involved in community conservation (see Chapter 8).

Definitions of philanthropy are often situational and selective, meaning that they overemphasize certain aspects of philanthropy such as purpose, process and so on, and also vary according to modes of giving. The angle from which philanthropy is defined is important for understanding conceptualizations of philanthropy and the critiques that flow from them. Conceptions of philanthropy also reflect the scale at, and sphere in, which philanthropic practice takes place. Definitions using the sphere of occurrence, for instance, often place philanthropy between the private and the public. Accordingly, Salamon considers philanthropy as 'the giving of time or valuables (money, securities, property) for public purposes', and as also 'one form of income of private non-profit organizations' (Salamon, 1992, p10).

For Adam (2004), philanthropy constitutes a third sector between the state and the market, but Adam warns us that this does not imply that it exists outside both, or is not influenced by both. This caveat signifies the difficulty in distinguishing between the public and private in the sphere of philanthropy. Accordingly, philanthropy's 'goal is to advance society by providing the *necessary* social, cultural, and educational services which are not provided by the state or the market for political or economic reasons, or which are provided by the state but not in a way that satisfies philanthropists' (Adam, 2004, p4, emphasis added). The notion of necessity is problematic since it shies away from the question of whether the service is necessary to the giver or recipient. In our view philanthropy constitutes a relationship between donor(s) and receiver(s). Others have emphasized one end of the spectrum of the private–public continuum. For example, Wolch considers philanthropy as 'charitable activities of individuals and private (for-profit and non-profit) corporations' (Wolch, 1990, p23). This definition of philanthropy asserts the autonomy of foundations hence it is referred to as an independent sector, especially in the US context (see Wolch, 1990).

It follows that philanthropy is also commonly defined in terms of its intentions and impacts. Sealander (2003), for instance, distinguishes between charity, which seeks to alleviate the sufferings of the poor, and philanthropy, which supposedly focuses on applying results from scientific research in order to address the root causes of poverty and to bring about permanent solutions to poverty and other 'social ills'. Others maintain that philanthropy only provides short-term solutions and fails to address the underlying causes of social problems – either unintentionally or deliberately (Lässig, 2004). As it will become clear below, most critiques of philanthropy focus on the intentions of philanthropists, especially the material and social gains that accrue from charity.

We suggest that philanthropy should be understood in its various contexts and the processes operating at the time. A sample of contexts such as religion, class formation, state and governance, and the expansion of global capitalism, demonstrates this point. It should be stated upfront that these contexts are intertwined and they are often simultaneously involved in shaping philanthropic practices. For example, philanthropy flowing from a business person with a strong religious orientation is likely to be shaped by both religious and business contexts. An institution such as a private sector organization could be acted upon by actors with different motives. Whereas governments might use the institution to leverage private funds and promote public administration, the business sector might use the same for private maximization. For ordinary citizens, the institution could provide the necessary platform for public discourse and civic engagement (Toepler and Mard, 2007). In the following section we reflect on these contexts, which are discussed in isolation in order to gain clarity on the roots of philanthropy. In so doing, we do not in any way assume that these contexts exist in isolation.

We see these contexts as providing the necessary background for engaging with philanthropy, especially environmental philanthropy.

Philanthropy and religion

Philanthropy has a long tradition, stretching back to ancient times, and appears a religious duty in nearly every religion. In his classic study of American philanthropy, Bremner describes how the religious Great Awakening in the third and fourth decades of the 18th century resulted, among other things, in 'the fostering of humane attitudes and the popularization of philanthropy at all levels of society, but especially among the poorer classes' (Bremner, 1980 [1960], p20). Among wealthy men in their later years, the motivation for philanthropy was not so much a matter of easing a sense of guilt for their wealth than 'to discharge the obligations of stewardship faithfully, so that, at the appointed hour, they might hear the joyful sound of "Well Done!" from the lips of their Divine Master' (Bremner, 1980 [1960], p43). Thompson and Landim note that 'in Latin America the idea of philanthropy is associated primarily with religious charity and with benevolence' (Thompson and Landim, 1998, p355). It would be naïve to assume that the influence of religion on philanthropy reflected the relationship between the self and God only. On the contrary, philanthropists also used beliefs as a context for their response to societal changes as the case of the Rockefeller Foundation demonstrates. John D. Rockefeller Jr's philanthropy was inspired by the Protestant mandate to extend the kingdom of God but was also a response to the secularization of the US in the 19th century (Schenkel, 1995). To be sure, whereas traditional philanthropy is rooted in religious beliefs that are less attentive to secular problems, Rockefeller's philanthropy sought to use modernity's tools for serving humanity while at the same time preserving Protestant moral values. This blending of Protestantism and progressivism is at the root of modern philanthropy (see Schenkel, 1995).

The foregoing suggests that a religious-based philanthropy is embedded in a particular cosmological vision (Ilchman et al, 1998). Nonetheless, religions vary in their emphasis on charity and philanthropy, and there are also variations in philanthropic practices that are attributed to local contexts. For example, whereas Anheier and Salamon have shown that Protestantism and Catholicism strongly emphasize charity, Jeong suggests that Korean Protestantism's disposition towards charity has been weakened by blending Christian doctrines with local shamanistic beliefs that emphasize material blessings (Anheier and Salamon, 1998; Jeong, 2010). Furthermore, Korean Buddhism's indifference to philanthropy is ascribed to the religion's emphasis on the welfare of future lifetimes (Jeong, 2010). In short, religion accounts for the ways in which an individual or a group understands and responds to the needs of others and also plays a critical role in drawing boundaries of groups that have access to certain types of charity. Such boundaries could distinguish a 'brother/sister' from a 'stranger'.

A question of relevance to the theme of this book is the influence that religion might have on environmental philanthropy. There are mixed research results concerning the impact of religion on attitudes towards the environment and the extent to which those attitudes translate into philanthropy. In other words, the correlation between religion and environmental attitudes and between religious orientation and spending on the environment is debatable. Greeley, for instance, found that a rigid religious orientation does not account for negative attitudes towards spending for the environment (Greeley, 1993). Instead, what matters are the mediating factors and their impact on religious values. The claim that religious and ritual activities can mediate human–environment relations implies that there are also strong possibilities for people to commit their resources and time towards looking after the environment (see Herva, 2006 on mediating conditions). The commitment of resources to a social cause is also manifested in the formation of classes in society.

Philanthropy and class formation

The relationship between philanthropy and class has a long pedigree. It is not our intention to document this pedigree here as much of the historiography of philanthropy is well documented elsewhere (see Shneewind, 1996). We refer to the connections between philanthropy and class in order to highlight the ways in which class identity matters in philanthropic endeavours. These connections have appeared in forms that differ from the past to the present. The contemporary association of individual philanthropy with prestige has a historical precedent. For example, the American Revolution in the early American Republic and the industrial revolution in Britain – which spread to the European continent – produced new forms of wealth and an upcoming social group of industrialists who used part of their newly acquired wealth to establish numerous charitable foundations. While many authors assume that modern philanthropy emerged in the US, Adam maintains that 19th century North American philanthropy was very much influenced by developments taking place in Europe (Adam, 2004). Wealthy North Americans started travelling to Europe to become more confident, learn about European art and culture, which, according to Adam served to give them a basis to claim 'membership of a superior social class' (Adam, 2004, p1). They recreated – in terms of philanthropy – what they saw and experienced in Europe. Developments in Berlin, London, Leipzig and Dresden produced 'blueprints for bourgeois philanthropic undertakings' (Adam, 2004, p1). Many historians believed that the German bourgeoisie did not develop feelings of responsibility for German society, since they expected the state to take responsibility for financing social and cultural public institutions, but Adam (2004) and Lässig (2004) argue that this only happened after the turn of the 20th century.

In line with Bremner's ideas about the need to justify one's place in society, Lässig also argues that for the emerging bourgeoisie, philanthropy also served as a cleansing mechanism (Bremner, 1980 [1960]; Lässig, 2004). In his essay *The Poor*, Simmel (1965 [1908]) describes how 'the motive for alms then resides exclusively in the significance of giving for the giver. When Jesus told the wealthy young man, "Give your riches to the poor", what apparently mattered to him were not the poor, but rather the soul of the wealthy man for whose salvation this sacrifice was merely a means or a symbol' (Simmel, 1965 [1908], p153). Lässig formulates it the following way: '[the members of the bourgeoisie] wanted to give back to the community that had made their fortunes possible. Above all, they had to cleanse themselves of the "stink" of new money and make themselves acceptable to society. A patron would be considered worthy and integrated once the state ... accepted his contribution' (Lässig, 2004, p213).

At the end of the 19th century in Europe, members of the newly emerging bourgeoisie sought to integrate themselves in the leading social and political elite, at the time still dominated by the aristocracy (Lässig, 2004). Devoting part of their accumulated capital to philanthropy provided a way into the elite, and allowed them to build up 'social wealth' in order to gain socio-political influence (see also Menninger, 2004; Anheier and Leat, 2006). Adam argues that economic capital was not sufficient grounds to be integrated into high society; only its exchange into cultural capital enabled wealthy citizens to be acknowledged by and integrated into the leading circles in society (Adam, 2004). These interpretations fit with Bourdieu's ideas on the 'exchange of capital', in which economic capital (i.e. money) can be exchanged for other forms of capital, such as cultural and social capital and vice versa (Bourdieu, 1983). These last two forms of capital provide people with societal recognition and status. This in turn leads to more power in philanthropic networks and configurations, which may lead to further accumulation of economic capital. Philanthropy served as a way to define social distinctions and social classes and therefore became part of the process of identity formation of the bourgeoisie (Adam, 2004). As such, one could argue that philanthropy was linked to processes of social change.

Lässig notes that 'philanthropy contributed to the socialization of the various factions within the bourgeoisie, especially in terms of consolidating the ideas of private ownership and education ... fulfilled an integrative and identity-building function for an otherwise heterogeneous group' (Lässig, 2004, p205). Nevertheless, this formation of a new elite identity did not always mean the delimitation of the bourgeoisie vis-à-vis other social classes or the complete integration of all possible members of the bourgeoisie. Instead, the bourgeoisie always played a game of inclusion and exclusion (Lässig, 2004). Exceptionally high philanthropic contributions were the basis for the emergence of new elites 'characterized by a specific self-awareness and code of honor' (Lässig, 2004, p206). These new elites then strengthened the fragmentary nature of the bourgeoisie.

Mechanisms of exclusion were also important at another level. As Menninger shows in a study of the rise of mercantile elites in Leipzig, cultural institutions funded through philanthropy were rarely accessible to lower classes (Menninger, 2004). For instance, the *Gewandhaus*, financed by and reliant on private funding, was closed to the lower classes; only after 1914 did the lower classes gain access to the music hall. As such, many philanthropic endeavours of the rising mercantile and industrialist classes, while stimulating their own rise in society, were at the same time maintaining a status quo concerning the position of the lower classes – this even applies to philanthropic endeavours directed at these very same classes. As Simmel argues, giving is both a symptom and a necessity of socio-structural inequities: 'to mitigate certain extreme manifestations of social differentiation, so that the social structure may continue to be based on this differentiation' (Simmel, 1965 [1908], p155). The social structure is either supported or weakened by institutions such as the state and the general mode of governing society.

The state and governance issues

The shifts in methods of governing society from centralized and bureaucratic government to governance has created a polycentric state in which sets of relationships between public, private and voluntary sectors restructure the public sphere (Morgan, 2007; Ball, 2008). Though the resultant bonds from this shift are not clearly articulated and often remain hidden below the surface, the governance structures through which they manifest are useful avenues for both philanthropic practice and influence. This is possible because philanthropists become part of a policy community that assumes multiple roles and also pursues public and personal motives when performing these roles. As Ball has noted 'giving or participation in policy events is a way of registering a presence and making purposeful relationships with contractors and opinion makers' (Ball, 2008, p753). This way philanthropy can be incorporated into state policy through the activities of philanthropic elites who are engaged with government in various ways.

The participation of a policy community in public affairs does not resolve the ambiguities between government spending and philanthropy. There are in fact competing views on the impact that public spending has on the non-profit sector's ability to deliver charity. A strongly held view is that public spending displaces or 'crowds out' private giving because it creates a dependency syndrome in formerly independent organizations; bureaucratizes the non-profit sector; turns non-profit organizations into quasi-public agencies; donors loose control over their activities; few people contribute voluntarily to government social programmes; and it is a disincentive to individuals whose tax benefits from charity are displaced by government spending (Brooks, 2000). A counterview is that public spending can actually encourage or 'crowds in' charity by providing public funds that act as seed money; state subsidy could act as proof of the quality or reputation of charity organizations; and as a guarantee of due diligence (Brooks, 2000).

The relationship between the state and non-profit organization becomes even more complex when philanthropy is situated within global and local political contexts. In their reading of philanthropy under colonialism, Lambert and Lester observe that:

> *colonial philanthropists were those people who believed, often passionately, that imperialism was about something more principled than the pursuit of military glory, personal riches or power, and who acted upon that belief in an attempt to influence official policy in the metropole and in the colonies themselves.* (Lambert and Lester, 2004, p323)

The logic here is that colonial philanthropy provided an alternative colonial tradition, which opened avenues for guilty westerners to make a contribution to the developmental cause in the (former) colonies (see Chapter 7). However, the end of formal colonialism ushered in new types and channels of philanthropy that paved the way for a neo-colonial environment necessary for maintaining metropolitan interests in the former colonies. The colonial present, as Gregory (2004) calls it, was expressed through, among other things, the links between state power and corporate philanthropy. Corporate philanthropy therefore served as the arm of the retreating empire and was used to legitimize imperial interests when coercion had lost its political relevancy (Newell, 2008). Clearly, the ways in which philanthropy was deployed were contingent on the nature of 'the road to independence'. It could be argued that where bloody armed struggles were waged to gain independence, the use of philanthropy of any kind immediately after independence was highly suspicious.

Outside colonial and post-colonial contexts, the rise of the post-war welfare state was accompanied by high public spending. The result was that business philanthropy relied on public sector funding, though philanthropy was largely peripheral to state services (Marinetto, 1999). Charitable practices under different political environments are referred to here to highlight that the nature of the state provides a useful context for understanding shades of philanthropy, drawing lines between philanthropic practices over time, and thinking through the ways in which philanthropy is both metamorphic and adaptive. Its adaptive strengths are vividly manifested in the economic domain.

Capitalist expansion

The intersections of capitalism and philanthropy occur in various forms of which the main one is corporate social responsibility, which, as Marinetto (1999) has cautioned, should be explained by recourse to changing social and political conditions. The replacement of the small family or individually owned enterprise by oligopolistic commercial organization meant that the idea of philanthropy as caring beyond one's family was to be carried out by corporations that in turn had to look after the interest of shareholders thereby placing 'significant limits on the ability of directors and managers to engage in socially responsible activities' (Marinetto, 1999, p1). It has also placed philanthropic practice within the ambit of a broad economic framework. Schramm (2006) observes that since philanthropic foundations in the US are a product of democratic pluralism and the free-market economy, they serve as a mechanism for the reconstitution of wealth and as an institutional entrepreneur. In this context, philanthropy 'is intended to apply wealth in ways that preserve democratic pluralism and a free-market economy, thereby promoting the "release of human possibilities" as intended by foundation donors' (Schramm, 2006, pp359–360).

There is a view that philanthropy reveals the tensions and contradictions in liberal capitalism and is a strategy used by capitalists to legitimize their actions since the market has not benefited the poor. In this regard, it is fair to suggest that inequalities in society have placed the poor into philanthropic focus as the conclusions of the Ninety-third American Assembly Report suggest: 'the most urgent and important contribution of philanthropy and the non-profit sector lies in focusing attention on the increasing economic inequality that afflicts us all' (cited in Clotfelter and Ehrlich, 1999, p512). It is on this basis that Sawaya has argued that 'the current version of philanthropy serves as a flashpoint for debates about liberal capitalism' (Sawaya, 2008, p202). In following the same logic, Newell opines that corporate social responsibility is 'ultimately and inherently a product of the neoliberal political economy from which it emerged and which it aims to legitimate and advance, reproducing its modalities, technologies of governance and failings' (Newell, 2008, p1069). These failings reflect the crisis of capitalism that is addressed through, among other things, philanthropic practices.

The activities of NGOs in countries where structural adjustment programmes were introduced provide useful hints on the deployment of philanthropy as a damage control strategy. Bornstein (2003) observes that the neo-liberal paradigm and its consequent structural adjustment in Zimbabwe meant that NGOs provided assistance to people suffering the consequences of the Economic Structural Adjustment Programme pushed by the International Monetary Fund (IMF) and the World Bank. In so doing, they allowed the adjustments to be implemented without too much resistance. In a similar vein, a report by the US National Committee on Responsive Philanthropy concludes that in the US conservative religious philanthropic foundations have consistently directed a majority of their funding to organizations and programmes that pursue an overtly ideological agenda based on industrial and environmental deregulation, the privatization of government services, reductions in federal anti-poverty spending and the transfer of authority and responsibility for social welfare from the national government to the charitable sector and state and local government (Covington, 1997).

Adam has argued that philanthropy in itself also serves as a way to produce more capital (Adam, 2004). The cultural and social capital acquired through philanthropy could be mobilized to generate more economic capital. Nineteenth century philanthropy was an economic system that competed with other organizational models such as cooperation and the social welfare state (Adam, 2004). In an analysis of the philanthropic endeavours of Sir Sydney Waterlow, who created a philanthropic housing enterprise in London in 1863, Morris (2004) claims that Sir Waterlow also considered it a business and expected a return of 5 per cent from his enterprise, and argued that only the connection of philanthropy with the market economy could solve the housing problem. Clearly, the economic lens offers insights into the working of capital and the relations between capital and philanthropy. However, it does not assist us to understand other equally important factors that account for philanthropy as a platform for civic engagement or as an outcome of and channel for social relations. A brief discussion on citizenship below clarifies this point.

Civic engagement and citizenship

The notion of citizenship and the practices it engenders have been a focus of attention in social theory, and have generated debates on the authenticity of citizenship, its agency, modes of exclusions, and its rights-based and duty-led orientation (see McEwan, 2005). Our concern in this book is on citizenship's duty-led outlook and how this creates an authorizing environment that is supported through charity. A sense of empowerment that is underpinned by the belief that it is within one's power to improve the welfare of others influences much of voluntarism. Nelson Mandela's injunction that 'it is in your hands to lift the burden of the poor', which was broadcast on 18 July 2010 to mark the United Nations International Mandela Day, captures the essence of individual empowerment and voluntarism. As society changes, ideas about the domains and roles of the individual, the public and the private alter. Accordingly, Schervish (1998) has argued that the connotation that philanthropy constitutes voluntary donations of time and resources needs to be questioned.

Lässig refers to the overlap between *Bürgerlichkeit* and liberalism around 1900 as 'one of the central axioms of Liberalism', which cherishes the importance of individual self-responsibility and the rejection of state regulation (Lässig, 2004, p201). This focus on the independent and industrious individual was linked to a system of privilege that proponents of liberalism defended fiercely. And, charitable behaviour was 'the result of this tension between bourgeois individualism and a fundamental sense of responsibility for the social structures of the city' (Lässig, 2004, p202). Lässig contrasts the proponents of liberalism, including the elites engaged in philanthropy, with the supporters of another ideology emerging towards the end of the 18th century, that of social democracy. She argues that while philanthropy provided only short-term solutions, social democracy saw poverty and unemployment as structural problems that could only be resolved through the reformation of the very foundation of society. Liberal politicians and patrons, by contrast, did not want to change the structures; they merely wanted to decrease the undesirable symptoms. Philanthropists defined entirely new tasks – such as social housing – for the state, and hence created new responsibilities for the state, yet they always acted in such a way that traditional social structures did not entirely erode. In other words, they attempted to decrease the negative social consequences of economic modernization without relinquishing their power (Lässig, 2004). Against the backdrop of an increasing popularity of social democracy, both liberalism and bourgeois philanthropy were promoted in such a way as to give them a decisively apolitical status (Lässig, 2004). In both counts, individual philanthropy is always performed within a broad socio-political context.

The Environmental Lens

The foregoing discussion provides a useful background for understanding dimensions of philanthropy and the forms that it might take in the environmental domain. It is in this domain that we have carved out the scope of this book. We use environmental philanthropy to refer to the contribution to the preservation or conservation of nature and the promotion of activities related to the general health of the planet by individuals, communities, NGOs and institutions. Thus, environmental philanthropy is broader than what Butler et al call 'wildlands philanthropy', which is limited to 'the intentional actions of people who worked hard to save wild country' (Butler et al, 2010, pxxii). Environmental philanthropy is a useful analytic for various reasons:

- It captures various forms of philanthropy from charitable contributions to bequests.
- The 'environmental' is a defining feature of our time to which philanthropy is expected to respond with a sense of urgency. The need for urgent action runs through findings from research on climate change and the campaigns lobbying governments to stop the collapse of the world and the 'end' of civilization, a message clearly conveyed by the movie *2012*. A combination of environmental concerns, increasing levels of education, the growing number of wealthy people and the mushrooming of environmental NGOs and groups make environmental philanthropy an important entry point to the study of philanthropy. Thus, environmental philanthropy is useful beyond the concerns with the environment as insights gained from charity towards the environment could be used to deepen our knowledge of philanthropy. It is our view that environmental philanthropy contributes to a terrain of knowledge relevant to the study of philanthropy and human actions towards the welfare of the environment.
- It offers possibilities for understanding channels of philanthropy and the networks necessary for its practice. These channels are useful for answering the basic questions of who gives and why.
- Environmental philanthropy is a useful avenue for understanding forces shaping global environmental agreements and the voluntary and non-voluntary commitments that flow from these agreements. These agreements and the environmental activities they engender at various scales shed light on agency and scale in environmental philanthropy.

- It offers fertile ground for evaluating a growing body of work that claims that the environmental dimension of neo-liberalism is inherent in the history of neo-liberalization (Heynen et al, 2007). Though the neo-liberal moment has profoundly shaped perspectives on environmental philanthropy it would be counterproductive to ignore the various forms in which philanthropy exists. Our point of departure is that philanthropic practices not only reflect the worldviews of the givers, but are also shaped by social, political and economic conditions to which philanthropy is meant to respond. Understanding these worldviews and conditions in the environmental domain requires that closer attention should be paid to philanthropy and its various permutations and logics.
- The involvement of local groups in the conservation of the environment opens avenues for understanding possibilities for philanthropy from the grassroots level.

Scope of the Book

This book grapples with two important sets of questions arising from the various contexts sketched above. The first set of questions relates to the form and content of philanthropy in the environmental arena: what constitutes environmental philanthropy? Who gives for which environmental cause and why? What are channels and directions of philanthropy? And, what are the outcomes of environmental philanthropy? The bulk of the book is devoted to engaging these questions. The second set of questions is a philosophical one and is concerned with the relevance of the environmental lens to the wider study of philanthropy. It focuses on how environmental philanthropy might shed light on the charity impulse and its agency, and on the implications that the current 'global economic crisis' could have for environmental philanthropy.

Outline of the Book

The content of the various chapters of this book is informed by the sets of questions referred to above. In Chapter 2 we discuss the concept of environmental philanthropy and situate it within the broad literature on philanthropy. In line with the broad view of philanthropy we adopt in this book, the chapter considers the division between environment, conservation and development less helpful in understanding environmental philanthropy. The main goal of the chapter is to highlight areas of 'the environment' that have attracted the attention of philanthropists. It also discusses the place of 'the environment' in the list of priorities for charity and relates these priorities to processes of social and environmental change. The chapter proceeds from the view that environmental philanthropy encompasses resources that individuals, communities, the business sector and foundations commit to the preservation of nature and the promotion of activities related to nature conservation and the general health of the planet. The networks through which charity flows are a subject of Chapters 3 and 4.

Actor-network theory is increasingly being used to understand how environmental networks are formed and how they operate once they are formed. It has been suggested that networks organize human and non-human actors but are also organized by human and non-human conditions (Robbins, 2004). This way the agency of networks is derived from the transformative interactions between human and non-human actors. We use network theorizing in Chapter 3 to understand points of connections and relationships in environmental philanthropy and to account for the flow of charity. The chapter combines elite theory and ideas about conspiracies to account for the connections between elites in ways that are often obscured from the public, yet the work of these elites in the environmental domain are publicly celebrated. The premise of the chapter is that particular historical moments provided conducive conditions for elites in South Africa Europe and North America to connect and that the environment facilitated some of those connections. It particularly reflects on how shifts and dynamics in the global geopolitical configurations have shaped environmental ideas, including the direction of philanthropic giving, particularly in South Africa. The growth of institutionalized private philanthropy and community foundations in Africa, Asia and Latin America, and the funding of conservation projects in different parts of the world by some of America's leading philanthropists make necessary the study of the South–North connections among environmental philanthropists. The connections forged by the elite cannot be understood outside the platforms on which the elite interact, dispense their wealth and influence public policy. Against this backdrop, Chapter 4 pays attention to the ways in which philanthropists connect and work through NGOs and community-based organizations (CBOs).

In Chapter 4 we engage the question of who gives for which environmental cause and why by looking at a sample of environmental NGOs (ENGOs) and CBOs. The focus of the chapter is on how the kinds of relationships discussed in Chapter 3 are operationalized through ENGOs and CBOs. These relationships and roles are understood from the vantage point of capitalism and conservation, which accounts for the growing trend of corporate involvement in conservation (Brockington and Duffy, 2010). The chapter draws on examples from the activities of the big ENGOs and small CBOs from developed and developing countries. It also teases out the role of NGOs in dispensing charity. It is logical to assume that, all factors being equal, the flow of environmental charity will be in accordance with pressing environmental issues that require urgent attention. It is for this reason that Chapter 5 focuses on the flows of philanthropy and environmental threats and how these threats are part of a discourse as well as an ecological reality.

In Chapter 5 we problematize the notion of environmental threats in order to understand why certain species and habitats are on the radar of philanthropists.

Our assumption is that the framing of environmental threats goes a long way towards promoting certain conservation efforts as more urgent, i.e. that there is a bigger 'threat' involved in relation to other issues, which in turn also configures the landscape for philanthropy. We refer to attempts to save the rhino in southern Africa to illustrate this and also to emphasize the need to understand philanthropy in (a socio-political and socio-economic) contexts. These contexts are relevant for evaluating the implications of, say, the Convention on International Trade in Endangered Species of Wild Fauna and Flora (CITES) for philanthropy in future studies. The discussion on the connection between environmental concerns with financial support is taken further in Chapter 6 where we show where the Global Environment Facility (GEF) has placed its emphasis in terms of focal areas and amounts of grants given to regions of the global South.

The focus in Chapter 6 is on the GEF's Small Grants Programme (GEF-SGP) and how it defines areas of environmental concern to which local action is mobilized through grants. The chapter proceeds from the creation of the GEF as a mechanism for supporting the protection of the biophysical environment in the global South. We see the GEF as the multi-donor funding mechanism operating at the global scale with specific areas of focus. These areas, in turn, limit the scope of participation and access to funding by CBOs and NGOs. The bulk of the chapter reflects on GEF-SGP projects in order to gain understanding of the connections between locally initiated environmental projects and the flow of global funds. The GEF-SGP is relevant for understanding these connections because, since it was launched in 1992, the programme has focused on community-level projects in developing countries. The chapter draws on data from a survey of 11,876 GEF-SGP projects in Africa, the Arab states, Asia and the Pacific, Europe and the Commonwealth of Independent States (CIS), and Latin America and the Caribbean. From this overview of local initiatives and global funding, the discussion moves to environmental actions and charity in Africa as a region.

In Chapter 7 we pay attention to why Africa has been attractive to conservationists and philanthropists over the years. We show that environmental philanthropy in the continent encapsulates the contexts and motives we outlined in Chapter 1 and also how its results are mixed when we consider the good and harm. The chapter shows that the image of Africa as a 'wild continent' accounts for much conservation activities in the continent. It also explains why philanthropy was motivated by this idea in different historical moments. The mapping of environmental philanthropy in the continent is based on two premises. The first is that the connections between philanthropists and ENGOs/CBOs discussed in the preceding chapters have a peculiar character in Africa. Their peculiarity is not so much about Africa as a unique place but is ascribed to several factors, including the abundance of, and threats to, Africa's rich biodiversity; the limited capacity of the state to implement complex and often expensive conservation plans and management regimes; the over-reliance of most governments on foreign aid; and sustained interests in Africa's natural resources. These and other factors account for the mushrooming of ENGOs and CBOs and the existence of a dense network of philanthropists and ENGOs/CBOs in the continent. The second premise is that environmental philanthropy can more appropriately be evaluated at the receiving end. Approaching it from this angle enhances prospects for decentring the broad study of philanthropy. The chapter is also used to refocus the discussion on philanthropy to experiences in the global South, hence the subsequent Chapter 8 pays attention to a broad range of conservation initiatives and the ways in which they are supported. We are conscious of the fact that the global South does not exist in isolation as the discussion on the support for locally initiated conservation projects shows in Chapter 6.

Implicit in the global funding of local initiatives (Chapter 6) and the dense network of philanthropists and local organizations (Chapters 4, 7 and 8) is the view that local conservation initiatives rely on external sources. In reality, this is not always the case as Chapter 8 shows that community-based conservation (CBC) initiatives have emerged in part as a response to unsustainable resource use, deteriorating environmental conditions and declining welfare conditions (Shukla and Sinclair, 2010). Some of these CBC initiatives have been awarded the Equator Prize because of the significant contribution they make towards environmental protection through sustainable development at the local level. It is worth noting that most CBCs recognized by the Equator Initiative are initiated by CBOs or local NGOs. The chapter notes that CBC initiatives are successful under certain conditions (see Seixas and Davy, 2008) and that they do not always require funding to get off the ground. The activities of CBOs raise important questions for philanthropy. The first question relates to the potential for a bottom-up philanthropy that benefits global biodiversity goals through locally self-initiated rather than imposed activities. This is where philanthropy can potentially do good as local communities define their objectives. What are the chances for local philanthropy to develop given that some of the contexts of philanthropy we referred to in Chapter 1 could still be relevant to communities involved in these efforts? What would be the necessary conditions for grassroots philanthropy to grow given the possibilities for cherry-picking by big external NGOs (Chapter 4)? What about national governments' role and plans regarding community involvement in caring for nature? The last question guides the discussion in Chapter 9.

The localness of the local has been a subject of much heated debates among social scientists, mainly as a result of the evidence that most local activities and agendas of all sorts are related to, or flow from, processes taking place at other scales (i.e. national, regional and global). For our purpose, the notion of networked scales implies that nature conservation plans in different localities are potentially linked to national plans, which have a global relevance. Questions that need to be addressed are the extent to which local conservation activities are driven by local communities, and whether those communities act as a conduit for external donations meant to shape national conservation outcomes. Chapter 9 draws on the experience from Australia's famous Landcare Programme to demonstrate the ways in which conservation activities of farming groups were integral to the national plan and also heavily depended on state funding.

Put together, the experiences from the global South raise the question of power relations in environmental philanthropy. Chapter 10 pays attention to these power relations and also paints the future of environmental philanthropy with a broad brush. The starting point in Chapter 10 is that since the boundaries between philanthropy and other interests have blurred over the years, the North–South flow of philanthropy cannot be taken for granted. This is more so in nature conservation where it has become difficult to ignore the upsurge of political and economic interests. It is therefore important to understand the goals of environmental philanthropy in nature conservation and the extent to which environmental philanthropy originating from the South can make a valuable contribution to nature conservation while at the same time protecting the interests of the South. We conclude that the future of environmental philanthropy is most likely to be shaped by three main factors:

- The current reassessment of philanthropy under global economic constraints. The reassessment is not only important for measuring the flow of funds towards an environmental cause but is also necessary for understanding the scale of interest behind the closed doors of corporate boardrooms.
- Heightened anxieties brought about by concerns with climate change and recent environmental disasters have certainly raised interest in the need to channel funds, time and energy towards the preservation and protection of the environment. We anticipate that environmental philanthropy will grow as a field of knowledge.
- The corollary to the growing anxieties with environmental problems and the need for practical solutions is most likely to lead to the production of technical knowledge rather than the enrichment of our knowledge of philanthropy. Expressed differently, the contribution that environmental philanthropy could make to the broad field of philanthropy is likely to be limited.

Understanding these factors and the direction of environmental philanthropy demands that we should first pay attention to the various ways in which philanthropy has a broad environmental scope. Our conceptions of environmental philanthropy are important for evaluating its outcomes as 'good' or 'bad' or a combination of both. Beyond this, environmental philanthropy offers a useful avenue for studying philanthropy in its various dimensions. In the chapter that follows, we highlight focal areas of environmental philanthropy against the backdrop of the theme of this chapter.

References

Adam, T. (2004) 'Introduction', in Adam, T. (ed) *Philanthropy, Patronage and Civil Society. Experiences from Germany, Great Britain, and North America*, Indiana University Press, Bloomington, pp1–12

Alterman, J. B. and Hunter, S. (2004) *The Idea of Philanthropy in the Muslim Contexts*, Centre for Strategic and International Studies, Washington DC

Anderson, L. (1998) 'Contextualizing philanthropy in South Asia: A textual analysis of Sanskrit sources', in Ilchman, W. F., Katz, S. N. and Queen II, E. L. (eds) *Philanthropy in the World's Traditions*, Indiana University Press, Bloomington, pp57–78

Anheier, H. K. and Leat, D. (2006) *Creative Philanthropy*, Routledge, London and New York

Anheier, H. K. and Salamon, L. M. (1998) 'Introduction: the nonprofit sector in the developing world', in Anheier, H. K. and Salamon, L. M. (eds) *The Nonprofit Sector in the Developing World*, Manchester University Press, Manchester

Aplet, G. H. (1999) 'On the nature of wilderness: Exploring what wilderness really protects', *Denver University Law Review*, vol 76, no 2, pp347–367

Ball, S. J. (2008) 'New philanthropy, new networks and new governance in education', *Political Studies*, vol 56, no 4, pp747–765

Berman, E. H. (1983) *The Ideology of Philanthropy: the Influence of the Carnegie, Ford and Rockefeller foundations on American Foreign Policy*, State University of New York, Albany NY

Bishop, M. (2007) 'What is philanthrocapitalism?', *Alliance*, March, p30

Bornstein, E. (2003) *The Spirit of Development*, Routledge, London

Bourdieu, P. (1983) 'The forms of capital', in Kreckel, R. (ed) *Soziale Ungleichheiten (Soziale Welt, Sonderheft 2)*, Otto Schartz & Co, Goettingen, pp183–198

Bremner, R. H. (1980)[1960] *American philanthropy (Second Edition)*, University of Chicago Press, Chicago

Brockington, D. and Duffy, R. (2010) 'Capitalism and conservation: The production and reproduction of biodiversity conservation', *Antipode*, vol 42, no 3, pp469–484

Brooks, A. C. (2000) 'Is there a dark side to government support for nonprofits?', *Public Administration Review*, vol 60, no 3, pp211–218

Brown, E. (1999) 'Patterns and purposes of philanthropic giving', in Clotfelter, C. T. and Ehrlich, T. (eds) *Philanthropy and the Nonprofit Sector in a Changing America*, Indiana University Press, Bloomington, pp212–228

Butler, T., Vizcaíno, A. and Brokaw, T. (2010) *Wildlands Philanthropy: the Great American Tradition*, Earth Aware, San Rafael, CA

Carnegie, A. (2006) *The 'Gospel of Wealth' Essays and Other Writings*, Penguin, London

Clotfelter, C. T. and Ehrlich, T. (1999) 'The world we must Build', in Clotfelter, C. T. and Ehrlich, T. (eds) *Philanthropy and the Nonprofit Sector in a Changing America*, Indiana University Press, Bloomington, pp499–516

Covington, S. (1997) *Moving a Public Policy Agenda: The Strategic Philanthropy of Conservative Foundations*, National Committee for Responsive Philanthropy, Washington DC

Damon, W. (2004) *The Moral Advantage: How to Succeed in Business by Doing the Right Thing*, Berrett-Koehler, San Francisco

Damon, W. (2006) 'Introduction: Taking Philanthropy Seriously', in Damon, W. and Verducei, S. (eds) *Taking Philanthropy Seriously*, Indiana University Press, Bloomington, pp1–11

Derrida, J. (1992) *Given time: I. Counterfeit Money*, University of Chicago Press, Chicago, IL

Dulany, P. and Winder, D. (2001) *The Status of and Trends in Private Philanthropy in the Southern Hemisphere*, Synergos, New York

Edwards, M. (2008) *Just Another Emperor? The Myths and Realities of Philanthrocapitalism*, Demos, London

Elias, N. (1971) *Wat is Sociologie?*, Uitgeverij Het Spectrum, Utrecht and Antwerpen

Godelier, M. (1999) *The Enigma of the Gift*, Polity, Cambridge, UK

Greeley, A. (1993) 'Religion and attitudes toward the Environment', *Journal for the Scientific Study of Religion*, vol 32, no 1, pp19–28

Gregory, D. (2004) *The Colonial Present: Afghanistan, Palestine and Iraq*, Blackwell, Oxford

Herva, V. P (2006) 'Flower lovers, after all? Rethinking religion and human–environment relations in Minoan Crete', *World Archaeology*, vol 38, no 4, pp586–598

Heynen, N., McCarthy, J., Prudham, S. and Robbins, P. (eds) (2007) *Neoliberal Environments: False Promises and Unnatural Consequences*, Routledge, London

Ilchman, W. F., Katz, S. N. and Queen, E. L. (1998) *Philanthropy in the World's Traditions*, Indiana University Press, Bloomington

Jeong, H. O. (2010) 'How do religions differ in their impact on individuals' social capital? The case of South Korea', *Nonprofit and Voluntary Sector Quarterly*, vol 39, no 1, pp142–160

Lambert, D. and Lester, A. (2004) 'Geographies of colonial philanthropy', *Progress in Human Geography*, vol 28, no 3, pp320–341

Lässig, S. (2004) '*Bürgerlichkeit*, patronage, and communal liberalism in Germany, 1871–1914', in Adam, T. (ed) *Philanthropy, Patronage and Civil Society. Experiences from Germany, Great Britain, and North America*, Indiana University Press, Bloomington, pp198–218

Marinetto, M. (1999) 'The historical development of business philanthropy: Social responsibility in the new corporate economy', *Business History*, vol 41, no 4, pp1–20

Mauss, M. (1924) *The Gift* [Translated by Cunnison, I.], Free Press, New York

McEwan, C. (2005) 'New spaces of citizenship? Rethinking gendered participation and empowerment in South Africa', *Political Geography*, vol 24, no 8, pp969–991

Menninger, M. E. (2004) 'The serious matter of true joy: music and cultural philanthropy in Leipzig, 1781–1933', in Adams, T. (ed) *Philanthropy, Patronage and Civil Society. Experiences from Germany, Great Britain and North America*, Indiana University Press, Bloomington

Morgan, K. (2007) 'The polycentric state: New spaces of empowerment and engagement?' *Regional Studies*, vol 41, no 9, pp1237–1251

Morris, S. (2004) 'Changing perceptions of philanthropy in the voluntary housing field in nineteenth- and early-twentieth-century London', in Adam, T. (ed) *Philanthropy, Patronage and Civil Society. Experiences from Germany, Great Britain, and North America*, Indiana University Press, Bloomington, pp138–162

Muukkonen, M. (2009) 'Framing the field: Civil society and related concepts', *Non-Profit and Voluntary Sector Quarterly*, vol 38, no 4, pp684–700

Newell, P. (2008) 'CSR and the limits to capital', *Development and Change*, vol 39, no 6, pp1063–1078

Philanthropy Roundtable (2006) 'Philanthropic freedom', www.philanthropyroundtable.org/content.asp?contentid=409, accessed 10 January 2010

Reich, R. (2005) 'A failure of philanthropy', *Stanford Social Innovation Review*, Winter, pp24–33

Reich, R. (2006) 'Philanthropy and its uneasy relation to equality', in Damon, W. and Verducei, S. (eds) *Taking Philanthropy Seriously*, Indiana University Press, Bloomington, pp27–49

Robbins, P. (2004) *Political Ecology: A Critical Introduction*, Blackwell, Oxford

Sahlins, M. (1972) *Stone Age Economics*, Aldine de Gruyter, New York

Salamon, L. M. (1992) *America's Nonprofit Sector: A Primer*, Foundation Center, New York

Sawaya, F. (2008) 'Capitalism and philanthropy in the (new) gilded age', *American Quarterly*, vol 60, no 1, pp201–213

Schenkel, A. F. (1995) *The Rich Man and the Kingdom: John D Rockefeller, Jr, and the Protestant Establishment*, Fortress Press, Minneapolis

Schervish, P. (1998) 'Philanthropy', in Wuthnow, R. (ed) *Encyclopedia of Politics and Religions*, Congressional Quarterly, Washington DC, pp600–603

Schramm, C. J. (2006) 'Law outside the market: The social utility of the private foundation', *Harvard Journal of Law and Public Policy*, vol 30, no 1, pp355–415

Schrift, A. D. (1997) *The Logic of the Gift: Toward an Ethic of Generosity*, Routledge, New York

Sealander, J. (2003) 'Curing evils at their source: The arrival of scientific giving', in Friedman, L. J. and McGarvie, M. D. (eds) *Charity, Philanthropy, and Civility in American History*, Cambridge University Press, Cambridge, pp217–240

Seixas, C. M. and Davy, B. (2008) 'Self-organization in integrated conservation and development initiatives', *International Journal of the Commons*, vol 2, no 1, pp99–125.

Shneewind, J. B. (ed) (1996) *Giving: Western Ideas of Philanthropy*, Indiana University Press, Bloomington

Shukla, S. R. and Sinclair, A. J. (2010) 'Strategies for self-organization: Learning from a village-level community-based conservation initiative in India', *Human Ecology*, vol 38, no 2, pp205–215.

Simmel, G. (1965) [1908] 'The Poor' [Translated by Claire Jacobson], *Social Problems*, vol 13, no 2, pp118–140

Sulek, M. (2010) 'On the modern meaning of philanthropy', *Non-Profit and Voluntary Sector Quarterly*, vol 39, no 2, pp193–212

Thompson, A. A. and Landim, L. (1998) 'Civil society and philanthropy in Latin America: From religious charity to the search for citizenship', in Ilchman, W. F., Katz, S. N. and Queen II, E. L. (eds) *Philanthropy in the World's Traditions*, Indiana University Press, Bloomington, pp355–372

Toepler, S. and Mard, N. (2007) 'The role of philanthropy within the United Nations System: The case of the United Nations Foundations', in Anheier, H. K., Simmons, A. and Winder, D. (eds) *Innovation in Strategic Philanthropy: Local and Global Perspectives*, Springer, New York, pp167–182

Wilkinson-Maposa, S., Fowler, A., Oliver-Evans, C. and Mudenga, C. F. N. (2005) *The Poor Philanthropist: How and Why the Poor Help Each Other*, University of Cape Town Graduate School of Business, Cape Town

Wolch, J. R. (1990) *The Shadow State: Government and Voluntary Sector in Transition*, Foundation Centre, New York

2

Environmental Philanthropy

INTRODUCTION

In the previous chapter we argued for environmental philanthropy as a useful analytic and as an additional lens through which we could deepen our understanding of philanthropy. In this chapter we expand on this analytic by highlighting its various attributes and meanings. Any meaningful discussion on environmental philanthropy should be attentive to the notion of the environment and how it permeates the categorization of NGOs through which charity is channelled and also implemented. The attention is warranted because the ways in which the environment is framed have a bearing on how the passion for and support toward 'saving nature' is understood, monitored and evaluated. At the core of the debate on the notion of the environment is the extent to which non-human qualities of the environment are distinguishable from human conditions and actions, and whether the non-human world can be preserved and protected without paying adequate attention to human conditions. Terminologies such as 'green environment' and 'brown environment' are reflective of that debate. Conservationists have particularly favoured the idea of the green environment in which the human contribution to, or benefit from, the non-human world is either marginalized or denied. The green environment is closely associated with ideas of pristine nature, wilderness and the like (cf. Duffy, 2000; Wolmer, 2007). This eco-centric perspective runs through organizations that campaign for the creation of new wilderness areas or the protection and extension of existing ones, and helps explain why philanthropy might follow a certain direction as the discussion below will show.

Scholarly work that sought to challenge green environmentalism has shown that humans have contributed to shaping what is often depicted as 'natural' (read: green) environments (Balée, 1989; Fairhead and Leach, 1996; McCann, 1999) and that the protection of the green environment is better served by a holistic approach towards people and the biophysical environment surrounding them (see resolutions to the World Parks Congress, IUCN, 2003). Critical scholarship has gone a long way towards demonstrating that the human and non-human worlds are inseparable in thought and practice (Castree and Braun, 2001). In conservation circles, green environmentalism was challenged by the argument that the protection of wild nature is unlikely to succeed if humans and their needs are not considered integral to the conservation enterprise (see also Chapter 4). Thus, the initial green environmentalist assumption that the poor degrade the environment and the threads of Malthusian doctrine that links the depletion of resources with population growth was turned on its head. Consequently, development and environmental protection were seen (though not always) as two sides of the same coin, hence the term 'green developmentalism'. To be sure, green developmentalism seeks to pursue the protection of nature and the promotion of human well-being simultaneously (Adams, 2001; see also Satterthwaite, 2003). Nowhere is the appreciation of this link more openly expressed than in the Equator Initiative, which we discuss in Chapter 8.

Though the divisions between brown and green environments have largely been rejected as conceptually flawed and practically ineffective, they continue to shape most of the discussion on environment-related topics, including charity toward the protection and preservation of nature. We attempt to move away from the green–brown binary by adopting the notion of environmental philanthropy, which is broader than conservation. This approach is necessary if we are to situate the passion for nature within broad concerns to which sponsorship respond. In our view, environmental philanthropy encompasses resources that individuals, communities, the business sector and foundations commit to the preservation and conservation of nature and the promotion of activities related to nature conservation and the general health of the planet. Using *environmental* philanthropy rather than *conservation* philanthropy allows us to capture the sponsorship of NGOs and CBOs that are involved in activities meant to promote the health of the planet in various ways. This way, we can begin to move away from dominant forms of conservation thinking. This is particularly relevant to our endeavour to show the emerging fertile ground for environmental philanthropy from the grassroots where local environmental challenges have spurred communities to self-organize and to mobilize their resources towards addressing these challenges (see Chapters 6 and 8). There is also a pragmatic reason for adopting environmental charity, namely, the NGOs involved in promoting the health of the planet are able to move from a narrow concern with the wild to broader environmental issues.

The chapter proceeds as follows. The first part explains why environmental rather than wildlands philanthropy is helpful in understanding the passion for nature and the charity that goes with it. This is followed by the second part that highlights areas of 'the environment' that have attracted the attention of philanthropists. The third part of the chapter provides a snapshot of the place of 'the environment' in the list of priorities for charity and points to the implications of the prioritization of philanthropy for the environmental cause.

WHETHER ENVIRONMENTAL OR WILDLANDS PHILANTHROPY

We proceed from the premise that efforts toward conservation are increasingly becoming indistinguishable from the wider concern with the biophysical environment on which human survival depends. The divide between the protection of the environment and conservation is artificial, as we show below. The links between conservation and broader environmental concerns can be traced back to the evolution of nature conservation and modern environmentalism. The nature conservation movement has its cultural origins in the introduction of liberal democratic ideals – human rights, personal liberty and social equality – in which modern environmentalism is embedded. In our view, nature conservation is concerned with the wild(erness) aspects of the biophysical environment. That is to say 'conservation and the environment' are conceptually and practically intertwined but the two can only be looked at from different vantage points depending on the aspects to be accentuated for analytical or pragmatic purposes. To this end, Worster (2008) asks a rhetorical question of whether the conservationist outlook of the rich supported the revolutionary triad of nature, freedom and equality, or whether their kind of conservation was a diminished and distorted shadow of its origin. Essentially, the question is related to how the rich only emphasized the conservation aspect of the biophysical environment. Thus, in the late 19th and early 20th centuries the elite were motivated to preserve the wild that they butchered because the numbers of wildlife were plummeting. They created NGOs to carry out the task of preserving the wild, and 'the goal of the penitent butcher was to use these associations to press for modest reforms centred on the creation of game reserves and parks' (Bryant, 2009, p1543). Though penitent butchers could be associated with a particular historical moment (i.e. the late 19th and early 20th century, see Chapter 7) in the evolution of game reserves and conservation NGOs, they do represent a good picture of the root of elite environmentalism that is being replayed through celebrities, as Dan Brockington (2009) has shown. The close relationships between NGOs and the elite account for views of environmental NGOs as both a product of elite environmentalism and an agency for eco-imperialism (see Bryant, 2009). It should be noted that elite environmentalism has been challenged by grassroots NGOs, which confronted environmental challenges occasioned by the activities of the elite (see Chapter 4).

Funding for open spaces, wildlife and wilderness for the enjoyment of the rich has been called 'environmental giving' by some (Delfin and Tang, 2007). Read from this angle, environmental giving is indistinguishable from wildlands philanthropy that has the protection of the wilderness as its main focus. In celebrating wildlands philanthropy in the US, Butler and others claimed that the natural heritage found in contemporary national parks, nature reserves and preserves, sanctuaries and so on were not simply spared by the juggernaut of industrial capitalism but are instead a result of courageous and foresighted women and men who stepped out to preserve remnants of the wilderness with their own resources (Butler et al,

2010). The preservation of the wilderness was associated with the advancement of civilization. As Roderick Nash (2001) noted, Americans used the idea of wilderness to give their civilization an identity and meaning – it was civilization that created wilderness. Nash's elaboration on this link is worth quoting at some length:

> *Evidence that civilization created wilderness is found in the attitudes of the 'Native Indians' that the European settlers found in the New World. It made no sense for them to distinguish wilderness from civilization or to fear and hate what they did not control in nature. Chief Standing Bear of the Ogalala Sioux explained that by tradition his people 'did not think of the great open plains, the beautiful rolling hills and the winding streams with their tangled growth as "wild". Only to the white man was nature a "wilderness" and… the land infested with "wild animals" and "savage" people'.* (Nash, 2001, pxiii).

Wildland philanthropy is preservationist in outlook and overemphasizes two important activities, namely, the acquisition of land for the wild and the protection of the wild from development projects and industrial interests.

Given the rise in the creation of ecological corridors that are meant to connect habitats and re-establish migratory routes of species in different parts of the world, this type of philanthropy is expected to grow stronger in years to come, as it contributes directly to contemporary nature conservation strategies. The links between ecological corridors as a conservation strategy and philanthropy are clearly captured by Walsh's description of the Redwoods to Sea conservation corridor, of which he said:

> *By helping to safeguard habitat continuity in the lowland forests of coastal California and create shared stewardship across the landscape, the Redwoods to Sea initiative is an excellent example of applied* wildlands philanthropy *that is informed by conservation science, instigated by opportunities, and fueled by the generosity of individuals and institutions who love the land.* (Walsh, 1999, p5, emphasis added)

The conservation science referred to here is 'corridor ecology', which is concerned with landscape elements that enhance the connectivity of habitats necessary for the reproduction, survival and protection of animal and plant species (see Bennett, 2003; Hilty et al, 2006). The various initiatives to connect habitats on the African continent through the creation of transfrontier conservation areas are another case in point (Ramutsindela 2004, Chapter 8; see also Peace Parks Foundation (no date a).

Since the focus of wildlands philanthropy is on conserving the wild, this kind of charity may as well be called conservation philanthropy. In fact it has been said that the need for wildlands philanthropy is greatest in the 21st century as it is required to complement strong public funding for *conservation* (Butler et al, 2010). The false distinctions between environmental and wildlands philanthropy also play out in the categorization of NGOs through which charity is channelled and philanthropic practice carried out on the ground. These NGOs are either classified as conservation NGOs or environmental NGOs. And, the two categories are sometimes used interchangeably. Brockington and Scholfield (2010) define conservation as activities concerned with conserving wildlife, habitat and protected areas in order to classify conservation organizations in sub-Saharan Africa. They also argue that conservation NGOs and environmental NGOs are separate groups. Proceeding from their definition of conservation referred to above, they:

> *excluded environmental organisations concerned with general soil or water protection and management, but included those supporting forest conservation, or those specifically working on the edge of protected areas to reduce pressure on land … included environmental education programmes where these were part of an NGO's larger conservation programme, but excluded NGOs whose sole focus was environmental education.* (Brockington and Scholfield, 2010, p9)

In the process of demarcating these lines, they excluded Roots and Shoots of the Jane Goodall Institute, because that NGO extends beyond sub-Saharan Africa and has a separate stand-alone education programme (Brockington and Scholfield, 2010).

We emphasize that *environmental* philanthropy is helpful in that it captures a diversity of activities and institutions that work towards a broader environmental cause than simply conservation. In fact, there has been a shift among environmental NGOs from narrow conservation objectives towards addressing contemporary environmental challenges that go beyond the traditional focus on creating national parks and nature reserves. That is to say, NGOs can move from one category to another. A case in point is the Sierra Club, which describes itself as 'America's oldest, largest, and most influential grassroots environmental organization. Inspired by nature, we are 1.3 million of your friends and neighbors, working together to protect our communities and the planet' (Sierra Club, 2011). This description masks a dense history of the transformation of the Club since its establishment in 1892. The Sierra Club changed from being a narrow conservation NGO to become a broad environmental organization, hence the Club has been described as 'a long-standing conservation organization that got caught up in one of the pivotal conservation battles of the early 1950s, and, in the process, transformed itself into a modern environmental group' (Young, 2008, p184).

The Sierra Club has its origin in the confrontation with the state over the building of two dams within the boundaries of the Dinosaur National Monument, but expanded its scope and activities beyond conservation principles to confront issues of economic development and their implications for the health of the planet. In addition to this factor, internal politics and institutional forces account for the transformation of the Sierra Club from a conservation organization to an environmental group (see Young, 2008 for details). This transformation of the Club supports our argument that drawing boundaries between conservation and environmental groups in absolute terms severely limits our analysis of these entities and the work they do.

Traditional conservation groups are increasingly defining themselves in broad environmental terms rather than as having an exclusive concern with nature conservation. The statements by World Wide Fund for Nature (WWF) and International Union for Conservation of Nature (IUCN) attest to this point:

> *WWF creates solutions that will solve our planet's BIG environmental challenges. We want people and nature to thrive together* (WWF, no date a, emphasis added)

This statement and the projects that WWF is involved with are proof that the organization has shifted away from its initial exclusive concern with wildlife from which its original acronym is derived. Its current mission is 'to stop the degradation of our planet's natural environment, and build a future in which humans live in harmony with nature' (WWF, no date b). By way of another example, consider the following statement from the International Union for Conservation of Nature (IUCN):

> *IUCN ... helps the world find pragmatic solutions to our most* pressing environment *and development challenges. It supports scientific research, manages field projects all over the world and brings governments, non-government organizations, United Nations agencies, companies and local communities together to develop and implement policy, laws and best practice. IUCN is the world's oldest and largest global* environmental network – *a democratic membership union with more than 1,000 government and NGO member organizations, and almost 11,000 volunteer scientists in more than 160 countries.* (IUCN, 2010, emphasis added)

By referring to these two statements we do not in any way suggest that all conservation groups have moved in this direction. On the contrary, there are organizations such as the Wildlife Society that have remained focused on narrowly defined conservation work.

We emphasize that focusing on conservation work alone becomes even more problematic when one considers that conservation NGOs and development NGOs are also closely related and have become something like hybrid NGOs. This is the case in developing countries where conservation and development are pursued on behalf of the rural poor and so-called weak states (Novellino and Dressler, 2010) (see Chapter 8). Brockington and Scholfield note that 'conservation NGOs which facilitate and respond to eco-tourism, or help local groups form cooperatives to manufacture and sell curios, or produce new markets or manage fish stocks, are part of the process of immanent development' (Brockington and Scholfield, 2010, p5). It is our view that 'the environmental' rather than a narrow conservation category offers a better chance for understanding the passion for nature and the charity that flows from it. It would appear that 'the environment' category is common in the public domain and that it is more likely to be used in various countries. The list of Japanese charities, for instance, refers to the environment rather than conservation though it includes non-profit organizations such as Conservation International Japan and the Nature Conservation Society of Japan (Charity Vault, no date). In fact, these are classified as environmental charities on the website. To return to the point, we prefer the notion of 'environment' over that of 'conservation' in order to capture the dimensions of philanthropy related to the passion for nature in different contexts. The concept of environmental philanthropy is helpful for understanding a variety of nature conservation-related activities to which we turn below.

Environmental Philanthropy in Practice

One of the main foci of research on philanthropy is the cause that the giver supports. As we have intimated above, the attempts to separate conservation from the environmental label is not helpful as the two are not only closely connected but also involve activities that cannot be confined to one end of the spectrum only. The category of 'conservation and the environment' that the US-based Chronicle of Philanthropy uses in its directory of contributors and beneficiaries is instructive of the difficulties associated with trying to separate these two in the domain of philanthropy. In other words, the category epitomizes attempts to draw the line between conservation and the environment while, at the same time, acknowledging that the two are not easily separable. Between 2005 and 2009, the Chronicle of Philanthropy (2010) listed the following philanthropic causes under the category of conservation and the environment:

- Protecting the forests from development;
- Monitoring environmental projects in developing countries;
- Conserving the Amazon;
- Purchasing land to be used for conservancies and nature reserves;
- Protecting state parks and forests;
- Building a marine animal hospital;
- Supporting training programmes;
- Researching sustainable energy;
- Conserving watersheds and river tributaries;
- Supporting youth and education programmes;

- Supporting conservation efforts in China;
- Establishing and supporting research centres;
- Promoting land conservation and economic development in Africa;
- Conserving the Appalachian Mountains;
- Planting and maintaining trees in public spaces;
- Supporting public housing development and schools;
- Funding educational programmes;
- Fundraising for land trusts.

The foregoing suggests that the support for an environmental cause comes in various forms including land donation, human resource development and mitigation:

- Land donation – land can be donated in the form of bequests or can be purchased from the market for environmental purposes. Despite Andrew Carnegie's dismissal of bequests as good philanthropy (see Chapter 1), conservation groups have benefited from land that had been bequeathed for an environmental cause. For example, Newell and Ann Meyer donated 374 acres of land in 2006 towards the establishment of the Newell and Ann Meyer Nature Preserve which is managed by the Nature Conservancy for the public good. The Nature Conservancy opened the reserve to the public in 2009 and is using the Meyers' gift to restore the land which had been used for agricultural production before the reserve was created (The Nature Conservancy, no date).

    In addition to land donation, the couple bequeathed $8.7 million to be used for the management and restoration of the Preserve (Chronicle of Philanthropy, 2010) . We do not cite this example because it is special in any way. Our attempt is to demonstrate the fact that conservation has benefited from philanthropy in the form of land donation. This act of philanthropy is not by any means limited to a particular country. Of significance to the study of philanthropy is the question of how much of conservation has actually relied on land donation.
- Land purchase – bequests in the form of funds and philanthropic donations can also be used to purchase land and this is increasingly becoming a popular route for charity for a number of reasons. First, land for conservation has become scarce due to industrial development and the expansion of human settlements, which are seen as threats to the remnants of wilderness. Generous givers who want to save the wild respond to these threats by funding the purchase of land as a way of securing space (Spierenburg and Wels, 2006). In this context, philanthropists act as the saviour of the wild. This sentiment is clear from Butler et al's (2010) description of American philanthropists as people who saved places.

    A telling example of this is Joseph Battell who bought property around Camel's Hump in Vermont in order to protect the forests from 'timber butchers, lumber merchants, and firebugs' (Butler et al, 2010, p11). The need to acquire land for the protection of nature accounts for the mushrooming of land trusts as a vehicle for environmental philanthropy. Land trusts are broadly defined as 'local, state, regional, and national nonprofit organizations that actively work to conserve land for the public benefit through a variety of means, including, most commonly, the acquisition of land and conservation easements by gift, purchase, or bargain purchase' (McLaughlin, 2002, p453). Though land trusts vary according to their specific objectives they all share a common feature, namely, the intention to protect land-related resources such as water, wetlands, farmland, woodlands, open spaces, historic sites and forests. They are considered the fastest growing arm of the environmental movement (Schear and Blaine, no date). The 2005 report of the Land Trust Alliance indicates that the total acres conserved by trusts increased by 54 per cent, the number of trusts increased by 32 per cent and the pace of conservation tripled between 2000 and 2005 (Aldrich and Wyerman, 2006). Of significance to the discussion of this chapter and the volume as a whole is that land trusts can also access land for conservation in private land through easements.

Land purchase is also crucial for new conservation strategies that seek to expand existing national parks and nature reserves or to create conservation areas across international boundaries. In both counts, there is a need to acquire more land. Practically, national parks and nature reserves can be expanded through the acquisition of land adjacent to these areas. A more ambitious project involves the expansion of conservation areas beyond state borders to create swathes of conservation land variously known as transfrontier conservation areas, transboundary biospheres, heartlands, transboundary natural resource management areas, peace parks, hotspots and so forth. The rationales and methods of expansion for these areas are couched in different terms. For example, hotspots are created around areas with the highest concentration of biodiversity while the focus of heartlands is on large landscapes of exceptional wildlife and natural value. However, both are concerned with the limitations that national parks and nature reserves have on the protection and management of biodiversity. The ecological rationales behind such expansions are that much of the biodiversity that requires protection and proper management is found outside existing protected areas; environmental problems are transboundary in nature; the management of watersheds and river basins shared by more than one country demands transboundary institutions and structures; and that most governments are unable to manage natural resources under their jurisdictions (Bennett, 2003; Hanks, 2003; Van Aarde and Jackson, 2007; Fenger, 2009; Flesch et al, 2009; Giordano, 2009; Leibenath et al, 2010). Others have argued that the expansion of protected areas is one particular expression of globalization and neo-liberalism (Zimmerer et al, 2004; Duffy, 2006; Büscher, 2010).

- Conservation easements – conservation easements are 'private land use restrictions designed to preserve open space and other environmentally significant resources' (Hollingshead, 1997, p321). They should be seen as an alternative to establishing nature reserves on private land without removing or disenfranchising the property owner (see Kiesecker et al, 2007). They are incentive-based conservation practices that enable the landowner to use his/her property for an environmental cause in perpetuity.

The incentives for easements are that landownership remains in private hands and the landowner benefits from a charitable income tax deduction equal to the value of the donated easement – where the tax system recognizes easements as charity (cf. McLaughlin, 2004). A landowner can receive 'an estate tax benefit in the form of the removal of the value of the conservation easement from the landowner's estate for estate tax purposes' (McLaughlin, 2002, p455). In the context of the US, tax is deducted when the easement is used for the preservation of land for public recreation or education; the protection of a relatively natural habitat of fish, wildlife, or plants; the preservation of open space that has scenic qualities benefiting the public or is consistent with clearly delineated governmental conservation policies; and the preservation of a historically important land area or a certified historic structure (McLaughlin, 2002). The US Congress extended the tax break for land-conservation gift in 2008 (Schwinn, 2008).

Easements contribute to conservation in that endangered species on habitats found on private lands are protected with minimal cost to the public. It has been estimated that 'some 95% of all federally threatened and endangered flora and fauna [in the US] is on private land, and 262, or 19%, of these species survive only on private parcels [of land]' (Merenlender et al, 2004, p66). Kiesecker et al (2007) also place the size of public land on which endangered species are found in the US at less than 10 per cent.

According to Hollingshead, 'the modern conservation easement is an amalgam of the ancient common law of easements, real covenants and equitable servitudes, as modified by the relatively recent state statutes designed to alleviate various problems created under this body of common law' (Hollingshead, 1997, p324). Easements are flexible and tailored to meet the needs of the parties involved; they are legally enforceable though not heavily dependent on law enforcement agencies; and can help the landowner to meet personal goals (Hollingshead, 1997; McLaughlin, 2002; Merenlender et al, 2004). For example, farmers wanting to pursue farming and conservation in tandem can do so, as in the case in New Zealand where 24 of the 26 covenantees[1] were actively involved in farming (Saunders, 1996). The motivation for conservation covenants or easements includes landholder demographics, knowledge of the programme, land tenure systems, financial circumstances, perceptions of risks involved and the beneficiation framework in use (Kabii and Horwitz, 2006).

To return to the point, the establishment of transboundary conservation areas requires the acquisition of land on both sides of the international border, especially where such land forms the link necessary for the creation of those areas

(Ramutsindela, 2007). By way of example, in 1997 it was estimated that the creation of the Gariep transfrontier conservation area between South Africa and Namibia would require the acquisition of 200,000 hectares (ha) on the South African side and 40,000ha in Namibia at the cost of $1.3 million (as of 14 June 2010) (Peace Parks Foundation, 1997). The attempts to create a continental conservation corridor in Australia would require the 'interconnection of natural lands of the southern parts of the 2800 kilometre north–south Great Escarpment of Eastern Australia with the Australian Alps' (Pulsford et al, 2003, p291).

Land under communal tenure could be acquired for these projects through outright removals often in the name of development, especially in developing countries (see Milgroom and Spierenburg, 2008; Dowie, 2009). This is possible because until recently, communal land rights were not validated as 'a perfectly legal way to acquire, hold, and transfer land' (Alden Wily, 2001, p77). Under these conditions people holding communal rights had a weak legal basis on which to challenge forced removals. In contrast to communal land, land in private hands can only be acquired through commercial transactions. Unsurprisingly, the primary target of the land trusts are private land owners who can either sell their properties or use them for purposes of conservation in the form of conservancies[2] or their equivalents. Thus, environmental philanthropy is likely to flourish under a private property regime that allows people to buy land for purposes of protecting nature. It should, however, be noted that communities owning ancestral land can also use that land to contribute to an environmental cause, especially when they have a strong attachment to land and a sense of stewardship over their resources (O'Garra, 2009).[3]

Environmental philanthropy also comes in the form of support for the development of the human resource necessary for managing natural resources and scenic sites being preserved. It is generally acknowledged that there is a need for well-equipped environmental practitioners and professionals if efforts to promote the health of the planet are to be successful. To this end, philanthropy is used to support the training of managers, hence centres of learning have been set up around the world with the intention to increase the number of professionals needed and also to prepare the human resources required to handle conservation and the management of natural resources in an increasingly complex world. For example, the College of African Wildlife Management was established in Mweka, Tanzania, in 1963 to train African wildlife managers. More recently, the World Wide Fund South Africa and the Peace Parks Foundation joined hands to establish the Southern African Wildlife College in 1997, the objective being 'to provide people of Africa with the required motivation and relevant skills to manage and conserve their protected areas and associated flora and fauna on a sustainable basis in cooperation with local communities' (Peace Parks Foundation, no date b).

More concerted efforts are also being made towards sponsoring activities that promote public awareness of environmental challenges and programmes designed to promote behavioural changes. Numerous studies have concluded that environmental education is crucial for improving human attitudes and behaviour towards the environment (Littledyke, 2008; Ferreira, 2009; Heimlich, 2010; Jin et al, 2010; Wyner and DeSalle, 2010). At the professional level, there is a growing recognition that knowledge of the biological sciences on which much of conservation practice relies should be equally matched by understanding of the societal issues impacting on conservation efforts. In arguing for consideration of human factors in environmental protection in the 1940s Neel stated that: 'in the field of sciences we stress the fact that trees cannot be grown in a few years and intimate that time is valuable in this relation but how often do we consider the significance of this in relation to the development of the human being?' (Neel, 1947, p247). This understanding is not new but has gained momentum in recent years as a result of complex socio-economic conditions that contemporary professionals have to deal with in developed and developing countries. In the absence of human dimensions, the training of natural resource managers becomes what Jacobson and McDuff call 'the training of idiot savants' – meaning 'individuals skilled in certain areas (in this case, the technical biological aspects of conservation) but largely inept in other aspects of the field' (Jacobson and McDuff, 1998, p263).

In emphasizing the need to blend the human dimension into the training of natural resource management, Jacobson and McDuff maintain that 'as conservation biologists in the field, we must gain an understanding of how human behaviors, values, and attitudes affect our respective research interests, from individual species to entire landscapes' (Jacobson and McDuff, 1998, p265). Against this backdrop, some philanthropists direct their funds towards environmental education and training of professionals. Beyond this, sponsorship is also directed towards educating the public through outreach programmes. Some such programmes are considered crucial where the protection of endangered species or habitats is considered urgent and the participation of local residents in conservation is required (Brewer, 2002). Thus, environmental education can be thought of as a strategy for conservation as the following quotation from WWF makes clear:

> *The trustees of [WWF] are of the opinion that an ever-increasing proportion of the Fund's income must be devoted to teaching people, and especially young people, the fundamental principles of conservation. In the end, it is the only way the peoples of the world will come to accept the ideals which brought the WWF into existence* (cited in Fien et al, 2001, p382).

Having sketched various forms in which the environmental cause is manifested, we move on to understand the place of *environmental* philanthropy within philanthropy. In other words, we seek to answer the question of how environmental philanthropy compares with other philanthropic concerns and commitments. The goal here is not to engage in comparative research. Rather, it is to have a sense of where environmental philanthropy is in the scheme of philanthropy. This understanding is necessary if we are to keep track of changes in giving and among givers.

Philanthropic Priorities: Implications for Environmental Philanthropy

No more useful or more beautiful monument can be left by any man than a park for the city in which he was born or in which he has long lived, nor can the community pay more graceful tribute to the citizen who presents it than to give his name to the gift. (Carnegie, 2006, p24)

Carnegie's statement might give an impression that he placed the sponsorship for parks above all other areas deserving philanthropy. Far from it, his main priority was a free library that he considered as the best gift to a community (Carnegie, 2006). The point here is that while leading philanthropists have shown interest in environmental matters, particularly conservation, they hardly consider supporting environmental activities as their main priority. The reasons for this require thorough research that we hope future studies will consider. For the moment we reflect on some current patterns of philanthropy.

A closer inspection on patterns of giving reveals that the environment has not received strong support from philanthropists. For example, the 50 most generous philanthropists recorded in *BusinessWeek* were more interested in supporting education and the arts than an environmental cause (Table 2.1). Though the environment appears high in terms of the frequency of donations (Table 2.1), the amount donated towards the environment is low compared to other areas receiving philanthropic support (Table 2.2.)

We are conscious that areas that philanthropists support vary from one person to another and that such areas are not fixed. There are philanthropists such as Donald Bren who have higher interest in nature conservation than, say, arts and culture. In fact, Donald Bren, who was ranked number nine in *BusinessWeek*'s list of *The 50 Top American Givers* in 2008, concentrates on education, research and conservation (BusinessWeek, 2008). In the context of environmental philanthropy, Donald Bren helped to secure 50,000 acres of land for wildlands, parks and trails in the Orange County and also supports the Irvine Ranch Conservancy. Despite efforts such as these, the general pattern of philanthropy is predominantly skewed towards areas of support other than an environmental cause. This statement is supported by statistics from the Chronicle of Philanthropy on philanthropic donations in the US, which places conservation and environment at the bottom of the pile (Table 2.2). This trend has been observed in other studies on philanthropy and NGOs. Everatt and Solanki (2008) found that the environment occupied the second lowest position in the list of philanthropic causes supported in South Africa.

Table 2.1 *Approximate areas and frequency of support by the 50 most generous philanthropists, 2009*

Areas of support	Frequency of support (%)
Education	25.75
Arts and culture	18.82
Health	9.91
Medical research	7.93
Environment	5.91
Social change	5.91
Global security	5.91
Jewish cause	2.98
Youth	2.98
Science	1.99
Free societies	1.99
Libraries	1.99
Deprivation and violence	1.99
Disabilities	1.98
Information access	0.99
Aquarium	0.99
Humanitarian	0.99
Community initiatives	0.99

Source: Compiled from *BusinessWeek* online (www.businessweek.com, accessed 2 June 2010)[4]

Table 2.2 *Philanthropic donations in the US, 2009*

Focal area	Amount in $ million
Colleges and universities	1890.1
Foundations	1094.4
Community foundations	831.1
Health	387.7
Arts	237.1
Public affairs	235
Education	143.4
Human and social services	110.7
Museums and libraries	57.1
Medical research	20
Zoos and aquariums	17.1
Children and youth	15.5
Conservation and environment	12.1
Religious groups	8
Other groups	6.6
Sports and recreation	2.5
Historic preservation	1.3

Source: Constructed from http://philathropy.com.stats/topdonors (accessed 1 June 2010)

In the Netherlands, environmental and animal rights issues occupied a sixth place in 2009 (Centre for Philanthropical Studies, 2010).

Put together, Tables 2.1 and 2.2 suggest that the possibilities for raising philanthropic support towards an environmental cause lie with foundations (including community foundations), since these receive a lion's share of donations. It should be emphasized that foundations are the main channel for all sorts of assistance, from development aid to assisting victims of disasters. Thus, the trajectory of environmental philanthropy can be understood by paying attention to foundations, more so because foundations have their own focal areas and geography. For example, whereas 'U.S. foundations' international grant-giving has doubled since 1998 and rose to $3.8 billion in 2005', the recipients of grants are highly concentrated in terms of geographic regions and countries (International Finance Team, 2006, p2). Approximately 90 per cent of grants from foundations are concentrated in three geographic zones (Africa, Asia and Latin America) and in the top emerging markets such as Brazil, China, India, Mexico, Russia and South Africa (International Finance Team, 2006). In the two chapters that follow we try to understand these links within the domain of environmental philanthropy.

NOTES

1   Outside the US, conservation easements are called conservation covenants.
2   These are 'areas of private property designated for special protection at the initiate of the landowner, in order to conserve the natural resources in the property' (The Nature Conservancy, 2001, p21). In the context of South and Southern Africa, the concept of (private wildlife) conservancies refers to landowners *pooling* their land and other resources for conservation purposes (Wels, 2003).
3   See for instance 'communal conservancies' in Namibia (Weaver and Petersen, 2008).
4   Some descriptions of the areas that are supported were grouped together into a category used in the tables. For example, support for the homeless, anti-poverty and the prevention of violence were grouped under deprivation and violence whereas hospitals, children's health and reproductive choice constituted the category of health.

REFERENCES

Adams, W. M. (2001) *Green Development: Environment and Sustainability in the Third World*, Routledge, London

Alden Wily, L. (2001) 'Reconstructing the African commons', *Africa Today*, vol 48, no 1, pp77–99

Aldrich, R. and Wyerman, J. (2006) *National Land Trust Census Report, 2005*, Land Trust Alliance, Washington DC

Balée, W. (1989) 'The culture of Amazonian forests', in Balée, W. and Posey, D. (eds) *Natural Resource Management by Indigenous and Folk Societies of Amazonia*, Advances in Economic Botany Monograph Series, vol 7, NY Botanical Garden, New York, pp1–21

Bennett, A. F. (2003) *Linkages in the Landscape: The Role of Corridors and Connectivity in Wildlife Conservation*, IUCN, Gland

Brewer, C. (2002) 'Outreach and partnership programmes for conservation education where endangered species conservation and research occur', *Conservation Biology*, vol 16, no 1, pp4–6

Brockington, D. (2009) *Celebrity and the Environment: Fame, Wealth and Power in Conservation*, Zed Books, London

Brockington, D. and Scholfield, K. (2010) 'The work of conservation organisations in sub-Saharan Africa', *Journal of Modern African Studies*, vol 48, no 1, pp1–33

Bryant, R. L. (2009) 'Born to be wild? Non-governmental organisations, politics and the environment', *Geography Compass*, vol 3/4, pp1540–1558

Büscher, B. (2010) 'Anti-politics as political strategy: Neoliberalism and transfrontier conservation in southern Africa', *Development and Change*, vol 41, no 1, pp29–51

BusinessWeek (2008) 'The 50 Top American Givers', http://images.businessweek.com/ss/08/11/1124_biggest_givers/10.htm, accessed 2 June 2010

Butler, T., Vizcaíno, A. and Brokaw, T. (2010) *Wildlands Philanthropy: The Great American Tradition*, Earth Aware, San Rafael, CA

Carnegie, A. (2006) *The 'Gospel of Wealth' Essays and Other Writings*, Penguin, New York

Castree, N. and Braun, B. (2001) (eds) *Social Nature: Theory, Practice and Politics*, Blackwell, Oxford

Centre for Philanthropical Studies, (2010), 'Giving in The Netherlands 2009', www.giving.nl, accessed 28 November 2010

Charity Vault (no date) 'Environment charities and non-profit organizations in Japan', www.charity-charities.org/Environmental/Japan, accessed 20 July 2010

Chronicle of Philanthropy (2010) 'Giving trends at big foundations', http://philanthropy.com/premium/stats/foundation/main.php?program, accessed 8 February 2011

Delfin, F. G. and Tang, S. (2007) 'Elitism, pluralism, or resource dependency: Patterns of environmental philanthropy among private foundations in California', *Environment and Planning A*, vol 39, no 9, pp2167–2186

Dowie, M. (2009) *Conservation Refugees: The Hundred-year Conflict between Global Conservation and Native Peoples*, MIT Press, Boston, MA

Duffy, R. (2000) *Killing for Conservation. Wildlife Policy in Zimbabwe*, James Currey, Oxford

Duffy, R. (2006) 'The potential and pitfalls of global environmental governance: the politics of transfrontier conservation areas in southern Africa', *Political Geography*, vol 25, pp89–112

Everatt, D. and Solanki, G. (2008) 'A nation of givers? Results from a national survey of social giving', in Habib, A. and Maharaj, B. (eds) *Resource Flows for Poverty Alleviation and Development in South Africa*, Human Sciences Research Council Press, Pretoria, pp45–78

Fairhead, J. and Leach, M. (1996) *Misreading the African Landscape*, Cambridge University Press, Cambridge

Fenger, J. (2009) 'Air pollution in the last 50 years – from local to global', *Atmospheric Environment*, vol 43, pp13–22

Ferreira, J. A. (2009) 'Unsettling orthodoxies: Education for the environment/for sustainability', *Environmental Education Research*, vol 15, pp607–620

Fien, J., Scott, W. and Tilbury, D. (2001) 'Education and conservation: Lessons from an evaluation', *Environmental Education Research*, vol 7, no 4, pp379–395.

Flesch, A. D., Clinton, W. E., Cain, J. W., Clark, M., Krausman, P. R. and Morgart, J. R. (2009) 'Potential effects of the United States–Mexico border fence on wildlife', *Conservation Biology*, vol 24, pp171–181

Giordano, M. (2009) 'Global groundwater? Issues and solutions', *Annual Review of Environmental Resources*, vol 34, pp53–78

Hanks, J. (2003) 'Transfrontier conservation areas in southern Africa: Their role in conserving biodiversity, socio-economic development and promoting a culture of peace', *Journal of Sustainable Forestry*, vol 17, no 1, pp127–148

Heimlich, J. E. (2010) 'Environmental education evaluation: Reinterpreting education as a strategy for meeting mission', Evaluation Programme Planning, vol 33, pp180–185

Hilty, J., Lidicker, W. and Merenlender, A. (2006) *Corridors Ecology: The Science and Practice of Linking Landscapes for Biodiversity Conservation*, Island Press, Washington DC

Hollingshead, J. L. (1997) 'Conservation easements: a flexible tool for land preservation', *Environmental Lawyer*, vol 3, pp319–361

International Finance Team, (2006) *Philanthropic Foundations: Actual Versus Potential Role in International Development Assistance*, World Bank Development Prospects Group (DECPG), Washington DC

IUCN (International Union for Conservation of Nature) (2003) *Proceedings of the Fifth World Parks Congress*, IUCN, Gland

IUCN (2010) 'About IUCN', www.iucn.org/about/, accessed 16 July 2010

Jacobson, S. K. and McDuff, M. (1998) 'Training idiot savants: The lack of human dimensions in conservation biology', *Conservation Biology*, vol 12, no 2, pp263–267

Jin, L., Zhiyun, O. and Hong, M. (2010) 'Environmental attitudes of stakeholders and their perceptions regarding protected area-community conflict: A case study of China', *Journal of Environmental Management*, vol 91, pp2254–2262

Kabii, T. and Horwitz, P. (2006) 'A review of landholder motivations and determinants for participation in conservation covenanting programmes', *Environmental Conservation*, vol 33, pp11–20.

Kiesecker, J. M., Comendant, T., Grandmason, T., Gray, E., Hall, C., Hilsenbeck, R., Kareiva, P., Lozier, L., Naehu, P., Rissman, A., Shaw, M. R. and Zankel, M. (2007) 'Conservation easements in context: a quantitative analysis of their use by The Nature Conservancy', *Frontiers in Ecology and the Environment*, vol 5, no 3, pp125–130

Leibenath, M., Blum, A. and Stutzriemer, S. (2010) 'Transboundary cooperation in establishing ecological networks: the case of Germany's external borders', *Landscape and Urban Planning*, vol 94, pp84–93

Littledyke, M. (2008) 'Science education for environmental awareness: Approaches to integrating cognitive and affective domains', *Environmental Education Research*, vol 14, pp1–17

McCann, J. (1999) *Green Land, Brown Land, Black Land: An Environmental History of Africa, 1800–1990*, James Currey, Oxford

McLaughlin, N. A. (2002) 'The role of land trusts in biodiversity conservation on private land', *Idaho Law Review*, vol 38, pp1–69

McLaughlin, N. A. (2004) 'Increasing the tax incentives for conservation easement donations – a responsible approach', *Ecology Law Review*, vol 31, pp1–115

Merenlender, A. M., Huntsinger, G., Guthey, S. and Fairfax, K. (2004) 'Land trusts and conservation easements: Who is conserving what for whom?' *Conservation Biology*, vol 18, no 1, pp65–76.

Milgroom, J. and Spierenburg, M. (2008) 'Induced volition: Resettlement from the Limpopo National Park, Mozambique', *Journal of Contemporary African Studies*, vol 26, no 4, pp435–448

The Nature Conservancy (no date) www.nature.org/wherewework/northamerica/states/wisconsin/preserves/art28210.html, accessed 8 February 2011

The Nature Conservancy (2001) *Private Land Management and Conservation: A Guide to Organizations*, The Nature Conservancy, Arlington

Nash, R. F. (2001) *Wilderness and the American Mind*, 4th Edition, Yale University Press, Yale

Neel, F. G. (1947) 'Conservation in education', *The Phi Delta Kappan*, vol 28, no 6, pp247–249

Novellino, D. and Dressler, W. H. (2010) 'The role of 'hybrid' NGOs in conservation and development of Palawan Island, The Philippines', *Society & Natural Resources*, vol 23, no 2, pp165–180

O'Garra, T. (2009) 'Bequest values for marine resources: How important for indigenous communities in less-developed economies', *Environmental & Resource Economics*, vol 44, pp179–202

Peace Parks Foundation (no date a) 'southern African Peace Parks', www.peaceparks.org/Parks_1022100000_0_0_0_0_0_Parks/htm, accessed 13 October 2010

Peace Parks Foundation (no date b) 'southern African Wildlife College', www.peaceparks.org/Content_1050100000_SA+Wildlife+College.htm, accessed 14 October 2010

Peace Parks Foundation (1997) *Annual Report*, Peace Parks Foundation, Stellenbosch

Pulsford, I., Worboys, G., Gough, J. and Shephered, T. (2003) 'A potential new continental-scale conservation corridor for Australia: Combining the Australian Alps and the Great Escarpment of Eastern Australia conservation corridors', *Mountain Research and Development*, vol 23, pp291–293

Ramutsindela, M. (2004) *Parks and People in Postcolonial Societies: Experiences in Southern Africa*, Kluwer and Springer, Dordrecht

Ramutsindela, M. (2007) *Transfrontier Conservation in Africa: At the Confluence of Capital, Politics and Nature*, CABI, Wallingford

Satterthwaite, D. (2003) 'The links between poverty and the environment in urban areas of Africa, Asia and Latin America', *Annals of the American Academy of Political Science*, vol 590, pp73–92

Saunders, C. (1996) 'Conservation covenants in New Zealand', *Land Use Policy*, vol 13, pp325–329

Schear, P. and Blaine, T. W. (no date) *Land Trusts CDFS-1262-98*, Ohio State University, Ohio

Schwinn, E. (2008) 'Congress extends tax break for land-conservation gift', http://philanthropy.com/article/Congress-Extends-Tax-Break-for/60842, accessed 14 October 2010

Sierra Club (2011) 'Homepage', www.sierraclub.org, accessed 8 February 2011

Spierenburg, M. and Wels, H. (2006) 'Securing space: Mapping and fencing in transfrontier conservation in Southern Africa', *Space & Culture*, vol 6, no 3, pp294–312

Van Aarde, R. J. and Jackson, T. P. (2007) 'Megaparks for metapopulations: Addressing the causes of locally high elephant numbers in southern Africa', *Biological Conservation*, vol 134, pp289–297

Walsh, D. (1999) 'Redwoods to Sea conservation corridor: Applied philanthropy helps unite over 130,000 acres', *Wild Earth*, vol 9, no 3, pp31–33

Weaver, C. and Petersen, T. (2008) 'Namibia communal areas conservancies', in Baldus, R. D., Damm, G. R. and Wolscheid, K. U. (eds) *Best Practices in Sustainable Hunting. A Guide to Best Practices from Around the World*, International Council for Game and Wildlife Conservation (CIC), CIC Technical Series Publication no 1, pp48–52

Wels, H. (2003) *Private Wildlife Conservation in Zimbabwe. Joint Ventures and Reciprocity*, Brill, Leiden

Wolmer, W. (2007) *From Wilderness Vision to Farm Invasions: Conservation and Development in Zimbabwe's South-east Lowveld*, James Currey, Oxford

Worster, D. (2008) *A Passion for Nature. The Life of John Muir*, Oxford University Press, Oxford

WWF (World Wide Fund for Nature) (no date a) 'How healthy is our planet?', www.wwf.panda.org, accessed 16 July 2010

WWF (no date b) 'WWF's mission, guiding principles and goals', www.wwf.panda.org/mission_principles_goals/cfm, accessed 16 July 2010

Wyner, Y. and DeSalle, R. (2010) 'Taking the conservation biology perspective to secondary school classrooms', *Conservation Biology*, vol 24, pp649–654

Young, M. (2008) 'From conservation to environment: The Sierra Club and the organizational politics of change', *Studies in American Political Development*, vol 22, pp183–203

Zimmerer, K. S., Galt, R. E. and Buck, M. V. (2004) 'Globalization and multi-spatial trends in the coverage of protected area conservation (1980–2000)', *Ambio*, vol 30, pp520–529

3

The South–North Connections

INTRODUCTION

In the previous chapters we argued that philanthropy should be understood as an impulse that is expressed in various forms and performed through channels that are dynamic and context specific. These channels are in turn embedded in complex relationships among individuals and between individuals and institutions/organizations. That is to say, understanding philanthropy and its flows demands that we should pay attention to both the motive of the giver as well as the global project in which the gift fits and feeds into, where this is applicable – not all gifts have this global dimension. Nowhere is the global context of the gift clearer than in sponsorships during the Cold War. Without over-generalizing, it is unlikely that high-profile philanthropy from the capitalist West turned a blind eye to the spread of communism. This is precisely the point we make in this chapter: the sponsorship for conservation in southern Africa became indistinguishable from the fight against communism in the region. We do not make this statement to suggest that the support for conservation projects in the region was motivated by anti-communist sentiments from the start. To do so would be to ignore a rich environmental history that predates the outbreak of the Cold War (see Beinart and Coates, 1995; Grove, 1995; Chapter 7). Our point is rather that Cold War geopolitics in the region provide a useful platform on which we can interrogate the geopolitics of conservation and its sponsorship. It is also a useful lens through which we can understand the web of interests among actors who were spread across continents, yet unified by a common vision for, and also imageries of, a southern Africa. More specifically, like-minded elites pursued conservation and political goals as two sides of the same coin. We use the case of Nick Steele in present-day KwaZulu-Natal (South Africa) to demonstrate this.

WORLD SYSTEMS THEORIES AND ELITE NETWORKING

Much of the writings on the connections between the South and North are informed by world systems theories and their variants. It is not our intention to engage with these theories here. However, we refer to them to highlight the importance of thinking about philanthropy in the context of the South–North power asymmetries. When the neo-Marxist dependency and world system theories were popular in the 1960s and 1970s, it seemed clear that the countries in the northern hemisphere were to be considered 'centre' and the countries in the southern hemisphere as 'periphery' (Gunder Frank, 1967; Wallerstein, 1974). It was an unequal power relation between the two, in which the capitalist North economically exploited the poor South to an extent that it was argued that the centre actively underdeveloped the periphery. In the unequal power relations between South and North, the periphery was only left with serving the centre with cheap raw materials, in the process sustaining the status quo (cf. Rodney, 1973). Nevertheless, developing the South was considered important by the North in order to prevent the South being overtaken by communism after World War II. This line of thinking led in Asia, for instance, to the development by a group of Commonwealth nations of the so-called Colombo Plan (as they gathered for this occasion in the capital of Sri Lanka). This plan entailed negotiations between industrial nations from the 'centre' and Asian countries in the 'periphery' to come to bilateral aid agreements (Brawley, 1995). The resulting economic development was to keep these countries away from the ideological seductions of communism. It was a time when the world in a way seemed almost conveniently and orderly organized in two rival camps, with a big divide in between that no one could pass without deflecting and betraying one's background. World systems theory, however, does not take elite networks into account in its analysis of the relationships between regions of the world. It pays less attention to elites and the power they have in shaping world futures, and is also silent on how the periphery 'talks back' and influences and challenges the centre through its own elites (Hannerz, 1992).

It is undeniable that some countries in the world are richer than others. It is also undeniable that many of the poorer countries are still geographically located in the southern hemisphere. In that sense we acknowledge this South–North divide in the world, but at the same time we are sceptical of the suggested separateness of the two blocks. Our scepticism is fed by classical elite theorists such as Vilfredo Pareto, Robert Michels, Wright Mills and Robert Putnam, who postulate that it is a relatively small number of people from the economic elite and policy planning networks, who heavily influence the directions and fate of policy processes in the world (Wright Mills, 1956; Putnam, 1976). Crucial in this perspective is not only that elites are influential, but also the notion that they exert this influence independently from state processes. In other words, they constitute a parallel universe to the state, far less visible but, according to elite theories, basically independent of and superior in influence to the official power bearers of the nation state.

Philanthropic foundations participating in or financing policy think tanks and other meeting places of elite networks are attributed an important role in elite theory (Faber and McCarthy, 2005). An example of this participation of philanthropic foundations in powerful elite gatherings is the annual Bilderberg conference. The first one was held in 1954 in the Bilderberg Hotel in Oosterbeek in the Netherlands, from which it derives its name, and was presided over by the late Prince Bernhard of the Netherlands, who had married Princess and later Queen Juliana of the Netherlands in 1937. The Bilderberg conferences, which continue to be organized, are meant as an annual meeting place for the highest ranking officials from the corporate sector, politics, media and royalty, to discuss current political and economic affairs, and any other subject of any significance to developments worldwide. Although the Bilderberg conferences do not have permanent members and participation is by invitation only, it is interesting to note that, for instance, David Rockefeller heir to the Rockefeller fortunes made in oil and banking and a world-renowned philanthropist (Hoffman, 1971) attended all the Bilderberg conferences between 1954 and 2006 (Aalders, 2007). Also the 'Ford Foundation has been part of the Bilderberg network right from the start' (Aalders, 2007, p34). John McCloy, president of the World Bank between 1947 and 1949 and chairman of Chase Manhattan Bank (part of the Rockefeller empire) between 1953 and 1960, was a trustee of the Rockefeller Foundation between 1946 and 1949 and between 1953 and 1958, and after that became the chairman of the Ford Foundation (Bird, 1992). The CIA (Central Intelligence Agency) financed the first Bilderberg conference in 1954. The first conferences were organized at a time when the transatlantic bonds were cooling after the end of World War II and in which plans for a united Europe were not met with much enthusiasm – much to the dislike of the Americans, who wanted a united Western Europe as a shield against the threat of communism. The Bilderberg meetings were basically meant to bridge the divide and bring a united Europe closer to realization, hence the CIA's interest in them. The Ford Foundation and Carnegie Endowment for International Peace later partly took over financing of the conferences (Aalders, 2007). In other words, philanthropic foundations have been part and parcel of elite networks and have been instrumental in getting them together around the world.

In relation to environmental philanthropy, the example of the Bilderberg network is of particular significance because of the involvement of Prince Bernhard, as he has also been deeply engaged with nature conservation through WWF International, of which he was president between 1962 and 1976. Together with his lifelong Afrikaner friend in South Africa, business tycoon Anton Rupert, Prince Bernhard developed the concept of the '1001 Club' in 1970. The club was meant to attract 1000 wealthy people from around the globe to donate $10,000 to help WWF cover its overhead costs. Member number 1001 was Prince Bernhard himself. It will probably not come as a surprise that many of its members consisted of persons from the banking sector, other business sectors, intelligence, the military and heads of states, i.e. the networks that also participated in the Bilderberg conferences (Aalders, 2009). Furthermore, quite a number of the members were part of the South African business sector that officially was the subject of a UN boycott (Spierenburg and Wels, 2010). The South and the North were here connected through philanthropy in a particular way. Both Prince Bernhard and Anton Rupert remained active in nature conservation and philanthropy until the very end of their lives. Prince Bernhard passed away in 2004, aged 93, and Anton Rupert in 2006, aged 90. Prince Bernhard and Anton Rupert also started the Peace Parks Foundation (PPF) in 1997, the major lobby organization for transfrontier conservation in South(ern) Africa (Ramutsindela, 2007). Again, they established a network of wealthy individuals, this time called the '21 Club', for which every member has to donate €1,000,000 (see Spierenburg and Wels, 2006, 2010, for further details).

The particular linkages between (parts of) the global Bilderberg elite network and wildlife conservation through the presidency of Prince Bernhard of WWF International, and the explicit links of WWF International to South Africa in the field of environmental philanthropy, make South Africa a particular strong case in point for exploring historical South–North connections in philanthropy. Although South Africa may seem a rather particularistic case because of apartheid and the special conditions that this system created for South Africa's position in the geopolitical world, it is at the same time a telling case of the (ethical) complexities involved in environmental philanthropy, especially when trying to interpret this type of philanthropy in terms of 'doing good' or 'doing harm' (and to what and whom) (see Chapter 1). 'Old fashioned' world system theory, blended with more recent theories on elite pacting and empirically founded on cases of longstanding and mutual relations in environmental philanthropy between people from 'the South' and 'the North' will further add to our careful assessment of environmental philanthropy as a Janus face (see Chapter 1). But before we present and explore the cases in this chapter in more detail and present our argument, it is necessary to explicate how we deal with the dangers of crossing the sometimes thin line between 'good science' and being carried away on the seducing waves of 'conspiracy theories'. How do we cope scientifically with the shrouds of secrecy that are part and parcel of the type of global elite networks that we describe? We do realize that the cases we describe here may be considered rather controversial, and for that reason not very representative of the general, common and everyday interactions in the field of environmental philanthropy. Then why do we deliberately focus on the controversial end of the spectrum? Part of the answer is that elsewhere in the book we do pay attention to the more everyday experiences and cases, and for that reason it might be considered balanced to analyse some more 'extreme' cases in this chapter to build our conclusions about the ambiguity of environmental philanthropy.

'Good Science' or 'Conspiracy Theories'?

One of the biggest dangers in writing about the type of elite networks and initiatives described above is that readers may accuse the authors of creating, participating or contributing to conspiracy theories. What adds to this sentiment is that many of these networks are shrouded in secrecy. Membership lists are often not publically available, and hardly ever are there minutes or well-structured reports of what is discussed at these meetings. Together this gives rise to all kinds of interpretations and often exaggerations of the influence and meanings of these elite networks for world affairs, political decision making and economic developments. Both Bilderberg and the 1001 Club have given rise to a multitude of conspiracy interpretations, in books but also on many internet forums (for instance, Estulin, 2007, on the Bilderberg; Beame, 2010, on the 1001 Club).

What exactly to consider a 'conspiracy theory' is not easy though. What we refer to here as examples of conspiracy theory can also be considered as 'excavations' and 'discoveries' of what is 'really happening' behind veils of secrecy. What complicates things further in distinguishing conspiracies from 'solid science' is that one of the key characteristics of a 'good conspiracy' is its 'academic credibility' (Aaronovitch, 2009, p5). In other words, a 'good conspiracy' may be difficult to disentangle from 'good science'. A 'good conspiracy' gives the reader lots of undifferentiated detail. All this detail from various more or less reliable sources is all similarly presented as 'indisputable truths' and presented as relevant and particularly crucial to understanding what 'really' happened. The footnotes to the argument indicate the finest details are almost too many to keep up with, an approach aptly described as 'death by footnote' (Aaronovitch, 2009, p12). If, on top of all this, the argument is presented to the reader in academic text-like formats, chances are considerable that many readers are seduced into accepting (at least parts of) the argument. It is therefore not surprising that '[it] has typically been the professors, the university students, the artists, the managers, the journalists and the civil servants who have concocted and disseminated the conspiracies'(Aaronovitch, 2009, p291). What might be key to distinguishing 'good science' from 'seductive conspiracy' is that which Aaronovitch presents as a kind of working definition of conspiracy theories: 'the attribution of deliberate agency to something that is more likely to be accidental or unintended' (Aaronovitch, 2009, p5). As scientists, the definition warns us, we must obviously be careful not to jump to firm conclusions too easily and try to explain as much as possible. Despite agency, plotting, networking and lobbying for certain outcomes in and through elite networks, social processes most of the time follow and develop unanticipated, unintended and coincidental paths and 'realities'. It is on this basis that we see the links between nature conservation and the anti-communism agenda in southern Africa as something that was not built into the initial enthusiasm for nature conservation in the region. Instead, the links emerged later from the need to ward off the spread of communism in the region.

What we are saying here is that there is a certain danger of falling into 'the conspiracy theory trap' in almost any interpretation of the influences and workings of (elite) networks in social and ideological processes. Especially the domain and types of networks that we are involved with in this book and the various names of well-known business and political people from around the world attached to them, lend themselves easily to accusations of conspiracy thinking. Nevertheless, despite Aaronovitch's warning against the seductions of conspiracy theories, he ends his book describing various conspiracy theories, mainly focusing on the Anglo Saxon world, and quoting Sam Smith saying that there is maybe still more to conspiracy theories than meets the eye if we read conspiracy theories the way a poet reads myths: 'the poet understands that a myth is not a lie but the soul's version of the truth' (Aaronovitch, 2009, p295).

With this quote in mind we can now turn our attention to the question of South–North relations, focusing on South Africa once more for reasons given in the introduction to this chapter. This is an interesting case because there is a particular moment in time when the relations between South Africa and the North changed considerably, which also had its major consequences for philanthropic relations between South and North in the field of nature conservation. This moment is the year 1994, when Nelson Mandela became the first democratically chosen black president of South Africa. Before that time and under apartheid, South Africa was one of the world's pariah states, isolated and excluded from almost all mainstream global and international activities ranging from a cultural and sports boycott to an economic boycott – though as will be shown below, this pertained far less to the domain of nature conservation. This all changed with the inauguration of Nelson Mandela on 10 May 1994, after which South Africa went across its borders into the world with confidence and an entrepreneurial spirit.

With a nose for branding and marketing, Anton Rupert, together with a globally networked Prince Bernhard started the PPF in 1997, with Nelson Mandela as its patron. The official launch took place at Palace Soestdijk in the Netherlands. Elite networks from the anti-apartheid struggle and old business networks from apartheid days came together in the superstructure of the PPF, the major promotion and executive institution of transfrontier conservation in southern Africa. It was a matter of 'elite pacting' as Draper et al (2004) argue (following Carmody's 2002 conceptualization), the cause of stimulating cross-border nature conservation bringing the old and new networks together. Not only the cause of nature conservation was important for this elite pacting, but physical nature in turn played an important role in creating the atmosphere and environment where former antagonists could meet and approach each other in an informal way. There is the now famous story of a fishing trip by Cyril Ramaphosa with the Nationalist Party's Roelf Meyer in 1992 when the Kempton Park negotiations about the transition from apartheid to democratic rule seemed to have come to a deadlock. Nature provided a way of bonding between the men, who discovered their mutual love for fishing, and their informal discussions resulted in the two men getting the peace process on the road again (Draper, 2002). This form of elite pacting in the political sphere through and in nature conservation coincided with elite pacting in the economic sphere (Bond, 2000). 'An increasing number of prominent ANC negotiators ended up joining the companies of members of the white business elite who also participated in the negotiations' (Draper et al, 2004, p344). The elite pacting at various levels and in various domains in South Africa also gave a particular twist to the South and North dimension of philanthropic giving for nature conservation, as it brought former antagonists together.

One of the first initiatives that Nelson Mandela took when he became the first democratically elected president of South Africa in 1994 was to ask a commission in October 1994 'to inquire into the alleged smuggling of ivory and rhino horn, particularly of Angolan and Mozambican origin, to and through South Africa' (Beame, 2010). The commission was led by Mr Justice Kumleben from whom the commission derived its name. The inquiry was to a large extent fuelled by allegations that the South African Defence Force (SADF) had been involved in large-scale ivory and rhino horn poaching. The Kumleben commission was able to verify these allegations, and concluded, among other things, that:

- *The SADF was directly involved in dealing in ivory and probably rhino horn from mid-1978 to the beginning of 1980.*
- *In 1980, the SADF established a front company called Frama which engaged in smuggling ivory and no doubt rhino horn from Angola to South Africa until about 1986. The SADF ensured that Frama vehicles were not searched on their journey through Namibia to South Africa. The SADF continued to transport ivory by air to South Africa during this period.*
- *The Military Intelligence Division was responsible for the above activities'.* (Cock, 1998)

In other words, the military had been responsible for reckless environmental destruction in the region of southern Africa (see also Ellis, 1994). It was condoned because it fitted very well with South Africa's destabilization policies with regards to its neighbouring states, as 'poaching and anti-poaching formed central elements in South Africa's destabilization programme' (Duffy, 2000). The WWF, in which Prince Bernhard and Anton Rupert were heavily involved, was also implicated in this particular configuration through Operation Lock, which we have extensively described and politically contextualized elsewhere (Spierenburg and Wels, 2010). This anti-poaching operation, through hiring British mercenaries to infiltrate the ivory and rhino horn networks, seemed to have become part and parcel of apartheid's counterinsurgency operations in the region. Why did Nelson Mandela, very much aware of this history, and known for his integrity and uncompromising principles, agree to become patron of Rupert and Bernhard's PPF in 1997?

It is widely known that Nelson Mandela had done his utmost best to integrate former antagonists into post-apartheid South African society, as is evident from the Truth and Reconciliation Commission, but to move from there to becoming a patron of PPF seems to stretch the principles of reconciliation a little too far. At least part of the reason could be that one of the main Dutch sponsors of the PPF, the Postcode Lottery, promised the Mandela Children Fund 500,000 guilders per year if he would become patron of the PPF (Bosman, 2007). Perhaps this seduced Nelson Mandela to join hands with former political opponents and to become almost the embodiment and convincing evidence of the 'elite pacting' in the new South Africa as described by Carmody (2002). It also shows once more that it is not possible to interpret the South–North dimension in philanthropic giving in simple bipolar terms. The South–North relation is a multi-faceted and ever dynamic and changing configuration of networks that link up and split up, depending on contexts. These configurations are too complex to judge only in terms of good and bad. This holds for the example of Mandela joining the PPF as described here, but also applies, for instance, to the role that military orientations play in nature conservation in general and in South–North relations in philanthropy in particular.

With 'the military' we refer here to both the military in South Africa and its role in nature conservation in South and southern Africa during the years of apartheid, but also to the broader military establishment in the North that was at the same time involved in combating communism all around the world. In this combination of the military protecting the apartheid regime, supporting the anti-apartheid struggle and struggling against communism, the boundaries between the various 'wars' that were being fought became intertwined and blurred. It is too easy to condemn anything the military in both the North and in South Africa did during the years of apartheid. Nonetheless, taking a nuanced perspective on the role of the military in South Africa during apartheid should not be construed as our appreciation of 'the good things' that the military did. On the contrary, our approach is to go beyond the simple dualism of good and bad. Our attempt here is to emphasize the need to understand the complexities of the South–North linkages through the lens of philanthropic giving for nature conservation, and to incorporate the broader global concerns at a given time in our analysis. In order to understand the role of the South African military in relation to nature conservation, we also look at the broader military context during the Cold War years, especially the widespread western fears of the communist threat and the socialist world economy that that ideology could bring about. An elaborate example is given here on the basis of empirical material presented for the very first time, concerning a well-known, controversial but at the same time influential conservationist in Natal and Zululand (now KwaZulu-Natal) in the 1970s and 1980s, Nick Steele. In order to understand the context in which Nick Steele was operating in South Africa, it is necessary to present Steele's ideas and actions in a rather extensive case study. It is furthermore necessary to paint a detailed picture in order to elucidate the intricacies and complexities of the South–North dimension in philanthropy and its relation to global military concerns and contexts.

NICK STEELE (1933–1997):
CONSERVATIONIST AND ANTI-COMMUNIST[1]

Nick Steele's life as a conservationist can be sketched on the basis of his involvement with the conservation and protection of the rhinoceros. At the beginning of his career, as a young game ranger in Umfolozi in the late 1950s and 1960s, he became the right hand man of Ian Player in one of the most ambitious rhino conservation projects then seen, Operation Rhino. Ian Player is considered one of South Africa's most famous conservationists, held responsible for saving the white rhino, but also celebrated as the great inspirational leader behind such initiatives as the Wilderness Leadership School and the World Wilderness Congresses.[2] In his book describing Operation Rhino, Ian Player (1972) refers to Steele all the time. In his report of a visit to a conference in San Diego on the role of zoos in international conservation of wild animals in 1966, Player mentions Steele first in his acknowledgements (Player, unpublished). They were obviously both equally committed to saving the rhino. Key to the whole operation was translocating rhinos from Umfolozi Game Reserve to locations around the globe: zoos in the US, the Netherlands, Portugal, Germany and others; national parks and game reserves elsewhere in Africa; 'Rhinos for Rhodesia' (*Natal Witness*, 1966),[3] and also for Mozambique, Botswana and Kenya; and of course to farms and reserves inside South Africa itself (Player, 1972). Of the various zoos, Ian Player himself considered the translocation and sale of rhinos to San Diego Zoo as the transaction that really got things started in Operation Rhino.[4] Operation Rhino surely 'catapulted the provincial conservationists to fame ... [and] opened global horizons' (Draper, 1998, p806). For Nick Steele this meant an entry into the world and (elite) networks of nature conservation. Not only in the proliferation of the private wildlife conservancy movement from South Africa to its neighbouring countries in the 1990s (cf. Wels, 2003) but throughout Steele's personal career in nature conservation, rhino conservation was key herein.

In the 1990s Steele became a member and chairman of the regional Southern African Development Community (SADC) Rhino Management Group (RMG) founded in 1989 by 19 conservation agencies and NGOs, and of the southern African Rhino and Elephant Security Group (RESG), a subcommittee of the RMG, focusing on security and founded in 1991 (Emslie and Brooks, 1999). The RMG's aim was to help and save the black rhino by implementing the 'Conservation plan for the black rhinoceros in South Africa and Namibia'. The RESG was particularly aimed at 'ensuring maximum cooperation between the conservation and law enforcement agencies' (Emslie and Brooks, 1999). It gave Steele the opportunity to network with all kinds of security-related organizations and security-oriented like-minded people inside and outside South Africa, who all used the discourse of the need for military-style conservation and preservation of Africa's wildlife, and particularly the rhino and elephant.

In terms of the history of ideas, these forums were predated in the 1970s by networks such as the Game Rangers Association (GRA) that gave the possibility to organize international linkages between like-minded military-oriented game rangers across Africa, although most members came from southern Africa.[5] The discourse among the members was constructed around the concept of 'wildlife wars' (cf. Leakey and Morell, 2001), which demanded and almost begged for a military-style answer. In his personal diary, in 1966 Steele already thought of a fitting war song to keep the conservation soldiers, game rangers and game scouts on the march:

> *Onward Conserve Soldiers*
> *Marching as to War*
> *With the Cross of Conservation*
> *Going on Before.*[6]

The GRA was set up in 1970 by Peter Hitchins, who was educated at Potchefstroom Boys High School, joined the Natal Parks Board (NPB) in 1961 and served most of his time in the Hluhluwe and Umfolozi Game Reserves (like Steele), before he was asked to join the research staff of NPB in 1968. His main task was to look at the ecology of the black rhinoceros in Hluhluwe Game Reserve. During the first five years of its existence, the GRA had its headquarters at Ubizane Game Ranch, a private wildlife initiative.[7]

In April 1972 Norman Deane was elected Chairman of the GRA. Steele and Deane knew each other well. As a junior warden at Hluhluwe Game Reserve, Steele was trained and mentored by the very military-like Norman Deane (Steele, 1992). The GRA wrote an occasional newsletter entitled, not surprisingly, *The Game Ranger*, to which Nick Steele was a frequent contributor. One of his contributions shows the ambivalences that have played such an important role in conservation history in southern Africa all along. It shows clearly how nature conservation in southern Africa has always been part and parcel of political agendas (at the time of white minority rule in Southern Rhodesia and South Africa) and how the rhetoric of conservation, and particularly the struggle against poachers often financed by philanthropists from the North, could be used for political ends. In this particular article in *The Game Ranger*, Steele describes how many game rangers in southern Africa have died in conflicts with poachers, who he labels as 'terrorists'. There seems to be only a thin line between anti-poaching activities and fighting the people struggling for democratic representation:

> *The ... modern ranger is the automatic-rifle toting type, adorned with ammunition pouches, who leads sticks [sic] of soldiers through the sizzling bush in search of 'terrs', as they are called. Many of these brave men have died in contacts in Southern Africa in the last decade. Others are still unobtrusively playing their part as game ranger-scouts in Zimbabwe-Rhodesia and South West Africa.* (Steele, 1980)

In communication with one of the game rangers, Willie Wilcox, he continues that 'Willie listed some of the items they require for anti-poaching patrols: an armoured car, FN machine guns, 60mm mortars ... They probably regard a black rhino or elephant charge as light relief from their grim task of confronting poacher-terrorists' (Steele, 1980).

The formulation above seems to suggest that every poacher is a terrorist and vice versa. This seems a major confusion running throughout the GRA: poachers threatening nature and wildlife and 'terrs' threatening the political status quo are considered one and the same person. From this perspective every game ranger is a political activist. In an undated edition of *The Game Ranger*, Derek Tomlinson pays tribute to the game rangers who fought and died in 'the terrorist war' in Rhodesia, actually confirming that anti-poaching operations of game rangers were at the same time politically motivated operations against black insurgents (Tomlinson, no date). He ends his two-page tribute by quoting, in capitals, a poem 'found scrawled in charcoal across a wall in a military base camp':

> *After all have come and gone*
> *We will remain shadows*
> *Of a forgotten past*
> *Those that follow*
> *After we are long forgotten*
> *Will say*
> *Here lived men of substance*
> *Therefore I pray*
> *God bless all sons of Rhodesia*
> *At least we tried, didn't we?*
> *Yet how did we fail*
> *When we were so sincere?* (Tomlinson, no date)

This military bravado, bench marking conservation and anti-poaching operations as part of the political agenda of the white minority regimes in southern Africa, is basically repeated years later when Nick Steele writes again in *The Game Ranger*, congratulating the GRA on its 21st anniversary, remarking that when a conservationist had stated on television that 'Military style game rangers marching up and down, saluting and carrying weapons, should be replaced by social scientists and women ... The Game Rangers Association should have immediately challenged this statement' (Steele, no date). These examples seem to tally with the earlier example we mentioned, where mercenaries from the UK Kilo Alpha Services (KAS) were involved in anti-poaching activities and ended up fighting 'ANC-terrorists' in Operation Lock. It led to a situation in which the logic behind conservation strategies was that to end poaching was to keep the status quo in the region intact; it meant that to fight *for* conservation was to fight *against* any black resistance fighting for equal and democratic rights. This was the unwritten ideological conviction of the type of military networks that Nick Steele got involved in across the world, and for which he attracted philanthropic sponsorship.

What united people in Nick Steele's network was a deep-felt fear of communism to the extent that they superimposed that fear on everything that was happening around them. This was a fear that was also all-consuming in the South African military: 'We soon believed that the good of the country took precedence over individual rights, and that all we had held sacred about our lives was under threat from the evil Communist empire that was brainwashing "our blacks" to raise up against us' (Thompson, 2006, p50). Whatever happened in the region, including in the domain of nature conservation, was only judged in terms of advancing or stopping the march of communism in southern Africa. Nothing could be seen in a detached way from this overriding concern.

Steele was particularly worried about what was happening in Mozambique. In November 1975 he wrote in his diary: 'I have been invited by the 2 i/c [in command] of the Umvote Mounted Rifles, Mr. Selwyn Meyer to accompany him on an inspection of his armoured car regiment camped in the field opposite the Mozambican FRELIMO [Front for the Liberation of Mozambique] border'. Not without a wry sense of humour he finishes this diary entry by saying that '(a)lthough it looks like being a long war against the Communists they will not find us easy to subdue, simply because we have our back to the ocean + it's a damn long swim to England, Holland + India'.[8] When he travels from Kosi Bay to the Mozambican border a month later, in December 1975, he writes in his diary: 'Gazing through the two border fences we saw the Frelimo camp with its civilian + military tents, flag post with Frelimo flag + several soldiers armed with A.K. machine guns. Communism has arrived at our doorstep in all its ugly colours'.[9] No wonder that all the game reserves bordering Mozambique were of particular relevance and interest to Steele and like-minded conservationists. There they could fight and keep the communist enemy at bay. Because of their many years of working together, Steele was probably also influenced by Ian Player's stern anti-communism:

> *[Player] spoke of the march of Communism + MPLA [Popular Movement for the Liberation of Angola] successes, of the ultimate fate of whites in South Africa if the land fell. "They would seek their retribution on us + I'd rather commit suicide than face that". His utterances provided a bleak picture of the future in Southern Africa. While I do not hold such a pessimistic view I feel more strongly by the day that the Afrikaner has led us all into the sea with his blind bloody stupid prejudice'.*[10]

It shows how almost all subjects in the end came together and were judged on the basis of what they did to favour or to stop communism in South Africa.

The African National Congress's (ANC) alliance and close cooperation with the South African Communist Party (SACP) and its worldwide linkages with communist networks supporting the struggle ideologically as well as through the training and provision of weapons to the ANC's armed wing rendered the ANC the ultimate threat to conservative and rather military-oriented conservationists. That is not presented here as an excuse for ignoring its dire consequences of human suffering, but it shows the various layers of complexities that are involved in trying to understand the influences of the South–North dimension of philanthropic money given to conservation in South and southern Africa. It makes clear why certain philanthropic money from the North (i.e. US) found its way to particular spots in the world where the 'threat' or advance of communism was considered greatest, and where anti-communist allies were prepared to try to stop 'the red danger'. Apartheid South Africa was an obvious choice for that money as it is clear from a book (Greig, 1977) of that time, published by the Southern African Freedom Foundation (SAFF), the South African branch of the International Freedom Foundation (IFF), an anti-communist think tank, established in 1986 in Washington DC[11] by lobbyist and businessman Jack Abramoff.[12] On the dust cover of the book the SAFF is presented as:

> *dedicated to the advancement of freedom and democracy in Africa through the creation of greater understanding of the issues and problems confronting the continent. The foundation believes that the economic welfare of all societies can best be served by the free enterprise system, and while it recognizes that inadequacies and lack of freedom do exist in our present systems, it seeks to expose the greater lack of freedom and dangers to the freedom of the individual in other systems – particularly the Communist system.* (Greig, 1977)

The book sketches a picture in which the communists are after world domination and are particularly on the rise on the African continent. The analysis is based on data on the build up of the military arsenal by the Soviets, derived from US military intelligence and North Atlantic Treaty Organization (NATO) sources (which is not surprising given IFF's roots in intelligence networks). But what is most worrying according to this analysis is not just the sheer numbers of weaponry, but the fact that 'the Soviet High Command has been switching the emphasis in its general strategic outlook and tactical doctrines from the defensive to the offensive' (Greig, 1977, p19). Southern Africa is one of the spearheads for this offensive, particularly by supporting what Greig throughout his book calls (between inverted commas), 'Liberation Movements'.

Greig presents the reader with 'Glimpses of some "Liberation Movements" in action'. In it he describes among others the MPLA, ZAPU (Zimbabwe African Peoples Union) and ZANU (Zimbabwe African National Union) in Rhodesia, SWAPO (South West Africa People's Organization), the ANC in South Africa and FRELIMO in Mozambique and their various military wings. Writing about the ANC he says:

> *the most potentially serious activity, thought to involve members of this [ANC] movement, would have seemed to take the form of a small scale guerrilla raid across the frontier from Moçambique into the Eastern Transvaal early in December [1976]. Although involving only four men, the raid was the first of its type and was presumably a consequence of the establishment of guerrilla training and base camps in the southern part of Moçambique with the aid of the South African Communist Party.* (Greig, 1977, p242)

Greig's very last lines of his book could have been written by Steele, as it seems to capture Steele's overriding urge for securing rhinos in South Africa:

> *to believe in the possibility of the birth of a new concert of mutual interest transcending racial issues which will at least point the way to the attaining of genuine freedoms, security, and prosperity for all the people of Africa, whilst holding at bay the efforts of alien Communism to use the 'liberation' of Africa as but a stepping-stone in its own proclaimed goal of world domination.* (Greig, 1977, p334)

Fighting the communists of the ANC also sprang from Steele's close friendship with Mangosuthu Buthelezi and his Inkatha Freedom Party (IFP). Waetjen and Maré summarize the history of Inkatha as follows:

> *The Inkatha National Cultural Liberation movement was formed in 1975. It was not the first campaign to give organisational form to Zulu ethnic nationalism during the twentieth century, nor even the first that was mobilised under the name Inkatha. In the 1920s, prominent isiZulu-speaking intellectuals, businessmen and local leaders established an organisation under the patronage of King Solomon kaDinuzulu. This earlier Inkatha sought to advance a range of political concerns and economic ambitions that were suffering under the assaults of legislated racial segregations and exclusions, beginning with the Act of Union in 1910.* (Waetjen and Maré, 2008, p353)

The ANC and IFP were outright enemies in Natal and the dynamics in that relationship must also have had its influence on Nick Steele. The IFP showed right from the start that it was basically an ethnic-based organization, representing Zulus instead of the whole of the South African population.[13] Nevertheless, 'when Buthelezi and others launched the *new* Inkatha to fight apartheid, this initiative was welcomed by exiled members of the ANC' (Waetjen and Maré, 2008, p354). Yet, within Natal, conflicts between IFP and ANC members continued.

The struggle between IFP and ANC in Natal resulted in tremendous violence and an estimated 11,600 people died because of it (Jeffery, 1997). A further conservative estimate 'is that 25,000 people have suffered injury in the conflict' (Jeffery, 1997, p2). The figure of people fleeing or being displaced because of the conflict is even higher and is estimated to be between 200,000 and 500,000 between 1984 and 1994 (Jeffery, 1997). It is not necessary here to give a complete account or overview of this 'civil war', but some aspects of it are worth mentioning to contextualize Nick Steele's work in conservation and more particularly his friendship with Buthelezi. Going into particular aspects of the fight between the ANC and IFP will clarify why Steele's involvement with the military was not only the result of his own fascination with military history or conviction that an almost military approach to conservation would save his beloved wilderness landscapes and animals. It also shows the alleged inter-linkages between the IFP, more particularly Buthelezi, with the SADF.

For the purpose of our argument it is interesting to note how over the years of the intensifying conflict with the ANC, the IFP became increasingly involved with the South African military (SADF) and police (South African Police, SAP). Despite convincing evidence to the contrary, this involvement has always been denied by Buthelezi, as much as he insisted that his cooperation with the apartheid government in Pretoria was a 'practical necessity, a means of dismantling apartheid from within' (Waetjen and Maré, 2008, p354):

> *Buthelezi has vehemently continued to deny Inkatha's relationship to the SADF, despite findings by the Truth and Reconciliation Commission (TRC) to the contrary. In 2003 he lost the suit he had brought against the TRC, which documents evidence of Inkatha units trained by the SADF in Namibia.* (Waetjen and Maré, 2008, p354)

Buthelezi's close relations with Pretoria and the military gave him tremendous benefits in securing his power base in Zululand, because Pretoria took care of a 'vast police force which buttressed notoriously fragile tribal homeland governments' (Waetjen and Maré, 2008, p354), including Zululand. Obviously, 'Buthelezi never found it easy to resolve the contradictions between sustaining anti-apartheid opposition and accumulating benefits from Pretoria's institutional bodies' (Waetjen and Maré, 2008, p354). The linkages with the defence force led to the procurement of weapons (Jeffery, 1997) and training of IFP youth in the Caprivi strip in Namibia via the SAP and SADF (Jeffery, 1997), which was of direct use in fighting the ANC in the 1980s. It led to accusations by the ANC of SADF and SAP involvement in 'third force' activities in the early 1990s that tried to fuel the conflict between IFP and ANC, in which the IFP was a more than willing participant according to the ANC (Jeffery, 1997). It was particularly the 'third force' activities that very much delayed and interfered with the first general democratic elections in 1994 (cf. Ellis, 1998).

These 'third force' activities coincided with Buthelezi's call for self-protection units (SPUs) (Jeffery, 1997, p391) for which the weapons came via Colonel Eugene de Kock, commander of the Vlakplaas unit of Koevoet (Jeffery, 1997). According to Buthelezi 'the SPUs were being trained "to protect rural communities against ANC-inspired violence"' (Jeffery, 1997, p391, quoting *The Citizen* of 10 November 1993). What becomes clear is that Buthelezi's IFP was probably quite involved with the central apartheid government in Pretoria, the SADF and the SAP. Although we must realize that many of the accusations come from the ANC, many of the issues were later also substantiated by the TRC. The IFP's involvement with the police and military parallels Steele's appreciation of the military; another point of convergence was that both can be situated on the right side of the political spectrum. This probably explains why Steele developed links with the IFP and, following Ian Player, became a friend to Buthelezi.

Nick Steele was part of a conservation network, with strong links to military and intelligence organizations around the world in order to keep communism at bay. These links favoured and served those involved by endowing prestige for their achievements in conservation, as if this concerned a politically neutral common good for mankind. Prince Bernhard for instance, as president of WWF International, awarded its most prestigious award, the Knight in the Order of the Golden Ark, to no less than four South Africans, of which Ian Player was one. The others were Colonel J. Vincent, Rocco Knobel and last but certainly not least Anton Rupert (Halbertsma, 1996). Both Prince Bernhard and Rupert, like Ian Player for that matter, were staunch anti-communists (see Klinkenberg, 1979; Domisse, 2005).

This anti-communist stance and network provided the basis for Steele's network within the military in South Africa, but also with other like-minded people outside the country, such as the 'fiercely anti-communist' Dr Robert Cleaves from the Wilderness Conservancy (WILDCON), which was founded in the US in 1992 (Petter-Bowyer, 2003). The endorsement of the network's anti-poaching programme came in 1993 via the Zoological Society of San Diego (remember that this is the zoo, according to Ian Player, that got Operation Rhino going). At that time, Cleaves was an attorney but he had also been a jet fighter pilot and test pilot for 36 years in the US Air Force. He represented President Ronald Reagan at the transition of Rhodesia to Zimbabwe in 1980, while he was known for his pro-Rhodesia stance (Petter-Bowyer, 2003). Together with Ian Player he was co-founder of the International Wilderness Leadership Foundation in 1974. Since 1968 he had been involved with anti-poaching activities in southern Africa, particularly by using aircraft.

Those in the top echelon of WILDCON are referred to as 'officers' and consist of an airline transport pilot, his wife and a secretary. The board of directors then consisted of five people of which two were retired lieutenant generals from the US Air Force and one retired deputy chief from the Los Angeles Police Department. Finally nine 'distinguished advisors' were listed, among which were Ian Player and Nick Steele. Three other advisors belonged to the highest ranking officials of the NPB in South Africa and the then acting director of the Department of National

Parks and Wildlife Management (DNPWLM) in Zimbabwe (who later became its director). In the foreword of its 1996 dossier WILDCON says that 'its main thrust has been in support of brave men who lay their lives on the line in the day-to-day war against poachers. And when I say "lay their lives on the line", I mean exactly that' (Cleaves, 1996). WILDCON's mission is defined as 'a direct-action foundation that provided hard assets to persons and organizations (governmental and non-governmental) with specific needs that cannot be addressed because funds are lacking', i.e. weapons and aircraft.

The logo of WILDCON speaks of its Air Force links by depicting a stylized Osprey, 'one of the most efficient of aerial hunters', with the motto written under it '*Pamwe Chete*', Shona for 'We are one', or 'all together' or 'forward together' (Cleaves, 1996). These words were the motto for the Selous Scouts in the 1970s, in what was then called Southern Rhodesia, an elite military unit, specifically geared towards and trained for the elimination of what were then considered 'terrorists'. The eponymous Frederick Courteney Selous was a military man and probably the most famous of the white hunters, a man of the wilderness; Selous serves both as a role model and a caricature of the British Empire (cf. Ryan, 1997). He died in Tanzania fighting against the German colonial *Schutztruppen* in 1917. Chapstick describes Selous as 'probably the most shining example of English manhood that the Victorian Empire could field in the Britain of those days' (Chapstick, 1992, p10).

The Selous Scouts were operational in Southern Rhodesia's bush war from 1973 to 1980, when it became independent Zimbabwe. Their charter mentioned: 'The clandestine elimination of terrorists/terrorism both within and without the country' (Serving History, 2011). The notorious Koevoet counter-insurgency unit of the SAP would follow their example later on in the border wars of South Africa in Angola and South West Africa, now Namibia (Stiff, 2004). WILDCON's choice of logo seems to suggest that its approach to those who are considered nature conservation's Enemy Number 1, poachers, is similar to the tactics that were employed by the Selous Scouts and Koevoet in their dealing with communist 'terrs'. WILDCON provided Nick Steele's KwaZulu Bureau of Natural Resources with a light aircraft 'used to patrol remote areas where rhinos and other wildlife have been hardest hit by poachers' (Cleaves, 1996, p2). It also provided the RESG of southern Africa with 14 Ruger rifles.[14] In the second half of the 1990s, WILDCON would also provide semi-automatic rifles to Shamwari Game Ranch, currently the biggest private game ranch in the Eastern Cape, based on the findings of a report by Ian Thomson, coordinator of the RESG of southern Africa, of which Steele was the chairman. To come full circle, the authors learned from a strictly confidential report (of which the authors have a copy) that Nick Steele's Department of Nature Conservation in KwaZulu Natal were giving the full training to the anti-poaching staff of Shamwari.

The involvement by conservationists in the geopolitics of the southern African region during the Cold War illustrates the relevance of context in analysing environmental philanthropy (see Chapter 1). As we have shown in this chapter, conservation activities and the support for nature conservation in the region were not insulated from anti-communism campaigns. Instead, they formed part and parcel of those campaigns, especially when the boundaries between poachers and 'terrorists' were blurred for ideological reasons. The networks that evolved during the Cold War provide further evidence of the influence of the elites on the futures of particular places while remaining outside the state. Most of the operations we have discussed in this chapter were carried out by organizations sometimes only loosely related to the state, and these organizations could operate with the financial support from sources other than the state. The lesson concerning environmental philanthropy here is that channels of philanthropy are characterized by actors and networks that operate across scales. This explains why philanthropic assets can be mobilized and distributed more quickly and sometimes through clandestine channels, as evident in Operation Rhino.

In the next chapter we discuss how ideas about the best ways to deal with the threat of poaching slowly changed. Conservationists increasingly started to realize that war-style confrontations were rather counterproductive, and that increased cooperation with local communities might offer better possibilities for fostering nature conservation. Taking place against the backdrop of the fall of the Berlin Wall and the ensuing fall of communism, the proposed linkages with local communities were interpreted and implemented in line with the increasingly dominant neo-liberal development paradigm.

NOTES

1. This part on Nick Steele is part of a broader research project of one of the authors, based on the personal diaries and archives of Nick Steele. A monograph on Nick Steele's role in particularly fostering *private* wildlife conservation in South and southern Africa is currently under preparation.
2. See for further details www.wild.org
3. They were aiming to translocate 100 rhinos to Rhodesia according to Steele's personal diary entry of 2 December 1966.
4. Interview Ian Player, 29 January 2009. Later see that the San Diego Zoo is an important factor for the philanthropic network and for the money that Nick Steele is able to mobilize for his conservation work.
5. Letter of invitation by Peter Hitchins, 26 February 1970. The first mentioned objective in the letter of invitation to join the GRA was '(t)o create and maintain contact between game rangers in all parts of Africa'.
6. Nick Steele, personal diary entry of 5 July 1966. Before and after the text is adorned with two music notes to indicate that it is a song text. It is based on the tune of the famous Presbyterian song 'Onward Christian Soldiers'.
7. Interview with Ian Player, 29 January 2009.
8. Nick Steele, personal diary, 27 November 1975.

9   Nick Steele, personal diary, 21 December 1975.
10 Nick Steele, personal diary, 17 February 1976.
11 In a *Newsday* article in 1995 (Olojede and Phelps, 1995), the IFF is depicted as a front for intelligence operators, working to prolong apartheid. It was also said in the same article that the IFF was funded by the South African government by $1.5 million a year. Funding was withdrawn by De Klerk in 1992 and its offices were closed down in 1993 (http://en.wikipedia.org/wiki/International_Freedom_Foundation#Funded_by_South_African_government, visited 15 July 2010).
12 Jack Abramoff was later convicted for three criminal felony counts. The SAFF was a follow up of the Democratic International of 1985 held at the UNITA (National Union for the Total Independence of Angola) Headquarters in Jamba, Angola, also organized by Abramoff.
13 'Inkatha's relationship with other anti-apartheid organisations quickly became contentious. The issue of ethnicity became the pivotal source of discord' (Waetjen and Maré, 2008, p354).
14 Letter by Ian Thomson, coordinator of the Rhino and Elephant Security Group Southern Africa to Dr Robert Cleaves, 22 December 1996.

References

Aalders, G. (2007) *De Bilderberg conferenties. Organisatie en werkwijze van een geheim trans-atlantisch netwerk*, Uitgeverij Van Praag, Amsterdam

Aalders, G. (2009) *De prins kan mij nog meer vertellen. Prins Bernhard – feit en fictie*, Uitgeverij Elmar, Rijswijk

Aaronovitch, D. (2009) *Voodoo Histories. The Role of the Conspiracy Theory in Shaping Modern History*, Jonathan Cape, London

Beame, J. (2010) 'De macht achter de macht: de 1001-Club, eugenetica en duistere kant van de milieubeweging', www.anarchiel.com (accessed 14 October 2010)

Beinart, W. and Coates, P. (1995) *Environment and History: The Taming of Nature in the USA and South Africa*, Routledge, London

Bird, K. (1992) *The Chairman. John J. McCloy and the Making of the American Establishment*, Simon & Schuster, New York

Bond, P. (2000) *Elite Transition: From Apartheid to Neoliberalism in South Africa*, Pluto Press, London

Bosman, M. (2007) 'Partnership for a southern Africa or "pre-colonial measures": A study on the Peace Parks Foundation and its corporate supporters', unpublished MA thesis, VU University Amsterdam, Amsterdam

Brawley, S. (1995) *The White Peril: Foreign Relations and Asian Immigration to Australia and North America, 1919–78*, University of New South Wales Press, Sidney

Carmody, P. (2002) 'Between globalisation and (post)apartheid: The political economy of restructuring in South Africa', *Journal of Southern African Studies*, vol 28, no 2, pp255–275

Chapstick, P. H. (1992) *The African Adventurers. A Return to the Silent Places*, St. Martin's Press, New York

Cleaves, R. (1996) *Dossier on Wilderness Conservancy*, Wilderness Conservancy, Los Angeles, CA

Cock, J. (1998) Introduction, in Cock, J. and Mckenzie, P. (eds) *From Defence to Development: Redirecting Military Resources in South Africa*, International Development Research Centre, Ottawa, pp1–24

Domisse, E. (in cooperation with Esterhuyse, W.) (2005) *Anton Rupert: A Biography*, Tafelberg Publishers, Cape Town

Draper, M. (1998) 'Zen and the art of garden maintenance: The soft intimacy of hard men in the wilderness of KwaZulu-Natal, South Africa, 1952–1997', *Journal of Southern African Studies*, vol 24, no 4, pp801–828

Draper, M. (2002) 'Going native? Trout and settling identity in a 'rainbow' nation', *Historia*, vol 47, pp55–94

Draper, M., Spierenburg, M. and Wels, H. (2004) 'African dreams of cohesion: Elite pacting and community development in Transfrontier Conservation Areas in southern Africa', *Culture and Organization*, vol 10, no 4, pp341–351

Duffy, R. (2000) *Killing for Conservation: Wildlife Policy in Zimbabwe*, The International African Institute in cooperation with: Weaver Press, Harare; James Currey, Oxford; Indiana University Press, Bloomington

Ellis, S. (1994) 'Of elephants and men: Politics and nature conservation in South Africa', *Journal of Southern African Studies*, vol 20, no 1, pp53–69

Ellis, S. (1998) 'The historical significance of South Africa's Third Force', *Journal of Southern African Studies*, vol 24, no 2, pp261–299

Emslie, R. H. and Brooks, M. (1999) *African Rhinos: Status Survey and Conservation Action Plan*, IUCN/SSC African Rhino Specialist Group, Gland

Estulin, D. (2007) *De ware geschiedenis van de Bilderberg-conferentie*, Kosmos-Z&K Uitgevers, Utrecht, Antwerpen

Faber, F. and McCarthy, D. (eds) (2005) *Foundations for Social Change: Critical Perspectives on Philanthropy and Popular Movements*, Roman & Littlefield, New York

Greig, I. (1977) *The Communist Challenge to Africa*, Southern African Freedom Foundation, Sandton

Grove, R. H. (1995) *Green Imperialism: Colonial Expansion, Tropical Island Edens and the Origins of Environmentalism, 1600–1860*, Cambridge University Press, Cambridge

Gunder Frank, A. (1967) *Capitalism and Underdevelopment in Latin America*, Monthly Review Press, New York

Halbertsma, N. (1996) *Natuurlijk Afrika*, Huis ter Heide, De Gouden Ark

Hannerz, U. (1992) *Cultural Complexity: Studies in the Social Organization of Meaning*, Columbia University Press, New York

Hoffmann, W. (1971) *David: Report on a Rockefeller*, Lyle Stuart, New York

Jeffery, A. (1997) *The Natal Story: 16 Years of conflict*, South African Institute of Race Relations, Johannesburg

Klinkenberg, W. (1979) *Prins Bernhard: een politieke biografie, 1911–1979*, Onze Tijd, Amsterdam

Leaky, R. and Morrell, V. (2001) *Wildlife Wars: My Fight to Save Africa's National Treasures*, St. Martin's Press, Gordonsville

Natal Witness (1966) 'Rhinos for Rhodesia', *Natal Witness*, 10 October 1966, p5, Durban

Olojede, D. and Phelps, T. M. (1995) 'Front for Apartheid', *Newsday*, 16 July

Petter-Bowyer, P. J. H. (2003) *Winds of Destruction: The Autobiography of a Rhodesian Combat Pilot*, Trafford, Victoria

Player, I. (1972) *The White Rhino Saga*, Collins, London

Player, I. (unpublished) *Internal report for Natal Parks Board on the role of zoos in international conservation of wild animals*, October 1966, p1

Putnam, R. D. (1976) *The Comparative Study of Political Elites*, Prentice Hall, Englewood Cliffs

Ramutsindela, M. (2007) *Transfrontier Conservation in Africa: At the Confluence of Capital, Politics and Nature*, CABI, Wallingford

Rodney, W. (1973) *How Europe Underdeveloped Africa*, Tanzanian Publishing House, Dar es Salaam

Ryan, J. R. (1997) *Picturing Empire: Photography and the Visualization of the British Empire*, University of Chicago Press, Chicago

Serving History (2011) 'Selous Scouts', www.servinghistory.com/topics/Selous_Scouts, accessed 5 May 2011

Spierenburg, M. and Wels, H. (2006) '"Securing space". Mapping and fencing in transfrontier conservation in southern Africa', *Space and Culture*, vol 9, no 3, pp294–312

Spierenberg, M. and Wels, H. (2010) 'Conservative philanthropists, royalty and business elites in nature conservation in southern Africa', *Antipode*, vol 42, no 3, pp647–670

Steele, N. (no date), *The Game Ranger*

Steele, N. (1980) 'The game ranger's lot', *The Game Ranger*, February

Steele, N. (1992) *Poachers from the Hills: Norman Deane's Life in Hluhluwe Game Reserve*, Nick Steele, Melmoth

Stiff, P. (2004) *The Covert War: Koevoet Operations in Namibia, 1979–1989*, Galago, Johannesburg

Thompson, J. H. (2006) *An Unpopular War, from Afkak to Bosbefok: Voices of South African Servicemen*, Zebra Press, Cape Town

Tomlinson, D. (no date) 'Rhodesian rangers in the front line', *The Game Ranger*

Waetjen, Th. and Maré, G. (2008) 'Shaka's aeroplane: the take-off and landing of Inkatha, modern Zulu nationalism and royal politics', in Carton, B., Laband, J. and Sithole, J. (eds) *Zulu Identities: Being Zulu, Past and Present*, University of KwaZulu-Natal Press, Scottsville, pp352–362

Wallerstein, I. (1974) *The Modern World System*, Academic Press, New York

Wels, H. (2003) *Private Wildlife Conservation in Zimbabwe. Joint Ventures and Reciprocity*, Brill, Leiden

Wright Mills, C. (1956) *The Power Elite*, Oxford University Press, Oxford

4

Philanthropists, Capitalists and Environmental NGOs

INTRODUCTION

The focus of this chapter is on how the kinds of relationships discussed in Chapter 3 and the changes therein in relation to changing geopolitical circumstances are operationalized through ENGOs and CBOs. These relationships are understood from the vantage point of the intersection between capitalism and conservation which in turn accounts for the growing trend in corporate involvement in nature (Smith, 2007). As we intimated in Chapter 1, the connection between conservation and capital interest has a long pedigree. Renewed scholarly interest in these connections can be ascribed to the intensity of capitalist penetration into nature; an increase in the diversity of forms of capitalist conservation; the mushrooming of sponsored ENGOs; and the belief in market-driven solutions to environmental problems (Brockington and Duffy, 2010). The ways in which capitalism penetrates nature conservation are understood in the context of neo-liberalism. On account of this, and in relation to the need to understand the permutations of global capitalism, a call has been made to reassess case studies from which general trends as well as specific manifestations of capitalism in nature may be comprehended (Castree, 2008a). To this end, Bakker (2005) provides us with concepts that could aid our understanding of neo-liberalized nature: privatization, commercialization and commodification. Given this knowledge of capitalism in nature, how do we explain environmental philanthropy? One way of answering this question is by drawing the links among capitalists, philanthropists and ENGOs and to understand how these links create new capitalist paths or reinforce existing ones.

Generally, there are different views on why the business sector donates funds to an environmental cause. Critics of environmental philanthropy argue that donors are elites who provide funds for creating open spaces, wildlife reserves and wilderness for the enjoyment of the rich. The assumption is that there exists a circle of elites between business and ENGOs, which, in turn, protects the status quo in society. Read from this angle, those ENGOs that call for radical changes that disrupt the interest of the business sector are most likely to fail to garner the support of philanthropic organizations or foundations (see Dryzek, 1996). The view of donors as elites could be ascribed to the adoption of a three-dimensional elite theory, which focuses on the composition, ideologies and impact of foundations. A counterview is that, consistent with pluralists and resource-dependency arguments, the pattern of environmental grant-making results from the donor's perception of the expertise and needs of the recipients rather than from collusion between elites in the foundations and ENGOs (Delfin and Tang, 2007).

Elite Theory Versus Plurality

Determining why people give to certain causes is quite difficult. Numerous surveys have been conducted (see Meijer et al, 2006), yet it is almost impossible to establish whether the answers provided by interviewees are politically correct or whether these truly reflect inner drives – provided the interviewees are conscious of their own motives. This renders theorizing about the motives for philanthropy quite complicated. In Chapter 1 we briefly touched upon this by referring to the debate about philanthropy as either a way to address social inequalities or as a way to maintain the socio-economic status quo. A common critique is that philanthropy serves as a way to promote the interests and dominance of elites (see Roelofs, 2003). Through their giving, philanthropists and the foundations they have established, set the agendas and influence the leadership of NGOs. In environmental philanthropy, attention is drawn to the fact that many of the patrons of environmentalism are drawn from the upper socio-economic strata; this could be referred to as compositional elitism (Delfin and Tang, 2007; cf. Morrison and Dunlap, 1986; see also Chapter 7). In a study published in 1999, Arnold argues that many of the big environmental grants provided by private foundations were allocated to large national environmental lobby groups in the US, whose leadership often overlaps with that of the foundations themselves. Other critics focus on the impact of elitism on environmental philanthropy, and point to the high priority accorded to nature preservation, in particular the focus on the creation of protected areas (see Brockington et al, 2008). Through this conservation strategy, the benefits of nature conservation are distributed to an elite community whose members can afford leisure time and travel away from their urban/industrial workplaces (Morrison and Dunlap, 1986). Indeed, most of the dominant and best-known environmental organizations, such as WWF and the Nature Conservancy, are mainly focusing on habitat and species protection (Chapin, 2004; Brockington et al, 2008), and many of the most influential national organizations in the US show similar concerns (Mitchell et al, 1991). Those who perceive a strong elite influence on environmental organizations argue that organizations or programmes related to other issues, such as pollution and climate change, which may touch directly upon the position of business and industrial elites, will experience difficulties in attracting funding (Dowie, 1996). For instance, in the 1980s, the Ford Foundation, fearing bad publicity from corporations, placed severe restrictions on the cases that could be dealt with by the environmental law firms they financed. It has been argued that this was one of the reasons why environmental litigation gradually became less aggressive and more focused on negotiation (Gottlieb, 1993). Mainstream environmental organizations, furthermore, are accused of ignoring the lack of citizen involvement in the decision making of corporations, regulatory agencies and other non-profit organizations such as the foundations funding them. According to Dowie (2001) this renders mainstream environmental organizations vulnerable to outside influences.

Others, however, point to the development and continued existence of more radical environmental organizations to question this elite perspective on environmental philanthropy, and signal the dramatic rise in grassroots activism – the main subject of this chapter – which according to them is hard to explain by referring to self-serving elites sponsoring nature conservation (Ingram et al, 1997). Morrison and Dunlap (1986) furthermore argue that compositional elitism of environmentalists is exaggerated, citing census data indicating that while environmentalists are typically above average in terms of socio-economic status, few belong to the upper class. These authors propose different perspectives on environmental philanthropy, such as pluralist and resource-dependency perspectives. The pluralist perspective is based on the idea that like-minded individuals will group together to pursue common interests, resulting in a proliferation of groups that are constantly competing and cooperating with each other in pursuit of their particular vision of what constitutes 'good society' (Delfin and Tang, 2007, p2169). Since foundation donors are believed to have diverse interests and motivations, proponents of a pluralist perspective expect giving to be diffused to a wide variety of causes. As a result, a diversity of issues such as air pollution, chemical waste, energy regulation and urban sprawl will also attract donors.

Resource-dependency theory explores how an organization's internal structure and behaviour are shaped by its external social and political context (Pfeffer and Salancik, 1978). Applied to NGOs, the focus often is on how giving influences patterns of accountability and the framing of the issues NGOs try to address (see Edwards and Hulme, 1996). Combining this theoretical perspective with an elite approach would explain how elites could dominate the agendas and problem framing of environmental organizations. Delfin and Tang (2007) however, argue that the resource dependency theory in combination with a pluralist perspective provides an alternative understanding that does more justice to the variety of environmental organizations that are active and actively supported. They argue that a variety of donors is looking to support those organizations they deem most capable of supporting the issues they consider important, and apply different funding strategies for different aspects of these issues.

There is indeed a wide variety of non-profit organizations focusing on environmental and animal-related issues. In the year 2000, the American Internal

Revenue Service recorded nearly 8700 such tax-exempt organizations with annual revenues above $25,000 – organizations with smaller amounts of revenues were not counted (Delfin and Tang, 2007). Nevertheless, it is widely recognized that there is a distinct set of organizations that are most visible and influential in environmental policy debates (Mitchell et al, 1991). Conservation-oriented organizations established in the late 1950s and early 1960s, such as WWF, the Nature Conservancy and the Conservation Foundation, are seen as belonging to the 'environmental establishment' (Delfin and Tang, 2007; see also Brockington et al, 2008; Chapter 7 of this volume). These organizations focus strongly on species and habitat protection and conservation. Their links with national and international policy making circles are quite strong, and legislative lobbying is a major strategy deployed. Furthermore, they favour research and education 'activities which large philanthropic donors have traditionally supported in other fields and which are deemed especially nonthreatening when it comes to environmental conflicts' (Delfin and Tang, 2007, p2172). Some of the organizations established in the late 1960s, early 1970s, such as Greenpeace and Friends of the Earth, have also become part of what are considered mainstream environmental organizations, despite the fact that these have a reputation of being anti-establishment. Bosso (1995) and Brulle (2000) argue that the substantive agendas of these organizations are less radical and quite similar to those of other mainstream organizations. Yet, the inclusion of these groups into the mainstream means that mainstream does not necessarily refer to an ideologically homogeneous group.

Following a pluralist perspective, Delfin and Tang (2007) posit that for national issues, foundations are more likely to fund mainstream national NGOs, for international issues, they turn to mainstream national and international NGOs, while some foundations would indeed be inclined to fund smaller local environmental groups to address issues at the local level. Funding strategies, according to this perspective, also depend on the specific issues addressed. Hence, donors are expected to be more likely to fund established (inter)national professional NGOs to address technically complex environmental subjects, while they would be more likely to support locally or regionally based NGOs when they want to fund grassroots mobilization, community projects or the protection of a local scenic area (Delfin and Tang, 2007). NGOs that have assumed the status of 'nationals' take up a large proportion of funds 'devoted to non-profit environmental advocacy and protection' (Dowie, 2001, p89).

Very few studies have actually tested the different perspectives and hypotheses on donations to environmental organizations. An exception is a study undertaken by Delfin and Tang (2007) in which they looked at patterns of environmental philanthropy in California for the year 2000. Some of their findings appear indeed more consistent with pluralist and resource dependency perspectives. One of the main conclusions of the study is that private foundations did not consistently favour mainstream national environmental organizations; on the contrary, only 11 per cent of grants were allocated to these organizations. However, the mean grant amount received by mainstream organizations was much higher than the mean grant amount allocated to other environmental organizations (Delfin and Tang, 2007). Grants for international issues awarded to mainstream organizations were higher than their share among others. The percentage of national grants awarded to mainstream organizations was also higher than their share among others. Finally, the share of local grants awarded to non-mainstream organizations was higher than that awarded to mainstream organizations. In terms of the environmental subjects addressed, there appeared no differences between funding awarded to mainstream and non-mainstream organizations in relation to land grants. However, grants to address the issue of toxins and waste were slightly more often awarded to non-mainstream organizations, while for atmospheric issues, mainstream organizations received more and higher grants (Delfin and Tang, 2007). These results suggest that 'donors deliberately channel their resources towards organisations with more expertise and competence in the area of giving interest' (Delfin and Tang, 2007, p2182). Nevertheless, one could question the grounds on which they assume that mainstream organizations have more expertise in atmospheric issues or in addressing national and international issues – though access to the national and international policy making circles may indeed be easier for these organizations. Delfin and Tang (2007) do admit that their study does not provide a conclusive proof in favour of a pluralist perspective, because mainstream organizations did indeed receive higher mean grant amounts in all grant categories. In addition, they conclude that arguments forwarded by elite theorists that foundations avoid funding NGOs that tackle more threatening issues appears to be valid for NGOs addressing problems with toxins and waste, yet, it is not true that they ignore all locally focused NGOs. Furthermore, NGOs deploying more confrontational tactics do receive – and are quite dependent on – grants, though Delfin and Tang (2007) do admit that these 'direct action' NGOs often have such small budgets that even small donations form a large share of their budgets.

Apart from the need to avoid looking at foundations and mainstream environmental organizations as ideological homogeneous blocks, McCarthy (2004) also draws our attention to the diversity *within* grant giving foundations. Staff within these foundations responsible for allocating funding quite often have a background in environmental activism, and may find ways to convince fellow staff to fund more radical activist groups. Furthermore, activist groups may also find ways to manoeuvre around some of the procedural restrictions placed on their self-determination by grant giving foundations.

The dependency of environmental organizations on funding provided by foundations also varies. Quite a large part of the environmental organizations' budgets studied by Delfin and Tang was dependent on foundations' and individual grants, about 40 per cent (Delfin and Tang, 2007). This is much higher than the percentages reported in the studies by Snow (1992), who cited 21 per cent, and Brulle (2000), who only quotes 19 per cent. Independent foundations were an important source of funding for the respondents, with 49.6 and 9.7 per cent of them claiming that 'most' or 'all' of their funding came from these foundations (Delfin and Tang, 2007). The study also found that community foundations provide more evenly distributed funds: 79 per cent of the respondents reported receiving some grants from community foundations. Older NGOs showed less dependency on grants and seem over time to have developed more diversified funding strategies (Delfin and Tang, 2007).

Furthermore, some of the mainstream environmental organizations, such as WWF and the African Wildlife Foundation (AWF), also rely very heavily on donations by individual citizens who are not part of the socio-political or economic elite. In some cases, these donations may overshadow other kinds of funding (Brockington et al, 2008). This diversity of funding may curb elite influence on environmental organizations. Bonner (1993) offers a detailed analysis of how in the early 1990s, WWF and AWF drastically reviewed their stance on sustainable use of wildlife and more specifically, their position on whether or not some African countries that had witnessed an increase in elephant populations should be allowed to engage in controlled ivory trading. While initially the organizations entered the debates preceding the negotiations on CITES supporting limited and controlled ivory trading, public outcry in the media and the threat of losing support from their many individual non-elite members, resulted in a change in their position and their advocacy for a total ban on the trade in ivory (Bonner, 1993). Yet, this popular support for the ban also showed a rift between popular support in the North for conservation, and the perceptions of those eking out a living in poor areas rich in wildlife. Gradually, however, acknowledgement of these – mainly but not entirely – southern perspectives on wildlife, led to new approaches to nature conservation, and hence also to new relations between ENGOs, donors and CBOs.

ENGOs, CBOs AND DONORS

While Delfin and Tang (2007) conclude that on the basis of their research it is difficult to favour either an elite or a pluralist perspective, the growth in number and importance of CBOs active in nature conservation may complicate matters further (see also Ingram et al, 1997). Especially since the late 1980s, the larger, 'mainstream' organizations increasingly cooperated with and/or donated funding to CBOs in the wake of the popularity of community-based conservation projects. A full discussion of community-based conservation is given in Chapter 8. For the moment, we focus on the links between conservation projects and donors.

Attempts to incorporate communities into conservation projects gained publicity and popularity in the 1980s. Until then, the protection of species and their habitats – those aspects of nature conservation that receive most funding, as was shown above – tended to exclude local communities. Especially in developing countries, antagonistic relations had often developed between conservationists and members of local communities. The establishment of protected areas had in many cases taken place at the expense of local land rights, and the eviction of local communities had been quite common (Dzingirai, 2004; Brockington and Igoe, 2006; Cernea and Schmidt-Soltau, 2006). In former colonies in Africa and Asia, nature conservation came to be associated with more general colonial policies of exclusion and exploitation (Anderson and Grove, 1987; Grove et al, 1998; Escobar and Alvarez, 1992; see also Chapter 7). In the Americas, conservation strategies sometimes pitted First Nation populations against conservation authorities, while in other cases, First Nation populations sought to conclude alliances with conservationists to protect their land rights from invasions by logging companies or migrating farmers (see Hoberg and Morawski, 2008; Brondizio and Siqueira, 1997). In Europe, as in some parts of North America, the situation was similarly complex, with some local residents opposing conservation authorities in reaction to restrictions placed on natural resource use, while in other cases local communities sided with conservation authorities in opposing encroaching industrial developments (Rootes, 2003). Nevertheless, many conservationists started to realize that antagonism with local residents had negative impacts on the management of protected areas, resulting in high costs to control trespassing, encroachment and poaching. When it became clear that this strategy was counterproductive and had become socially unacceptable, conservation organizations started advocating strategies to generate benefits for communities in proximity of protected areas and sometimes even community participation in the management of these areas (see Adams and Hulme, 2001). This new approach was often referred to as 'moving beyond the fences' and was developed in the wake of the Bali declaration of 1982.

Another important influence was the publication by the Brundtland Commission Report 'Our Common Future' in 1987. The commission was installed in 1983 to address growing concerns over the accelerating deterioration of the human environment and natural resources and the consequences of that deterioration for economic and social development (Brundtland Commission, 1987). The solution was sought through a focus on sustainable development that would allow the use of natural resources but with respect for future generations. The underlying idea was that by allowing local communities to benefit economically from natural resources, they would develop an interest in protecting these resources. In this vein, a number of so-called community-based natural resource management (CBNRM) projects were started, and many of the larger environmental organizations such as WWF and IUCN started to propagate this approach (McNeeley, 1992), so much so, that Adams and Hulme (2001) argue that CBNRM became the dominant narrative in conservation circles from the late 1980s onwards.

In order to implement the new strategy of protected areas outreach and CBNRM projects, public–private partnerships or community–public–private partnerships were promoted (see Ramutsindela, 2007). Especially in developing countries, high hopes were placed on these partnerships. Fakir (2001), then director of IUCN South Africa, initially considered such partnerships of the utmost importance to contribute to both environmental conservation as well as poverty alleviation, though at a later stage he became more critical (Fakir, 2004). Within the region of southern Africa, a number of pioneering initiatives had already been taken and now received political backing and international acclaim. Conservationists in southern Africa were leading the way in this respect with groundbreaking projects in the field of community conservation, such as ADMADE in Zambia (Gibson, 1999), LIFE in Namibia and CAMPFIRE in Zimbabwe (Hulme and Murphree 2001; see also Kiss, 1990). These projects allowed communities to benefit from wildlife through tourism – hunting and ecotourism. Similar projects were undertaken in other parts of the world. Tourism has been a main focus of many protected areas and CBNRM projects, but forestry projects have also been quite popular (see Brechin et al, 2002; Chatre and Saberwal, 2006; Hoberg and Morawski, 2008).

Projects such as those described above often involve the collaboration of environmental and development NGOs (local and international) with state agencies and private sector companies (Saidel, 1991). Edwards et al (1999) argue that these projects provide NGOs with an opportunity to exert more influence on development policies. Problematically, this remark assumes that the NGOs involved have similar objectives and interpret sustainable development in the same way, which is often not the case (Roué, 2003; Chapin, 2004; Draper et al, 2004). Furthermore, Edwards et al (1999) seem to suggest that NGO influence on development and environmental policies is unequivocally positive, which is equally debatable. Whereas Escobar (1995) considers the rise of NGOs in itself as a counterpoint to the dominant neo-liberal discourse, others argue that the growing importance of NGOs contributes to neo-liberalism (Levine, 2002; see below). The NGO sector is not homogeneous and its involvement in protected area outreach and CBNRM projects is likely to have contradictory effects on the position of communities, which are not homogeneous either, thereby further complicating the issue. While some authors maintain that these projects have shown a good track record in terms of nature conservation and local socio-economic benefits, Suich et al (2009) argue that the results are much less positive, especially in terms of local development. The plethora of organizations active at the local level may result in communities loosing control over their natural resources (Ribot, 2004; 2007). Chapin (2004) argues that environmental organizations often refuse to support local communities in their struggles to claim land rights. While many of the environmental organizations funding or involved in these projects are larger, international ENGOs, with significant funds available and international contacts and reputations, those organizations promoting local economic development are often smaller, locally based NGOs or CBOs (see Spierenburg et al, 2008). While these can benefit from their cooperation with the ENGOs, it is often the priorities of international ENGOs that dominate. Differences in negotiating skills, funds available and dependency relations as a result of unequal access to funds, result in complicated power relations (see Hulme and Edwards, 1997). Similar complications can be discerned concerning the role of the private sector in TFCAs (Transfrontier Conservation Areas). On the one hand, its involvement can generate economic benefits for communities. On the other hand, the sector's greater experience with negotiation processes and legal contracts can reduce these benefits and diminish communities' control over land.

Differences in capacities, resources and power are not only an issue in the relation between the state, the private sector and the communities, but also between different state agencies and between the different states involved. As Glick-Schiller (2006) aptly remarks, there is a tendency in many transnational studies to treat all nation-states as if they were equal and sovereign players. However, many scholars of nature conservation allude to differences in power between 'the South' and 'the North' and the consequences of a capitalist penetration from the North (see also Chapter 7). As Glick-Schiller (2006) argues, this analysis should be complemented by a study of the rivalry between competing and colluding imperial and sub-imperial powers.

Furthermore, in the 1990s, there began to be changes in the operations of large foundations active in nature conservation. The basis for this development was laid in the 1980s when the influence of government on environmental policies and programmes waned in Europe and the US, under the influence of the Reagan administration and Thatcher's government. This resulted in a renewed support for conservation by local groups and large foundations (Hulme and Edwards, 1997; Delfin and Tang, 2005; Entwistle and Martin, 2005). In the 1990s, the stock market boom resulted in huge increases in the assets of foundations (see for the US, Ferris and Sharp, 2002). Several authors noticed that the 'venture capital culture' (Delfin and Tang, 2005, p2) resulted in changes in the philanthropic sector, emphasizing the leveraging of philanthropic funds, high levels of engagement with grantees and performance measurement. Cobb (2002) refers to these emerging trends in the 1990s as 'new philanthropy', Letts et al (1997) use the term 'venture philanthropy', while Delfin and Tang (2005) speak of strategic philanthropy. While these authors use different terms, they do seem to agree on a number of characteristics of these new and/or strategic ways of doing philanthropy. These new ways included the willingness to engage with grantees for longer term periods, and working more closely with the grantees to ensure that the activities and programmes funded would have a (measurable) impact. These higher levels of engagement also meant that philanthropists were willing to fund organizational capacity building and overhead costs, which hitherto had been difficult to obtain funding for. Furthermore, the emphasis was on constructing sustainable initiatives, and the preferred structure consisted of (public–private) partnerships, with foundations actively looking for intermediary organizations that could assist the grantees.

As Delfin and Tang (2005) show in a study of the Conserving California Landscape Initiative (CCLI), funded by the David and Lucile Packard Foundation – established by one of the founders of Hewlett-Packard – these partnerships may render conservation more democratic, since more stakeholders are involved in the planning and implementation of such projects, but may also render conservation initiatives less stable. The process of establishing and maintaining partnerships can be quite complex and costly (see Brinkerhoff, 2002).

The CCLI started in 1998 as a five-year $175 million programme to conserve 250,000ha of land in three key areas in California. The Foundation involved many different stakeholders in the planning process, drawing on the interests of a wide variety of groups, including for instance landowners, administrative agencies, scientists and non-profit organizations. This bottom-up approach, Delfin and Tang (2005) argue, contrasted sharply with the hitherto quite prescriptive behaviour of foundations involved in conservation, and can be linked to the new CBNRM initiatives that had become popular worldwide. Instead of the Foundation buying up the land – as had been common in earlier land conservation initiatives sponsored by philanthropic foundations – under the CCLI, land easement payments were made to landowners that did allow them ownership of the land but bound them to restrictions concerning the development of the land. Furthermore, the Foundation offered low-interest loans to non-profit organizations and public agencies to buy land coming up for sale on the market to add to the conservation initiative. The Foundation required matching funds from other sources, thereby minimizing its financial risk, but also argued that this would increase the partners' commitment and viability of the initiative. In regions where conservation support was conceived to be weak, the Foundation assisted in the creation of organizations to serve as an intermediary between the philanthropic community and the area's smaller non-profit organizations. Furthermore, an important focus of the Foundation was the provision of capacity-building grants to existing non-profit organizations. The implementation of the project was subcontracted to an independent organization, the Resources Law Group, which included in its staff some of the most renowned conservationists in the region, with long-term conservation experience, both within and outside government.

The Foundation claims the project was a huge success, and in 2003 announced it had secured much more than its initially set land target of 342,355 acres. Of this land, 72 per cent was purchased using Foundation grants, while the remaining 38 per cent was acquired through the bridging loans; 45.6 per cent of the land was subject to direct title deeds obtained, and 54.3 per cent of the land was conserved through easements (Delfin and Tang, 2005). Furthermore, the project had attracted interest from individuals, other foundations and government agencies, who had added about $700 million to Packard's initial $175 million. The Foundation, however, admitted that its capacity-building activities showed rather mixed results.

Interviews conducted by Delfin and Tang (2005) with those involved in the process showed that many stakeholders appreciated the Foundation's attempt to involve government, other foundations and the landholders, arguing that such a large project could not be funded or organized by just one organization. Nevertheless, they also indicated that the process of identifying stakeholders was a complicated matter. The interviewees furthermore indicated that the collaborative planning meetings were often dominated by the conservationists, and that landowners and development initiatives were marginalized. Tensions also arose between the need to take time to establish cooperation between the different stakeholders and the need to quickly respond when land became available on the market. Some of the land deals lacked transparency – related to circumstances pertaining to the land market – which was an extra problem when part of the funding was public. Despite the experienced domination of conservation interests, post-acquisition policies and activities were felt to be lacking, and there was some resentment that the Foundation did not want to fund more radical activist groups that wanted to take action to ensure that acquired lands were indeed used for conservation purposes or lobbied for local land users' development needs.

These findings show that in strategic philanthropy we find the same somewhat contradictory mix of, on the one hand, a domination of conservation interests over local empowerment and development interests, and, on the other hand, a dominance of market interests. Brockington et al (2008) also noted this, and argue that the links between capitalism and conservation have a direct impact on the way landscapes are changed and categorized; they are also changing attitudes towards wildlife and landscapes, introducing markets in nature conservation and commodifying nature (Brockington et al, 2008; see also Ramutsindela, 2007). Brockington et al (2008) argue that the global expansion and proliferation of protected areas and related conservation strategies can be directly related to these increasingly tight links. Protected areas are transformed from places to protect the elite's trophy animals (Beinart and Coates, 1995) to places that can be marketed as 'tourist habitat' (Brockington et al, 2008).

The trend of commodifying conservation is part of a more general political economic process that is often referred to as 'neo-liberalizing nature' or simply 'neo-liberalization' (McCarthy and Prudham, 2004; Castree, 2008b). Neo-liberalization, according to McCarthy and Prudham is '… an *environmental* project, and it is *necessarily* so' (McCarthy and Prudham 2004, p277). They argue that 'classical liberalism' – neo-liberalism's direct ancestor – made the natural environment centre stage. McCarthy and Prudham point to the normative arguments of people such as John Locke and Thomas Malthus, which were articulated with reference to the enclosure, ownership and commodification of land, forests, watercourses and other natural resources; those individuals who labour with nature, add value to it and should accordingly gain private entitlement over that part of nature. Ideal-typical characterizations of neo-liberalism combine this idea with specific state-led actions to enhance the process of marketization and privatization of nature, hence, it leads to both de- and re-regulation to bring nature under the control of markets (Castree, 2008b). Neo-liberalization as a principally environmental project entails a (re) shaping of boundaries between nature, society, market and state. Yet, exactly how neo-liberalization operates is a moot point. Neo-liberalization does not operate uniformly across the world; path dependency is important in studying de- and re-regulation processes (Castree, 2008b). Brenner and Theodore (2002) posit that in practice there are different but interconnected neo-liberalizations at a variety of spatial scales. What has become evident though, is that the role of the state in nature conservation is increasingly complemented or even replaced by the private sector, both for-profit and non-profit (Brockington et al, 2008). Non-profit organizations, such as ENGOs, become increasingly dependent on the private sector for funding (MacDonald, 2010).

The degree to which ENGOs depend on corporate funding varies. Among the large mainstream ENGOs, The Nature Conservancy has been quite successful in obtaining funding from corporations, between 1993 and 2007 8.4 per cent of its funding was derived from this source. Conservation International raises 11 per cent of its funding from the corporate sector. For WWF the percentage amounts only to 3 per cent, but it must be said that the organization appears to be quite hesitant to devolve information about its corporate sponsors (Brechin, 2008). Eyebrows have been raised about some of the corporate sponsors; for instance, oil companies feature prominently among the contributors to Conservation International, while The Nature Conservancy has a multi-year agreement with General Motors (Brechin, 2008) and IUCN cooperates with Shell (MacDonald, 2010), leading to accusations that the organizations team up with polluters. The organizations' leadership argues that the organizations are assisting the companies with greening their practices, yet the question remains whether they should accept funding from these sources. The Environmental Defence Fund also assists companies in rendering their practices more environmentally friendly but does not accept funding from the companies it assists (Brechin, 2008). However, as competition for funding increases, and the organizations' ambitions increase – also linked to the changing role of the state (see below) – ENGOs increasingly turn to the corporate sector. As Brockington and Duffy (2010) argue, conservation is using capitalism as much as capitalism is using conservation as an instrument.

This leads us to the increasingly commonly voiced critique that the whole focus on sustainable development – and its concomitant protected areas outreach and CBNRM projects – are the result and expression of the dominance of the private sector in conservation debates. Sklair (2001) argues that at present the corporate sector is dominating the debates on strategies towards nature conservation to an extent we have not witnessed before (cf. MacDonald, 2010). He poses and analyses the existence of a transnational capitalist class – composed of corporate executives, merchants, professionals, bureaucrats and politicians – striving for global economic growth and a global adoption of a neo-liberal economic model. It does so through, among other things, a profit-driven cultural ideology of consumerism, which it tries to promote at international development and environmental policy forums, which it has been dominating for quite some time (see Carroll and Carson, 2003). Special sessions have been allotted to the corporate sector at for instance the meetings of the Conference of Parties of the Convention on Biological Diversity (MacDonald, 2010), the World Summit on Sustainable Development,[1] and for the Millennium Ecosystem Assessment, in which one of the authors participated, the corporate sector was defined as an important 'user group'. The transnational capitalist class, however, also tries to resolve the ecological crisis that arises from its drive towards global economic growth, but without compromising its economic goals. Linking up with the discussions initiated by the Brundtland Report 'Our Common Future', its focus is on sustainable development – albeit in a piecemeal fashion focusing on separate, 'manageable' problems rather than a wholesale transformation of the corporate sector – arguing that consumption is not only reconcilable with sustainable development, but even a prerequisite. The marketing of protected areas as 'tourist habitat' is directly connected to this (Brockington et al, 2008).

While CBNRM and other multi-stakeholder approaches arose out of the sustainable use paradigm, recently there is increasing evidence that there is a movement back to the barriers. Chapin (2004) argues that this is a result of an increased involvement of private sector philanthropy (see also Hutton et al, 2005) but also shows that many environmental organizations have become disappointed with what they perceive as a 'lack of a buy-in' by local communities who prioritize development over conservation. He further suggests that dealing with development needs is indeed complicated, and that many environmental organizations lack the expertise to deal with development (Chapin, 2004). As a result – and stimulated by corporate philanthropy – environmental organizations increasingly focus on large-scale conservation initiatives, which are transnational in character. This focus on transnational conservation initiatives poses challenges to the nation state – though it cannot completely bypass the role of the nation state (Duffy, 2000, 2006). Yet, it seems to be indeed a move away from local communities (see also Dzingirai, 2003; Brockington et al, 2008; Spierenburg et al, 2008). Nevertheless, many conservation organizations still maintain that the socio-economic development interests of local communities are served by these new initiatives, claiming legitimacy for their projects (Spierenburg et al, 2006). However, the focus seems to lie more on the marketing of conservation areas and the creation of tourism enterprises than on forming partnerships with local communities. Recent fieldwork in Madikwe, a national park in northwest South Africa (conducted by one of the authors in cooperation with Sarah Bologna), seems to point to a shift away from partnering with local communities to defining community issues as corporate social responsibility (CSR).

Growing Importance of CSR and New Initiatives in the South

The growing dominance worldwide of neo-liberalization has resulted in less government regulations and restrictions concerning the corporate sector and a blurring of the boundaries between the private and the public (Karppi and Haveri, 2009). At the same time, increasing global flows of information also allow for a closer scrutiny of the corporate sector by NGOs and activist groups, and more effective ways of communicating critique to a wider audience (Burchell, 2006).

Controversies surrounding the sinking of the Brent Spar and Shell's activities in Nigeria show the power of 'watchdog' environmental organizations, including some of the mainstream conservation organizations such as WWF and Greenpeace. Pressure is put on the corporate sector to take responsibility in relation to fostering sustainable development (Arts, 2002; Michael, 2003). In the North, during the 1990s, governments stimulated the development of partnerships between the state and the private sector, explicitly including the non-profit sector, to enhance development and service delivery (Edwards et al, 1999; Entwistle and Martin, 2005). Furthermore, aided by tax regulations, the corporate sector was stimulated to develop CSR programmes.

Indeed many corporations – both large-scale transnational and small and medium enterprises – have developed and are developing CSR programmes (Elbers, 2004; Enderle, 2004). In a recent internet study, Dahlsrud (2008) found that the most commonly used definitions of CSR in the corporate sector come from the Commission of the European Communities in 2001: 'a concept whereby companies integrate social and environmental concerns in their business operations and in their interaction with their stakeholders on a voluntary basis'; and from the World Business Council for Sustainable Development in 1999: 'the commitment of business to contribute to sustainable economic development, working with employees, their families, the local community and society at large to improve their quality of life'.

The voluntary character of CSR leaves quite some room for the corporate sector to interpret their responsibilities towards the wider society and context in which they operate. Through lobbying organizations such as the World Business Council for Sustainable Development, the corporate sector has quite some influence on the way the concept of CSR is shaped, and has used this to its own advantage (Carroll and Carson, 2003; Burchell, 2006). CSR is implemented in many different ways and for many different reasons. CSR can be viewed in a highly instrumental way, 'greening' a company's image and resulting in positive public relations (PR) (Garriga and Melé, 2004, Burchell, 2006). It may also help to improve relations with local communities whose cooperation is necessary to maintain or improve production. Ethical motivations and concerns may indeed also play a role (Garriga and Melé, 2004). Furthermore, CSR programmes may concern activities that touch upon the core of the business – such as attempts to change production methods to render them less polluting – or relate to the business' direct social context, but they may also involve more charity-like activities in subject and geographical areas far removed from the business.

Recently, a renewed interest in CSR stimulated the search for alternative concepts that move away from the voluntary character of most CSR interpretations. Corporate citizenship is one such concept that stresses the duties of businesses towards society. Through state regulations and audits as well as close scrutiny by civil society, attempts are made to increase pressure on the corporate sector (Garriga and Melé, 2004; Burchell, 2006). The renewed interest in CSR has also broadened the premise on which CSR is founded. It is now widely understood that the business sector operates in relation with other sectors as its interests affect and are affected by not only economic, but also cultural, environmental and social interests in society. For business, CSR involves the understanding and management of these relationships. As societies are different, CSR can have different faces in different societal contexts (Dobers and Halme, 2009). Welford et al (2007) found that agendas for CSR differ in different parts of the world, but there are also differences in which companies respond to these agendas, and differences in capacities of organizations and their managers to understand and address CSR issues (Dobers and Halme, 2009).

CSR programmes no longer only involve North–North and North–South flows of funding and activities, but increasingly also South–South flows. The emergence of the so-called BRIC countries (Brazil, Russia, India and China) as an economic bloc is changing the world economy, especially since 2000 when the countries established a formal trade organization (Dobers and Halme, 2009; Alon et al, 2010). In search of (natural) resources, these new economic powers are engaging with countries in the South – as witnessed by the recent deal concluded between Brazil and Mozambique concerning the acquisition of land for the production of biofuels (Friends of the Earth, 2010). Yet, the interests move beyond the search for natural resources. About 750,000 Chinese have moved to Africa to engage in business, agriculture and mining. Sino–African trade is expected to surpass that of US–African trade in 2010 with over $100 billion predicted (Dobers and Halme, 2009). In early 2008, the Industrial and Commercial Bank of China announced a $5.5 billion investment to gain a strategic 20 per cent share in the South African Standard Bank (Blume and Grill, 2008), indicating an interest in a wider interconnection with the African economy (Dobers and Halme, 2009).

There is increasing attention paid to the possible negative consequences of such deals for the environment and society. Pressure is mounting also on the corporate sector in the South to engage in CSR. These demands are not only coming from international 'watchdog' organizations, but also from NGOs and the states within the South. Some authors argue that CSR has a longer history in some Asian countries than many assume, calling attention to community activities companies have been involved in before the concept of CSR became popular (Gonzalez III, 2005). However, there is a difference between CSR practices in countries with strong institutional environments and those with weak institutional environments. In some emerging economies and developing countries, characterized by weak institutional environments with sometimes arbitrary enforcement of law, insecurity of property rights and corruption, CSR may get a different twist (Jamali and Mirshak, 2007; Kuznetsov et al, 2009). In reaction to this, the United Nations Development Programme (UNDP) and the World Business Council for Sustainable Development promote a new approach to CSR. Instead of 'polishing' existing business to become (or seem) more socially responsible, companies are asked to go for CSR innovation (Dobers and Halme,

2009), which involves taking a social problem as a source of innovating new business, such as the Grameen microfinance banks. NGOs are also increasingly adopting these ideas to their own activities.

One area where CSR as a business opportunity is becoming increasingly popular is the area of carbon sequestration. In relation to reducing emissions from deforestation and forest degradation (REDD) policies, claims are made on large tracts of forests, mainly in the South, increasing the value of such areas not least because of expected subsidies (Ferguson, 2009). Furthermore, 'off-setting' is becoming a popular way of exercising CSR: damage done in one area is 'off-set' by the creation of protected areas elsewhere. One such project is described by Harbison (2007) and involves Rio Tinto Mining. This corporation has received criticism for its destructive mining activities in Madagascar. In reaction, the company started to work together with a number of international environmental organizations active in Madagascar, such as Conservation International and WWF, funding a major land deal between these organizations and the government of Madagascar for the establishment of conservation areas. While this deal has been hailed as a great success for the conservation of biodiversity, the initiative undermines land rights of those residing in those areas, thereby adding another disadvantaged group to the one already suffering from Rio Tinto's mining practices.

Hence, in relation to CSR, the same remarks apply that have been made in relation to CBNRM initiatives. Attention should be paid to the interconnections between society and the environment, and to the relations between the different stakeholders involved. Power relations are an often neglected aspect (cf. Brinkerhoff, 2002), and it is important to study these in relation to CSR activities. While CSR activities can have positive effects on environmental problems, they can also easily lead to the appropriation of resources by the corporate sector to the detriment of local land rights and development needs.

In conclusion, CSR and the capitalist foundation on which it operates could be explored as an avenue for understanding capitalist interests in the environment and why this interest is growing rapidly in the 21st century. In addition to the various dimensions of CSR we discussed in this chapter, we also see CSR as a vehicle by which the corporate sector 'performs' philanthropy. CSR collapses philanthropy and capitalism together to give capitalism a supposedly human face. This way the love of humankind – being responsible to society – and the love of money – profit-making – are packaged together to promote companies and to give them a competitive edge. Environmental philanthropy becomes an avenue through which the 'bundle of love' is expressed. Read together with our discussion on land acquisition and tax incentives in Chapter 2, the sponsorship for nature conservation through CSR represents a neo-liberal moment in which the business sector saves while increasing its profit margins in ways that have a strong social appeal. As we show in the next chapter, a great deal of framing of environmental problems is required to give philanthropy a particular direction.

Note

1 See www.wssd.org

References

Adams, W. and Hulme, D (2001) 'Conservation and community, changing narratives, policies and practices in African conservation', in Hulme, D. and Murphree, M. (eds) *African Wildlife and Livelihoods. The Promise and Performance of Community Conservation*, James Currey, Oxford, pp9–23

Alon, I., Lattemann, L., Fetscherin, M., Li, S. and Schneider, A. (2010) 'Use of public corporate communications of social responsibility in Brazil, Russia, India and China (BRIC)', *International Journal of Emerging Markets*, vol 5, no 1, pp6–22

Anderson, D. and Grove, R. (1987), 'The scramble for Eden: Past, present and future in African conservation', in Anderson, D. and Grove, R. (eds), *Conservation in Africa: People, Policies and Practice*, Cambridge University Press, Cambridge, pp1–12

Arnold, R. (1999) *Under Influence: Wealthy Foundations. Grant-driven Environmental Groups, and Zealous Bureaucrats that Control Your Future*, Free Enterprise Press, Bellevue, WA

Arts, B. (2002) '"Green alliances" of business and NGOs. New styles of self-regulation or "dead-end roads"?', *Corporate Social Responsibility and Environmental Management*, vol 9, pp26–36

Bakker, K. (2005) 'Neoliberalizing nature? Market environmentalism in water supply in England and Wales', *Annals of the Association of American Geographers*, vol 95, no 3, pp542–565

Beinart, W. and Coates, P. (1995) *Environment and history, the taming of nature in the USA and South Africa*, Routledge, London

Blume, G. and Grill, B (2008) 'Afrikas Neue Freunde', *Die Zeit*, no 3, pp11–15

Bonner, R. (1993) *At the Hand of Man: Peril and Hope for Africa's Wildlife*, Vintage Books, New York

Bosso, C. J. (1995) 'The color of money: environmental groups and the pathologies of fund raising', in Cigler, A. J. and Loomis, B. A. (eds) *Interest Group Policies*, CQ Press, Washington, pp101–130

Brechin, S. (2008) 'Private sector financing of international biodiversity conservation: An exploration of the funding of large conservation NGOs', paper presented at the Capitalism and Conservation Symposium, University of Manchester, 8–10 September

Brechin, R. S., Wilshusen, R. P., Fortwangler, L. C. and West, C. P. (2002) 'Beyond the square wheel: Toward a more comprehensive understanding of biodiversity conservation as social and political process', *Social and Natural Resources*, vol 15, pp41–64

Brenner, N. and Theodore, N. (2002) 'Cities and the geographies of "actual existing neoliberalism"', *Antipode*, vol. 34, pp349–379

Brinkerhoff, J. M. (2002) 'Government non-profit partnership: A defining framework', *Public Administration and Development*, vol 22, pp19–30

Brockington, D. and Duffy, R. (2010) 'Capitalism and conservation: The production and reproduction of biodiversity conservation', *Antipode*, vol 42, no 3, pp469–484

Brockington, D. and Igoe, J. (2006) 'Eviction for conservation: A global overview', *Conservation and Society*, vol 4, no 3, pp424–470

Brockington, D., Duffy, R. and Igoe, J. (2008) *Nature Unbound: Conservation, Capitalism and the Future of Protected Areas*, Earthscan, London

Brondizio, E. S. and Siqueira, A. D. (1997) 'From extractivists to forest farmers: Changing concepts of Caboclo agroforestry in the Amazon estuary', *Research in Economic Anthropology*, vol 18, pp233–279

Brulle, R. J. (2000) *Agency, Democracy, and Nature: The US Environmental Movement from a Critical Theory Perspective*, MIT Press, Cambridge, MA

Brundtland Commission (1987) *Our Common Future, Report for the World Commission on Environment and Development*, Oxford University Press, Oxford

Burchell, J. (2006). 'Confronting the "corporate citizen"', *International Journal of Sociology and Social Policy*, vol 26, no 3, pp121–137

Carroll, W. K. and Carson, C. (2003) 'Forging a new hegemony? The role of transnational policy groups in the network and discourses of global corporate governance', *Journal of World-Systems Research*, vol 6, no 1, pp67–102

Castree, N. (2008a) 'Neoliberalising nature: Processes, outcomes and effects', *Environment and Planning A*, vol 40, no 1, pp153–173

Castree, N. (2008b) 'Neoliberalising nature: The logics of deregulation and reregulation', *Environment and Planning A*, vol 40, no 1, pp1–22

Cernea, M. M. and Schmidt-Soltau, K. (2006) 'Poverty risks and national parks: Policy issues in conservation and resettlement', *World Development*, vol 34, vol 10, pp1808–1830

Chapin, M. (2004) 'A challenge to conservationists', *World Watch* (December), pp17–31.

Chatre, A. and Saberwal, V. (2006) *Democratizing Nature: Politics, Conservation, and Development in India*, Oxford University Press, New Delhi

Cobb, N. K. (2002) 'The new philanthropy: Its impact on funding arts and culture', *Journal of Arts Management, Law, and Society*, vol 32, no 2, pp125–143

Dahlsrud, A. (2008) 'How corporate social responsibility is defined: An analysis of 37 definitions', *Corporate Social Responsibility and Environmental Management*, vol 15, no 1, pp1–13

Delfin, F. and Tang, S. Y. (2005) *Strategic Philanthropy, Land Conservation Governance, and the Packard Foundation's Conserving California Landscape Initiative*, Research Paper 21, Center on Philanthropy and Public Policy, University of California, Los Angeles

Delfin, F. and Tang, S. (2007) 'Elitism, pluralism, or resource dependency: Patterns of environmental philanthropy among foundations in California', *Environment and Planning A*, vol 39, pp2167–2186

Dobers, P. and Halme, M. (2009) 'Editorial, corporate social responsibility in developing countries', *Corporate Social Responsibility and Environmental Management*, vol 16, pp237–249

Dowie, M. (1996) *Losing Ground: American Environmentalism at the Close of the Twentieth Century*. MIT Press, Cambridge MA.

Dowie, M. (2001) *American Foundations: An Investigative History*, MIT Press, Cambridge, MA

Draper, M., Spierenburg, M. and Wels, H. (2004) 'African dreams of cohesion: Elite pacting and community development in Transfrontier Conservation Areas in southern Africa', *Culture and Organization*, vol 10, no 4, pp341–353

Dryzek, J. S. (1996) 'Political inclusion and the dynamics of democratization', *American Political Science Review*, vol 90, pp474–487

Duffy, R. (2000) *Killing for Conservation: Wildlife Policy in Zimbabwe*, James Currey, Oxford

Duffy, R. (2006) 'The potential and pitfalls of global environmental governance: The politics of transfrontier conservation areas in Southern Africa', *Political Geography*, vol 25, no 1, pp89–112

Dzingirai, V. (2003) 'The new scramble for the African countryside', *Development and Change*, vol 34, no 2, pp243–263

Dzingirai, V. (2004). *Disenfranchisement at Large. Transfrontier Zones, Conservation and Local Livelihoods*, IUCN/ROSA, Harare

Edwards, M., Hulme, D. and Wallace, T. (1999) 'NGOs in a global future: Marrying local delivery to worldwide leverage', *Public Administration and Development*, vol 19, no 2, pp117–136

Edwards, M. and Hulme, D. (1996) 'Too close for comfort? The impact of official aid on non-governmental organizations', *World Development*, vol 24, no 6, pp961–973

Elbers, W. (2004) *Doing Business with Business*, Radboud University, Nijmegen

Enderle, G. (2004) 'Global competition and corporate responsibilities of small and medium-sized enterprises', *Business Ethics: A European Review*, vol 13, no 1, pp51–63

Entwistle, T. and Martin, S. (2005) 'From competition to collaboration in public service delivery: A new agenda for research', *Public Administration*, vol 83, no 1, pp233–242

Escobar, A. (1995) *Encountering Development: The Making and Unmaking of the Third World*, Princeton University Press, Princeton, NJ

Escobar, A. and Alvarez, S. (eds) (1992) *The Making of Social Movements in Latin America: Identity, Strategy and Democracy*, Boulder Press, Westview, CA

Fakir, S. (2001) 'CPPPs a way forward in CBNRM', *IUCN Policy Think Tank*, no 5

Fakir, S. (2004) 'Globalisation and its influence on poverty and environment', *IUCN Policy Think Tank*, no 17

Ferguson, B. (2009) 'REDD comes into fashion in Madagascar', *Madagascar Conservation and Development*, vol 4, no 2, pp132–137

Ferris, J. M. and Sharp, M. (2002) 'California foundations: trends and patterns', *The Center on Philanthropy and Public Policy*, vol 2, no 1, (January)

Friends of the Earth (2010) 'EU-Brazil biofuels deal: *land-grabbing charter*', www.foei.org/en/media/archive/2010/eu-brazil-biofuels-deal-land-grabbing-charter, accessed 24 February 2011

Garriga, E. and Melé, D. (2004) 'Corporate social responsibility theories: Mapping the territory', *Journal of Business Ethics*, vol 53, pp51–71

Gibson, C. C. (1999) *Politicians and Poachers. The Political Economy of Wildlife in Africa*, Cambridge University Press, Cambridge

Glick-Schiller, N. (2006) 'Introduction: What can transnational studies offer the analysis of localized conflict and protest?', *Focaal, European Journal of Anthropology*, vol 47, pp3–17

Gonzalez III, J. L. (2005) 'Is there room for more social responsibility in Asia's business and economic turn around?', *Asia Pacific Perspectives*, vol V, no 2, pp1–15

Gottlieb, R. (1993) *Forcing the Spring: The Transformation of the American Environmental Movement*, Island Press, Washington DC

Grove, R. H., Damodoran, V. and Sangwan, S. (eds) (1998) *Nature and the Orient: The Environmental History of South and Southeast Asia*, Oxford University Press, Oxford, Delhi, Calcutta, Chennai, Mumbai

Harbison, R. (2007) *Development Recast? A Review of the Rio Tinto Ilmenite Mine in Southern Madagascar*, PANOS, London

Hoberg, G. and Morawski, E. (2008) 'Policy change through sector intersection: Forest and aboriginal policy in Clayoquot Sound', *Canadian Public Administration*, vol 40, no 3, pp387–414

Hulme, D. and Edwards, M. (1997) 'NGOs, states and donors: An overview', in Hulme, D. and Edwards, M. (eds) *NGOs, States and Donors: Too Close for Comfort?*, Macmillan Press, London

Hulme, D. and Murphree, M. (eds) (2001) *African Wildlife and Livelihoods, the Promise and Performance of Community Conservation*, James Currey, Oxford

Hutton, J., Adams, W. M. and Murombedzi, J. (2005) 'Back to the barriers? Changing narratives in biodiversity conservation', *Forum for Development Studies*, vol 2, pp341–370

Ingram, H. M., Colnic, D. H., and Mann, D. E. (1997) 'Interest groups and environmental policy', in Lester, J. P. (ed) *Environmental Politics and Policy: Theories and Evidence*, 2nd edition, Duke University Press, Durham NC, pp115–145

Jamali, D. and Mirshak, R. (2007) 'Corporate social responsibility (CSR): Theory and practice in a developing country context', *Journal of Business Ethics*, vol 72, pp243–262

Karppi, I. and Haveri, A. (2009) 'Publicity: Policy push in the age of privatisation', *The Service Industries Journal*, vol 29, no 4, pp491–502

Kiss, A. (ed) (1990) *Living with Wildlife: Wildlife Resource Management with Local Participation in Africa*, World Bank, Washington DC

Kuznetsov, A., Kuznetsova, O. and Warren, R. (2009) 'CSR and legitimacy of business in transition economies: The case of Russia', *Scandinavian Journal of Management*, vol 25, no 1, pp37–45

Letts, C., Ryan, W. and Grossman, A. (1997) 'Virtuous capital: What foundations can learn from venture capitalists', *Harvard Business Review*, vol 75 (March–April), pp2–16

Levine, A. (2002) 'Convergence or convenience? International conservation NGOs and development assistance in Tanzania', *World Development*, vol 30, no 6, pp1043–1055

MacDonald, K. I. (2010) 'The devil is in the (bio)diversity: private sector "engagement" and the restructuring of biodiversity conservation', *Antipode*, vol 42, no 3, pp513–550

McCarthy, D. (2004) 'Environmental justice grant making: Elites and activists collaborate to transform philanthropy', *Sociological Inquiry*, vol 74, no 2, pp250–270

McCarthy, J. and Prudham, S. (2004) 'Neo-liberal nature and the nature of neo-liberalism', *Geoforum*, vol 35, pp275–283

McNeely, J. A. (ed) (1992) *Parks for life. Report of the IVth World Congress on National Parks and Protected Areas*, IUCN, Gland

Meijer, M., de Bakker, F. G. A., Smit, J. H. and Schuyt, T. (2006) 'Corporate giving in the Netherlands 1995–2003: Exploring the amounts involved and the motivations for donating', *International Journal of Nonprofit and Voluntary Sector Marketing*, vol 11, pp13–28

Michael, B. (2003) 'Corporate social responsibility in international development: An overview and critique', *Corporate Social Responsibility and Environmental Management*, vol 10, pp115–128

Mitchell, R. C., Mertig, A. G. and Dunlap, R. E. (1991) 'Twenty years of environmental mobilization: Trends among national environmental organizations', *Society & Natural Resources*, vol 4, no 3, pp219–234

Morrison, D. E. and Dunlap, R. E. (1986) 'Environmentalism and elitism: A conceptual and empirical analysis', *Environmental Management*, vol 10, pp581–598

Pfeffer, J. and Salancik, G. R. (1978) *The External Control of Organizations: A Resource Dependence Perspective*, Stanford University Press, Stanford

Ramutsindela, M. (2007) *Transfrontier Conservation in Africa: At the Confluence of Capital, Politics and Nature*, CABI, Wallingford

Ribot, J. C. (2004) *Waiting for Democracy: The Politics of Choice in Natural Resource Decentralization*, World Resource Institute, Washington DC

Ribot, J. C. (2007) 'Representation, citizenship and the public domain in democratic decentralization', *Development*, vol 50, no 1, pp43–49

Roelofs, J. (2003) *Foundations and Public Policy: The Mask of Pluralism*, State University of New York Press, Albany, NY

Rootes, C. (2003) *Environmental Protest in Western Europe*, Oxford University Press, Oxford

Roué, M. (2003) 'US environmental NGOs and the Cree. An unnatural alliance for the preservation of nature?', *International Social Science Journal*, vol 178, pp619–628

Saidel, J. R. (1991) 'Resource interdependence: The relationship between state agencies and nonprofit organizations', *Public Administration Review*, vol 51, pp543–553

Sklair, L. (2001) *The Transnational Capitalist Class*, Blackwell, Oxford

Smith, N. (2007) 'Nature as accumulation strategy', in Panitch, L. and Leys, C. (eds) *Coming to Terms with Nature: Socialist Register 2007*, New Monthly Review, New York, pp17–36

Snow, D. P. (1992) *Inside the Environmental Movement: Meeting the Leadership Challenge*, Island Press, Washington DC

Spierenburg, M., Steenkamp, C. and Wels, H. (2006) 'Resistance of local communities against marginalization in the Great Limpopo Transfrontier Area', *Focaal – European Journal of Anthropology*, vol 47, pp18–31

Spierenburg, M., Steenkamp, C. and Wels, H. (2008) 'Enclosing the local for the global commons: Community land rights in the Great Limpopo Transfrontier Conservation Area', *Conservation and Society*, vol 6, no 1, pp87–97

Suich, H., Child, B. and Spenceley, A. (2009) (eds) *Evolution and Innovation in Wildlife Conservation: Parks and Game Ranches to Transfrontier Conservation Areas*, Earthscan, London

Welford, R., Chan, C., and Man, M. (2007) 'Priorities for corporate social responsibility: A survey of businesses and their stakeholders', *Corporate Social Responsibility and Environmental Management*, vol 15, no 1, pp52–62

5

Framing Environmental Threats: Implications for Funding

INTRODUCTION

Whereas the links between elites and NGOs/CBOs (see Chapter 4) reveal the complexity of networks, another way of evaluating the intentions of philanthropists in nature conservation would be to measure the flow of resources against the nature or considered severity of the environmental threat, a task that this chapter aims to tackle. The chapter does this by starting with a comparison and analysing how in South(ern) Africa, conservation-oriented discourses centre on perceived threats and how these are related to pledges for philanthropy. It is the academic community that primarily seems to feed these discourses with ongoing presentations of scientific developments and findings. As an example we describe and present a historical example of a French scientist participating in and feeding alarmist discourses. This approach fits with our conceptualization of *environmental* philanthropy presented in Chapters 1 and 2, particularly its socio-political contextualization. With this basic framework in mind we start travelling further around the globe, following in the footsteps of the various predictions of species on their way to extinction. Our focus in this chapter is on the notion of environmental threats. Environmental threats are often conceived and even presented in numerical terms. This emphasis on numbers is understandable given that much of conservation was and still is driven by concerns with shrinking habitats and disappearing flora and fauna. We posit that the work of biological and social scientists should be brought together to shed light on various dimensions of environmental threats. This would assist us in understanding why certain threats matter more than others when it comes to funding environmental projects. In other words, analysing environmental threats is helpful for understanding the direction of philanthropic impulses, especially in environmental philanthropy. In the context of CSR (see Chapter 4) these threats help us to understand how the corporate sector reads and responds to particular environmental problems, and how its responses fit into its profit-maximizing projects and plans.

Under Severe Threat

In *White Writing*, Nobel laureate J. M. Coetzee (1988) introduces the term 'dream topography'. Barnard (2007, p26) describes the concept as 'a kind of social dream work, expressing wishes and maintaining silences that are political in origin'. Nature conservation organizations are always very vocal and explicitly express their dreams and wishes for Edenic and Arcadian landscapes and everything that they hold and contain in terms of flora and fauna. The most recent such dreams in southern Africa are those involving TFCAs, which are presented as Mandela's dream for Africa. Another version of this dream is the creation of TFCAs in which Africa's cultures and landscapes would form a unique tapestry in the tourist landscape (Ramutsindela, 2007). Many of the websites of conservation organizations teem with really beautiful pictures of various Edens around the world in need of conservation and protection (see Brooks et al, in press). According to these organizations, those areas and landscapes need and deserve protection because almost all are under some form of (human) threat of destruction or even worse, ultimate extinction. Brantlinger (2003) describes this white 'extinction discourse' with regard to 'primitive races' and 'savages' in their encounters with the 'civilized' white colonial powers, but the discourse seems to run parallel, or is even part and parcel of a similar and broader discourse in the biological sciences. The extinction discourse on race in Europe was rooted in a particular interpretation and social application of Darwin's theories on human evolution in biology, known as 'social Darwinism'. It has led to the most shameful scientific legitimation of exploiting people in the European colonies through slave trade and other means (Magubane, 2007). Similar discourses in biology and the social sciences are also of interest to understand Nazi ideology with regard to nature conservation and their ideas about race (cf. Bruggemeier et al, 2005). In more recent times, interesting parallels can be drawn between a strong focus in biological and ecological sciences on the threat of 'invasive species' in the 'new' South Africa and increasing xenophobia and fear of the consequences of globalization (cf. Comaroff and Comaroff, 2001). It is a discourse of threat and fear, considered necessary to get measures started against the described doomsday tidings. It seems that the more severe the apocalyptic message of eternal loss, the more philanthropists seem to be prepared to donate for measures to be taken (urgently of course) that promise to prevent this irreversible destruction. An informative example of extinction discourse where biological and social sciences seem to run in tandem is the predictions and scenarios formulated around the survival chances of the rhinoceros (both black and white).

The Idea of Rhino in European History and Conservation

A rhino is both an animal and an idea; a rhino is both a fact and a fantasy. Rhinos are living legends, combining physiological and imaginary aspects in their huge bodies. It is the embodiment of fictions about extinction and a major 'pin up' for philanthropic campaigns, like the one that led to the ban on rhino horn trade in 1979 and new campaigns in reaction to the alleged recent upsurge in rhino poaching in southern Africa.[1] At the launch of the WWF on 11 September 1961, its initial fundraising for the IUCN 'began with a front-page story in the London *Daily Mirror* featuring a black rhinoceros and its calf under a banner headline reading "DOOMED to Disappear from the Face of the Earth due to Man's FOLLY, GREED and NEGLECT". A week later, WWF had sixty thousand pounds in the bank' (Dowie, 2009, p49, emphasis original). Where do the biological and social sciences meet in rhino conservation? How do rhinos as biological classified species fit into the European idea and imagery (cf. Mudimbe, 1994) of Africa?

The European idea of rhinos is probably best represented by one of the most famous French naturalists and zoologists, Georges Cuvier (1769–1832). His full name was Georges Léopold Chrétien Frédéric Dagobert Cuvier. His name is one of the 72 that are engraved in the Eiffel Tower in Paris. In the 19th century, naturalists like Cuvier built on the images of rhinos that were transmitted in stories and images from the ancient times of Rome and Greece, when live rhinos were shown to audiences gathered in the arenas. In the Circus Maximus in Rome complete landscapes were depicted in which rhinos along with lions and leopards were showcased (Enright, 2008). They all were imported to Greece or Rome from Africa. Interestingly enough not a single rhino came to Europe between the 3rd and 16th centuries (Enright, 2008). For more than a thousand years there were no live specimens of rhino brought into Europe. Nevertheless in 1515, Albrecht Dürer drew a picture of a rhino, without ever having seen a live one. In itself it is quite amazing to see how much 'rhinoness' can be seen in Dürer's drawing.[2] The creature is definitely recognizable as a rhino. Dürer's drawing would dominate the European image of the rhino for the next 200 years (Enright, 2008). It represented the (imagined) rhino as a heavily armoured warrior, an armed soldier. Only when Douwemout van der Meer, a Dutch sea captain took a live Indian rhino to Europe in the mid-18th century was Dürer's image adjusted and the rhino became contextualized in 'the fashion for the exotic' (Enright, 2008, p37).

European exoticism was basically represented in two ways. On the one hand, the rhino was presented as the 'sublime in nature', i.e. romantic nature, without a specific location (Enright, 2008, p43). It is a notion that seems to run straight through into our current day and age. In an advertisement for computer wall papers in the *Holland Herald* of February 2010, the monthly flight magazine of the Dutch national carrier KLM, for instance, a rhino is depicted almost in the style of Dürer amidst other decorative items, entitled 'the *essence* of nature' (*Holland Herald*, 2010; emphasis added). Here the rhino is a kind of 'unplugged' embodiment of unspoiled nature. On the other hand, the rhino was represented as embodying the exotic, the native and far-away places, in much the same way (human) 'natives' were portrayed (Magubane, 2007). It is therefore significant to note that Georges Cuvier is, aside from his romantic depiction of the rhino and his academic contribution to the so-called theory of 'catastrophism' in geological processes (Huggett, 1997), probably most notorious to Africanists for his important role in the anatomical research of the 'Hottentot Venus', Saartjie Baartman, and depicting this Khoisan woman as closer to animals than to humans. It is a line of research and bio-politics that finds its modern day continuation in primatology, which is, according to Haraway (1989), structured around the two axes of sex/gender and nature/culture in which 'monkeys and apes have a privileged relation to nature and culture' (Haraway, 1989, p1) as they constitute the 'border zones' between human and non-human animals. At the time of Cuvier, a commonly held assumption was that 'the more primitive the mammal, the more pronounced the genitalia and the bodily enticements to procreation. There was a strong tendency to see hyper sexuality and uncontrolled drives in the female Hottentot body' (Crais and Scully, 2009, p133). The 'proof' of this animality lay in what was called the 'Hottentot apron' or the 'elongated outer labia that would provide anatomical proof of the unrepressed sexuality and essential animal character of the Hottentot' (Crais and Scully, 2009, p133–134). Saartjie never allowed Cuvier's inspection of her private parts when she was still alive, but Cuvier got his chance when she died at an early age, probably of pneumonia in Paris in December 1815. 'Now she could no longer resist their entreaties. Spreading her legs open, the men examined Sara's genitals, to their delight discovering her "apron"' (Crais and Scully, 2009, p140). Cuvier could now 'scientifically' conclude and confirm the already existing European belief that the Hottentot (women) were closer to animals than to humans. Saartjie became an icon of a racialized imperial European imagery of Africa and Africans (cf. Hobson, 2005; Strother, 1999). Initiated by Nelson Mandela in 1995, only one year after his installation as first black president of South Africa, Saartjie's remains were brought back to South Africa in 2002, in a grand display of 'returning home' and South African national identity politics. Then President Mbeki quoted Cuvier's report on Saartjie's dissection extensively. 'On hearing this gruesomely pornographic, bigoted descriptions spoken by the president, several youngsters in the audience wept and fainted' (Holmes, 2007, pp179–180). Stories such as these raise serious questions concerning the classifications of humans, which groups are considered part of environmental threats and how these threats are framed.

In representing the rhino and Saartjie Baartman, Cuvier made himself icon and spokesperson of a time and age of (upcoming) European expansion, masculine and sexist imperialism and colonialism. This European identity is primarily created by contrasting and mirroring Europe and its people in dichotomies with other people and cultures, such as between civilisation and savagery (cf. Corbey, 1989), Christian and heathen (cf. Magubane, 2007) or, in the sphere of nature conservation, between white and Western conservationist versus the black and native 'poacher' (cf. Adams, 2004; Anderson and Grove, 1987). It is strong dichotomies like those presented here that seem to go together or even kick-start philanthropic pledges in the Western world. These processes of identity formation are violent (and virulent) and are as much about the physical and tangible as it is about the imaginary and the symbolic. Every physical representation stands at the same time for something imaginary. A rhino is flesh, bones, blood, and at the same time stands for an image of times immemorial and a romantic notion of unspoilt wilderness landscapes and nature. The same holds for depicting humans, as Saartjie's example shows. The physical cannot be analysed or understood without its imaginary associations, as the physical is interpreted in the context of the imagery, as Cuvier's example makes abundantly clear. That is why biology 'needs' social sciences as much as the other way around. It is therefore important to present and analyse the campaign to save the rhino in South and southern Africa as a response and consequence of its predicted physical extinction, but it is equally important to interpret that notion in the context of what the 'rhino in Africa' stands for in the conservationists' and environmental philanthropists' imagery.

In Africa there are two types of rhinoceros, the black rhino (*Diceros bicornis*) and the white rhino (*Ceratotherium simum*) (Emslie and Brooks, 1999). Both the black and white rhino were (are) allegedly on their way to extinction. The first and primary reason for this was excessive hunting by European hunters. According to Ian Player (1972), by the end of the 19th century there were hardly any rhino left in southern Africa. The famous hunter Frederick Courtenay Selous was already talking of *total* extinction around the 1890s (Player, 1972). Readers are given the impression that they literally have to think in terms of a few remaining animals. On its website, the WWF notices the near extinction of the rhino in southern Africa, where 'once' the African savannah 'teemed with more than a million white and black rhinos' (WWF, 2008). Notwithstanding all this, there were too many rhinos in South Africa's Umfulozi Game Reserve in the 1950s. So many, that the reserve's management either had to cull them or find another solution. Nick Steele, speaking on behalf of Ian Player at a conference in San Antonio in the US in 1967, told his audience that 'during the eventful years since the start of [Operation Rhino] no less than *five hundred* White Rhino were captured' (Steele, 1967, p1, emphasis added) (see Chapter 3). And, this in Umfulozi Game Reserve alone! Following, or despite, the success of Operation Rhino and other initiatives to save the rhino worldwide, the WWF reports that in the 1970s, the shipments of 'huge quantities' of rhino horn to the 'lucrative markets in the Middle East and Asia' were causing a 'crisis' that could only be stopped by an 'Appendix I listing' of the rhino on the list of CITES, which 'inhibited all trade of rhino parts or products' (WWF, 2008). When a game ranger from Zimbabwe in his memoirs laments the current political and economic meltdown in the country causing so much human suffering, he refers in his afterword to a report of the Zimbabwe Conservation Task Force, starting with the words '(o)ur *biggest* concern is for the fate of the rhino in Zimbabwe [because of an increase in poaching]' (Tredger, 2009, p311; emphasis added), adding again to the image of conservationists as putting animals before people. The rhinos are always presented as being under the threat of extinction. Nevertheless it seems rather difficult to add up the various available figures: a few individual rhinos at the end of the 19th century, an abundance in Umfolozi in the 1960s, a crisis in the 1970s, rhinos in Zimbabwe in 2009 wiped out? This chapter and the book as a whole are not meant to unpack rhino statistics on the issue, or any other related statistics for that matter, but we can safely conclude on the basis of the above that it is difficult to decide about the actual state of rhino populations in the world. This small tour around the issue of (predicted) rhino extinction shows at least that there is a multitude of confusing voices and interpretations about the actual state of rhino numbers in the world. But most agree that the species is under severe threat of extinction and that their biggest enemy is humans. This line of reasoning feeds the call for philanthropic giving. With extinction just around the corner, concrete protective measures and actions in the field are urgently required.

No matter how grim the picture is for rhinos worldwide and despite the fact that it is mankind that seems to have an unstoppable appetite for rhino products, philanthropists and conservationists, almost paradoxically, have great faith that their financial contribution will, once used to finance concrete actions in the field, be able to protect, undo and ultimately have the power to stop these processes of destruction and the road to extinction. Even stronger, they assume that their philanthropic giving will directly turn the tide and prevent further destruction and even recreate what was almost lost; this is human-inflicted destruction versus human engineering. Rhinos are only one of the many examples of this paradox of environmental threat related to philanthropic giving, and below we list some other examples from around the globe that seem to follow this same mechanism or route, where philanthropic giving is considered to be the ultimate saviour and last resort of otherwise vanishing flora and fauna, of otherwise considered irreversible processes of destruction and extinction. But how do philanthropists deal with prioritizing which extinction to tackle first? On the basis of our analysis of secondary material we conclude this chapter with an informed reflection on the question of whether environmental threats can be ranked according to their severity.

OTHER PREDICTED EXTINCTIONS

One of the most referenced sources when speaking about the rate of extinctions of particular species is 'The IUCN Red List of Threatened Species' (IUCN, 2010). The very name even seems to be in need of protection as it is trade marked, with the well-known small letters in superscript '™'. Here we can find our rhino listed, but also many other species, neatly divided in various categories indicating the degree of threat to a particular species, or how close they are to extinction. The categories range from 'Least Concern' or 'LC' to 'Extinct' or 'EX'. In between are the categories of 'Vulnerable' (VU), 'Endangered' (EN) and 'Critically Endangered' (CR) species. Another well-known source is CITES.[3] CITES is an international agreement between governments that the 'international trade in specimens of wild animals and plants does not threaten their survival' (IUCN, 2010). CITES distinguishes three categories or Appendices I to III, which list the different species and the degree to which they are threatened. Appendix I contains the species that are threatened with extinction and are subject to a trade ban; trading in these species is only allowed in very exceptional cases. Appendix II contains species that are threatened but which can be traded under very strict and specific conditions. Appendix III contains species that are protected in at least one country that has asked other CITES Parties for assistance in controlling the trade. All together the three appendices list about 5000 animals and some 28,000 plants. To get species listed is a highly political process with much lobbying by stakeholders.

Some mediagenic species receive much media attention (which helps the lobbying tremendously) when proposals are tabled to list them under Appendix I. The most famous example of this probably being the elephant in the second half of the 1980s, when it got Appendix I status in 1989 (Bonner, 1993). Especially the burning of a huge pile of ivory by then Kenyan president Daniel Arap Moi, carefully staged by a Washington-based lobby organization and a pyrotechnist who specialized 'in creating fires for movie sets', stands out as a powerful image in the international memory. In a dramatic appeal to the world the president stated at the occasion in Nairobi National Park: 'To stop the poacher, the trader must also be stopped and to stop the trader, the final buyer must be convinced not to buy ivory ... I appeal to people all over the world to stop buying ivory' (*New York Times*, 1989).

In the further process and political skirmishes to get the elephant in the first category of CITES, all kinds of elephant specialists and scientists were asked for their expert opinions on the actual number of elephants that were remaining in the various parts of Africa. It is interesting to see how many different estimates were presented, all of them 'scientifically grounded' and just how much they differ from each other, just like the rhino estimates we referred to above. The *Elephant Status Report* of 2007 states quite straightforwardly that:

> (p)opulation estimate data entered into the AED [African Elephant Database] vary in quality from the identification of individual animals to plain guesswork. The addition of population estimates of varying quality in national, regional and continental total is, from a statistical viewpoint strictly invalid and produces misleading results. (Blanc et al, 2007)

Despite this acknowledgement the reason for still using them is, according to the authors, because 'discarding low-quality estimates would produce equally misleading estimates, as high-quality survey estimates are not available for most areas in which elephants are found' (Blanc et al, 2007, p11). It suggests that it is better to knowingly base and make decisions on invalid data and information than on nothing at all.

We could continue here listing various other species that over the years have drawn worldwide media attention, such as tigers,[4] whales,[5] pandas,[6] rhinos,[7] etc., all counting on and asking for generous philanthropic giving to save and protect these iconic species. It is interesting to see how all conservation organizations emphasize on their websites the importance of further scientific research on the species and habitat. The production of (scientific) knowledge seems a *sine qua non* for adding credibility and scientific legitimacy to campaigns set up to save particular species. But as we have seen with the example of the elephant, it also implies that the outcomes of scientific research become highly politicized (Dickson and Adams, 2009). Scientific doubt and political positions hardly ever go together well and therefore the 'surviving numbers game', with all its nuances and statistical intricacies, is actually not fit for the political arena. Nevertheless, scientists are called in all the time to make statements about numbers, and as they are committed to their research they will probably continue to do so.

Further to worries about particular species becoming extinct, there is a broad spectrum of charities and organizations that lobby and warn against the destruction and therefore extinction of complete ecosystems. The climax of this way of thinking is no doubt the enormous scientific and political attention that is now being paid to the concept of 'global warming' and 'climate change', not least because of the efforts by Al Gore through his film *An Inconvenient Truth*, for which he was awarded the Nobel Peace Prize in 2007. The road to this global political concern about the state of the environment and its effects on global climatic patterns was paved in the 1980s and 1990s by more habitat-specific worries and concerns, more particularly desertification in Africa and the destruction of the world's rainforests, particularly in Latin America. The 'prophet' of this latter movement[8] was Norman Meyers with his 1992 book *The Primary Source: Tropical Forests and Our Future*, which led the way and developed the concept of 'biodiversity hotspots'. The local hero in this campaign was the Brazilian Chico Mendes, 'a name synonymous with the battle to save the rain forest' according to an international book site (AbeBooks.com, no date), a self-made man and rubber tapper from the Amazon, who fought for the rights of his profession against the 'invasion' of cattle farmers:

> *His struggle caught the attention of international environmentalists who saw Chico's resistance movement as a fight to save the rainforest. Chico and the ecologists worked together for a short period, but then Chico was murdered by ranching interests in late 1988. This news… appeared on the front page of the* New York Times.

Andrew Revkin (1990) wrote a book on the murder of Chico Mendes, which became a New York Times Bestseller.

On desertification there is no specific iconic author that can be mentioned, but the threat of it was not less felt because of that. Estimates of how a 'threatening' desert (Grainger, 1990) was overtaking once fertile grounds were abounding, especially in the Sahel region in Africa. Deserts were said to be 'moving' (Global Greenhouse Warming.com, no date) and 'marching' (NASA Earth Observatory, 2010) and were 'eating up' cultivated soils (El-Baz, 1990). What organizations that fought against deforestation and desertification share with the species-specific organizations we described above is that they all seem to suggest that the processes are irreversible if we don't do something about it NOW! It is not presented as 'just a threat', but usually as a matter of life and death, starting tomorrow. It is five minutes to twelve. Death follows if we do not act NOW and start donating money to the cause immediately. This 'crisis narrative' appears a dominant and effective mobilization tool in policy making and philanthropic fundraising (see Roe, 1994).

Underlying, grounding and informing much of this hectic contemporary campaigning for species or habitat survival though is a much more prolonged, longitudinal and culturally aesthetical informed trend with regard to nature and why it would be worth saving. Restricting ourselves to the Anglo Saxon world, this road is primarily paved by British romantic poets such as William Wordsworth and Samuel Taylor Coleridge, American environmentalists such as Henry David Thoreau, Ralph Waldo Emerson and Aldo Leopold, and artists such as John Constable and Joseph Mallard Turner. It is a 'picture of nature as a place of eternal order, balance and separate purpose, a place whose very survival depends on the absence of man and his works' (Budiansky, 1995, p6). In short, nature as 'wilderness'. The Wild Foundation, which is home of the World Wilderness Congress, defines wilderness:

> in contrast with those areas where man and his works dominate the landscape, [wilderness] is hereby recognized as an area where the earth and its community of life are untrammeled by man, where man himself is a visitor who does not remain. An area of wilderness is further defined to mean in this Act an area of undeveloped federal land retaining its primeval character and influence, without permanent improvements or human habitation, which is protected and managed so as to preserve its natural conditions and which:
>
> - Generally appears to have been affected primarily by the forces of nature, with the imprint of man's work substantially unnoticeable;
> - Has outstanding opportunities for solitude or a primitive and unconfined type of recreation;
> - Has at least two thousand hectares (five thousand acres) of land or is of sufficient size as to make practicable its preservation and use in an unimpaired condition; and,

- *May also contain ecological, geological or other features of scientific, educational, scenic or historical value.* (Wild Foundation, no date)

This definition is very close to the categorization and classification that the IUCN gives to 'wilderness', as a 'Category Ib protected areas [which] are usually large unmodified or slightly modified areas, retaining their natural character and influence, without permanent or significant human habitation, which are protected and managed so as to preserve their natural condition' (IUCN, 2009).

It is a romantic influence that runs through much of European and American (landscape) ideas of national identities and culture (resp. cf. Wylie, 2007; cf. Buell, 1995). What is interesting to note in this regard though is that the very first World Wilderness Congress in 1977 did not take place in Europe or the US but in South Africa, and that Ian Player (the man behind the success of Operation Rhino), together with Robert Cleaves from WILDCON (both introduced and described in Chapter 3) were the most important founding fathers of World Wilderness Congress. It was the centre that was dependant on the periphery; it was the periphery that had to stand up in order to facilitate the centre's soul searching. Just like in colonial days, the centre was once again dependent on the periphery for its identity construction (cf. Maxwell, 1999). Ian Player is a self-declared romantic (Draper, 1998) who ascribes much of his spiritual sense for and understanding of nature to his Zulu-mentor during his years in the game reserves in Zululand (now KwaZulu-Natal), Magquba Ntombela (Magquba Ntombela Foundation, no date). This romantic notion has a powerful influence on many if not most people active in nature conservation, in whatever way. Interestingly again, the daughter of the late Prince Bernhard and Queen Juliana (see Chapter 3), Irene van Lippe-Biesterfeld, is also very much involved in this romantic and spiritual appreciation and interpretation of nature (Van Lippe-Biesterfeld, 2005), and has a game farm devoted to those principles in South Africa, close to Graaff Reinet, where also Anton Rupert was born. She also teaches what she preaches in her Nature College.[9]

What (white) romantics in Europe and the US share is that they are very worried on the one hand about what is happening around them and what mankind is doing to nature, but on the other hand and at the same time they are always able to present a message of hope that things can be turned around for the better (see for example one of the most famous fundraisers for the cause of animals, Jane Goodall, 1999, 2009).[10] This hope runs parallel to the paradox we presented earlier on in this chapter, where it became evident that although extinctions seem to loom everywhere, through philanthropic giving organizations we should be able to turn the tide. The paradox is fuelled by this spiritually and romantically informed hope of better times to come, at least as long as we donate gifts. Theoretically this paradox can be interpreted along the lines of reciprocal altruism, in which, both in the biological and in the social sciences, a gift is considered key to building trust, peace and cooperation. With the gift always comes the hope and expectation that things will (re)turn out for the better (resp. cf. Bekoff and Pierce, 2009; cf. Schrift, 1997).

To round up this discussion, we must note that this chapter is not intended to give a full exposé of all the environmental threats that have played a role in world news or in scientific debates. We do not touch on fascinating debates on the impact of the growth of world populations on the environment or resource depletion with regard to fossil energy, or the engaged debates on matters of pollution, ranging from plastic in the oceans to the recent oil spill in the Gulf of Mexico. What we have tried to make clear and illustrate here is that the notion of catastrophic threat is all-pervasive in almost all presentations of causes for conservation, ranging from species to habitats to planet earth as a whole. It serves a purpose of giving ultimate urgency to the issues at hand, and with that comes the inevitable question to everyone willing to read about the issues, 'please donate for this good cause'. In other words and concluding, at least in the minds of the presenters and providers of this information, there is a sense that the level of urgency, almost always bordering or on its way to extinction or utter destruction, will influence the level of giving in a positive way. The motto seems to be that the more urgent the cause can be presented, the bigger the philanthropic gifts will be. Not only because of the urgency but also because the gifts are indicative of the level of hope that is expressed through the gift: that the people asking for the gift will take action in order to drag the particular cause off the rim just in time from its predicted doomed end. Urgency and hope are paradoxically related here: the more urgent the matter, the more hope is needed, and that hope can be expressed in the amount of philanthropic giving. This is not at all a matter of the amount of (scientific) proof that is given for the amount of threat. The amounts of philanthropic giving are not in that sense related to the seriousness of the threat. This qualitative conclusion seems to be in line with quantitative studies in philanthropic giving that show that there is a host of factors responsible for what and how much people and organizations are prepared to give in time and money. Factors such as gender (Wiepking and Bekkers, 2010), education (Bekkers, 2004), class (Habib and Maharaj, 2008), stock market fluctuations (Strom, 2002) and religion (Bremner, 1980), all have their individual and combined and intertwined influences on the amount of philanthropic giving. Suggesting monocausal influences like the nature of the environmental threat on the flow of resources does not seem to be able to capture the complexities of the processes of philanthropic giving. This explains in part why the environment has not attracted much philanthropic funding despite the numerous images of a pending disaster (see Chapter 2). It can be suggested that what all nature conservation causes have in common is that they picture huge, if not catastrophic environmental threats, and that seems to do the trick to stimulate people and organizations to keep on donating (generously) to philanthropic causes.[11] Our emphasis on environmental threats and philanthropy should not be misconstrued as suggesting that environmental philanthropy is driven by concerns with environmental threats alone. On the contrary, we acknowledge other triggers and incentives. In the chapters that follow we present other dimensions of philanthropy and channels for funding conservation.

Notes

1. See www.savingrhinos.org and www.rhinoresourcecenter.com/, visited 19 July 2010.
2. An interesting case of the power of a particular kind of 'indirect knowledge' as used by Jansen (2009), following Hoffman (2004). Here the indirect knowledge concerns an 'image-ined rhino', as transmitted over many generations in Europe between the 3rd and 16th centuries.
3. See www.cites.org, accessed 21 July 2010.
4. See www.savethetiger.org, visited 21 July 2010. Interesting here is that this lobby organization for saving tigers was started by the foundation of the Exxon oil company (now ExxonMobil Foundation), well-known for its tiger logo and catchphrase, 'Put a tiger in your tank', together with WWF.
5. See www.wdcs.org (Whale and Dolphin Conservation Society), visited 21 July 2010.
6. Although the panda is probably best-known as logo of the WWF, the major conservation and lobby organization is to be found under www.pandasinternational.org (visited 21 July 2010), proudly displaying on its homepage that they were awarded 'Best of America' by Independent Charities of America.
7. See www.rhino-irf.org, visited 21 July 2010.
8. See www.wrm.org.uy, with WRM being the World Rainforest Movement, focusing on local peoples' rights over their forests and territories and environmental conservation.
9. See www.natuurcollege.nl/welcome-to-nature-college, visited 21 July 2010.
10. Note how the subtitle of Jane Goodall's 2009 book refers to the discourse of extinction.
11. However, it seems that it is not the severity or 'size' of the disaster that ultimately decides how much people are prepared to give or donate. The great effort to ask people to donate money for the victims of the catastrophe in Pakistan in August 2010 made this catastrophe look more severe than the tsunami in 2004 or the earthquake in Haiti in 2010; the two disasters which failed by far to bring in the expected amounts of money (see http://blog.mcf.org/2010/08/19/pakistan-floods/, a blog on the site of the Minnesota Council on Foundations). It shows at least that the reasons for philanthropic giving are manifold and still to be researched in more detail.

References

AbeBooks.com (no date) 'Community', www.abebooks.com/docs/Community/Featured/amazonBooks.shtml, visited 21 July 2010

Adams, W. M. (2004) *Against Extinction. The Story of Conservation*, Earthscan, London

Anderson, D. and Grove, R. (eds) (1987) *Conservation in Africa. People, Policies and Practice*, Cambridge University Press, Cambridge

Barnard, R. (2007) *Apartheid and Beyond. South African Writers and the Politics of Place*, Oxford University Press, Oxford

Bekkers, R. (2004) 'Giving and volunteering in the Netherlands: Sociological and psychological perspectives', unpublished PhD dissertation, Utrecht University, Utrecht

Bekoff, M. and Pierce, J. (2009) *Wild Justice. The Moral Lives of Animals*, University of Chicago Press, Chicago

Blanc, J. J., Barnes, R. F. W., Craig, G. C., Dublin, H. T., Thouless, C. R., Douglas-Hamilton, I. and Hart, J. A. (2007) *African Elephant Status Report. An Update from the African Elephant Database*, IUCN, Gland

Bonner, R. (1993) *At the Hand of Man: Peril and Hope for Africa's Wildlife*, Vintage Books, New York

Brantlinger, P. (2003) *Dark Vanishings. Discourse on the Extinction of Primitive Races, 1800–1930*, Cornell University Press, Ithaca

Bremner, R. H. (1980) [1960] *American Philanthropy (Second Edition)*, University of Chicago Press, Chicago

Brooks, S., Spierenburg, M. and Wels, H. (in press), 'The organization of hypocrisy? Juxtaposing tourists and farm dwellers in game farming in South Africa', in Van Beek, W. E. A., Schmidt, A. (eds) *African hosts and their guests: Cultural dynamics of tourism in Africa*

Bruggemeier, F. J., Ciok, M. and Zeller, Th. (2005) *How Green were the Nazis?: Nature, Environment, and Nation in the Third Reich*, Ohio University Press, Ohio

Budiansky, S. (1995) *Nature's Keepers. The New Science of Nature Management*, Phoenix Giant, London

Buell, L. (1995) *The Environmental Imagination. Thoreau, Nature Writing, and the Formation of American Culture*, Harvard University Press, Cambridge, MA

Coetzee, J. M. (1988) *White Writing: On the Culture of Letters in South Africa*, Yale University Press, New Haven

Comaroff, J. and Comaroff, J. L. (2001) 'Naturing the nation: Aliens, apocalypse and the post-colonial state', *Journal of Southern African Studies*, vol 27, no 3, pp627–651

Corbey, R. (1989) *Wildheid en beschaving. De Europese verbeelding van Afrika*, Ambo, Baarn

Crais, C. and Scully, P. (2009) *Sara Baartman and the Hottentot Venus. A Ghost Story and a Biography*, Princeton University Press, Princeton

Dickson, P. and Adams, W. A. (2009) 'Science and uncertainty in South Africa's elephant culling debate', *Environmental Planning C: Government and Policy*, vol 27, pp110–123

Dowie, M. (2009) *Conservation Refugees. The Hundred-year Conflict between Global Conservation and Native Peoples*, MIT Press, Cambridge, MA

Draper, M. (1998) 'Zen and the art of garden maintenance: The soft intimacy of hard men in the wilderness of KwaZulu-Natal, South Africa, 1952–1997', *Journal of Southern African Studies*, vol 24, no 4, pp801–828

El-baz, F. (1990) 'Do people make deserts?', *New Scientist*, 13 October, pp41–44

Emslie, R. H. and Brooks, M. (1999) *African rhinos: Status Survey and Conservation Action Plan*, IUCN/SSC African Rhino Specialist Group, Gland

Enright, K. (2008) *Rhinoceros*, Reaktion Books, London

Global Greenhouse Warming.com (no date) 'Deserts and desertification', www.global-greenhouse-warming.com/deserts.html, visited 21 July 2010

Goodall, J. (with Berman, Ph.) (1999) *Reason for Hope. A Spiritual Journey*, Thorsons, London

Goodall, J. (2009) *Hope for Animals and their World: How Endangered Species are Being Rescued from the Brink*, Icon Books, Cambridge

Grainger, A. (1990) *The Threatening Desert: Controlling Desertification*, Earthscan, London

Habib, A. and Maharaj, B. (eds) 2008) *Giving and Solidarity. Resource Flows for Poverty Alleviation and Development in South Africa*, HSRC Press, Pretoria

Haraway, D (1989) *Primate Visions. Gender, Race and Nature in the World of Modern Science*, Routledge, London

Hobson, J. (2005) *Venus in the Dark. Blackness and Beauty in Popular Culture*, Routledge, London

Hoffman, E. (2004) *After Such Knowledge: Where Memory of the Holocaust Ends and History Begins*, Secker and Warburg, London

Holland Herald (2010) 'The essence of nature', *Holland Herald*, February

Holmes, R. (2007) *The Hottentot Venus. The Life and Death of Saartjie Baartman, born 1789 – Buried 2002*, Jonathan Ball, Johannesburg

Huggett, R. (1997) *Catastrophism. Asteroids, and other Dynamic Events in Earth History*, Verso, London

IUCN (International Union for Conservation of Nature) (2009) 'Category 1b wilderness area', www.iucn.org/about/work/programmes/pa/pa_products/wcpa_categories/pa_category1b/, visited 21 July 2010

IUCN (2010) 'The IUCN Red List of Threatened Species', www.iucnredlist.org/, accessed 19 July 2010

Jansen, J. D. (2009) *Knowledge in the Blood: Confronting Race and the Apartheid Past*, Stanford University Press, Stanford

Magquba Ntombela Foundation (no date) 'Tribute to Magquba Ntombela', www.mnf.org.za/tribute.php, visited 21 July 2010

Magubane, B.M. (2007) *Race and the Construction of the Dispensable Other*, UNISA Press, Pretoria

Maxwell, A. (1999) *Colonial Photography and Exhibitions. Representations of the "Native" and the Making of European Identities*, Leicester University Press, London

Meyers, N. (1992) *The Primary Source: Tropical Forests and our Future*, Norton, London

Mudimbe, V. Y. (1994) *The Invention of Africa. Gnosis, Philosophy, and the Order of Knowledge*, Indiana University Press, Bloomington

NASA Earth Observatory (2010) 'Defining desertification', http://earthobservatory.nasa.gov/Features/Desertification/, visited 21 July 2010

New York Times (1989) 'Kenya, in gesture, burns ivory tusks', *New York Times*, 19 July 1989, www.nytimes.com/1989/07/19/world/kenya-in-gesture-burns-ivory-tusks.html, accessed 21 July 2010

Player, I. (1972) *The White Rhino Saga*, Collins, London

Ramutsindela, M. (2007) *Transfrontier Conservation in Africa: At the Confluence of Capital, Politics and Nature*, CABI, Wallingford

Revkin, A. (1990) *The Burning Season: The Murder of Chico Mendes and the Fight for the Amazon Rainforest*, Island Press, Washington DC

Roe, E. (1994) *Narrative Policy Analysis: Theory and Practice*, Duke University Press, Durham

Schrift, A. D. (1997) *The Logic of the Gift: Toward an Ethic of Generosity*, Routledge, New York

Steele, N. (1967) 'The future of the white rhino', Big Game Hunters and Fishermen's Conference, San Antonio, Texas, United States of America, 31 March 1967

Strom, S. (2002) 'Charities find donors scarce as market losses compound', *The New York Times*, 30 July

Strother, Z. S. (1999) 'Display of the body Hottentot', in Lindfors, B. (ed) *Africans on Stage. Studies in Ethnological Show Business*, David Philip, Cape Town

Tredger, N. (2009) *From Rhodesia to Mugabe's Zimbabwe. Chronicles of a Game Ranger*, Galago, Alberton

Van Lippe-Biersterfeld, I. (with van Tijn, J.) (2005) *Science, Soul, and the Spirit of Nature: Leading Thinkers on the Restoration of Man and Creation*, Bear and Company, Rochester

Wiepking, P. and Bekkers, R. (2010) 'Does who decides really matter? Causes and consequences of personal financial management in the case of larger and structural charitable donations', *Voluntas*, vol 21, no 2, pp240–263

Wild Foundation (no date) 'Wilderness as a protected area classification', The Wild Foundation, www.wild.org/main/about/what-is-a-wilderness-area/wilderness-as-a-protected-area-classification/, visited 21 July 2010

WWF (World Wide Fund for Nature) (2008) 'More of Africa urged to boost rhino numbers', WWF, www.panda.org/who_we_are/wwf_offices/mozambique/?127280/More-of-Africa-urged-to-boost-rhino-numbers, visited 20 January 2010

Wylie, J. (2007) *Landscape*, Routledge, London

6

The Global Environment Facility: Financing Conservation in the Global South

Research and popular literature on philanthropy overemphasize the importance of either the individual philanthropists or foundations, or the combination of the two (see Salamon, 1992; Clotfelter and Ehrlich, 1999). Such an emphasis might give the false impression that philanthropy can best be understood by studying foundations through which philanthropists channel their gifts. In this chapter we suggest that attention should also be paid to other channels, especially those involving the state. States, too, channel their resources towards a humanitarian cause, the education of other nations and communities, the protection of the environment, and so on, to countries other than their own. While it is odd to call states philanthropists, the work they do to help others outside their areas of jurisdictions could be similar to that performed by philanthropists and may even flow from similar kinds of impulses. It could also be suggested that in some instances, the politics of foreign assistance is not dissimilar to that of philanthropy. Our point here is that channels for philanthropy can also be found in formal structures and institutions. We do not see such formal structures as a contradiction to the clandestine philanthropic channels and networks we discussed in Chapter 3. For us, formal and informal channels manifest the different dimensions of philanthropy we presented in Chapter 1.

Whereas Chapters 3 and 5 presented ethnographic material to account for networked philanthropy, this chapter relies on quantitative material to demonstrate the actual grants and projects that are funded. The point we make by using these different types of data is that the South–North connections are real, irrespective of the type of data one uses and the perspective from which such connections are analysed. In other words, we bring together ethnographic and quantitative material to validate our points. We interrogate the South–North alignment of environmental donations through formal channels such the World Bank's GEF. The GEF is one of the most ambitious mechanisms through which funds can be channelled to CBOs and NGOs that pursue the environmental cause in low- and middle-income developing countries. Between 1990 and 2010, the GEF invested $9.2 billion and spent $40 billion in co-financing some 2,700 projects in 165 countries, making it – according to its latest publication – 'the world's leading public financial fund dedicated to smart environmentally sound choices that boost local economies and protect the planet' (GEF, 2010, p1).

The GEF-SGP, in particular, provides the clearest example of global donations that are used to support an environmental cause at the local level (GEF, 2006). The GEF-SGP was created in 1992 as an arm of the GEF. The SGP (Small Grants Programme) was specifically designed:

> *to develop community-level strategies and implement technologies to reduce threats to the global environment, to gather and communicate lessons from community-level experience, to build partnerships and networks with community-based organizations (CBOs) and Non-governmental Organizations (NGOs), and to ensure that conservation and sustainable development strategies and projects that protect the global environment are understood and practiced by communities and other stakeholders.* (GEF and UNDP, 2008, p5)

The SGP currently operates in 122 countries, and the programme has awarded more than 12,000 grants to support environment-related projects that are run by CBOs and NGOs in developing countries. In terms of the theme of this book, the SGP should be understood as both a channel for donor funds and the opportunity for locals to engage with global donors and their intended environmental goals. In this context, Gan sees the GEF as providing Southern NGOs with the opportunity to 'express their concerns, and even to impose their influence and values' (Gan, 1993, p267). This chapter proceeds from the premise that the GEF-SGP is a practical expression of the broad goals of the GEF. A brief discussion on GEF below will assist us to understand this.

GEF: Greening of the World Through Funding Mechanisms

Young (2002) traces the history of the GEF from 1982 when the United Nations Environment Programme (UNEP) undertook a ten-year review of the Stockholm Conference, which laid the foundation for the creation of the World Commission on Environment and Development (WCED) in late 1983. The Commission was created by the UN General Assembly with the goal of providing concrete actions for resolving the environment–development problematic; strengthening international cooperation on environmental and development projects; and raising levels of commitment to the environment by voluntary organizations, the business sector, governments and individuals. The Commission's Tokyo Declaration of 27 February 1987 emphasized eight key areas necessary for building a 'secure' future for all: improving economic growth, working towards distributive justice, conserving and enhancing the resource base, ensuring a sustainable level of population, re-orientating technology and managing risks, integrating environment and economics in decision making, reforming international economic relations and strengthening international cooperation (WCED, 1987).

These objectives could only be met with substantial funding at the global level as the following statement from the Commission makes it clear: 'there is a need to increase the financial resources for new multilateral efforts and programmes of action for the environmental protection and sustainable development' (WCED, 1987, p340). The Commission also noted that voluntary contributions by governments have limited multilateral scope, are discretionary and unpredictable, short term and largely support the administrative and operating costs of organizations working on environmental and development projects. Of significance to the theme of this chapter is that the Commission revived earlier efforts to set up international financing mechanisms for protecting the environment. Earlier efforts included the 1977 Plan of Action to Combat Desertification, which called for the establishment of a special account for the purpose of financing actions on the ground. Following on the need for financing mechanisms, the WCED suggested that revenue derived from the use of international commons and natural resources should be used to support strategies towards a common future of the world and its people. The revenue was to be derived from ocean fishing and transportation, seabed mining, Antarctic resources and parking charges for geostationary communications satellites. The use of taxes on international trade was also mooted (WCED, 1987). It is for this reason that the WCED report of 1987 is regarded as the foundation of the GEF (Mittermeier and Bowles, 1993).

ENGOs, mostly those based in Washington DC, not only appreciated the WCED's vision for a 'healthy' relationship between development and environmental protection, but, more importantly, viewed the mechanisms for financing that vision as crucial for their funding needs as well. To be sure, ENGOs were lobbying for the consolidation of existing disparate multilateral conventions under a common institutional framework (Young, 2002). These conditions were conducive to the creation of a global funding instrument. Indeed, the renewed attempt towards creating such an instrument came in the form of an International Conservation Financing Programme (ICFP). It was initially thought that the ICFP would be financed by the World Resources Institute's brain child, the International Environmental Facility that was established in 1987 (World Resources Institute, 1989). The Institute's 1989 report on *Natural Endowments: Financing Resource Conservation for Development* proposed that international environmental facilities should be used to identify and support conservation projects, and create synergies between governments, bilateral aid agencies, multilateral development banks, NGOs and intergovernmental organizations (Mittermeier and Bowles, 1993).

The proposal for the ICFP and its facility is ascribed to, among other things, the influential position and role of the US economist, Robert Repetto, and Michael Sweatman. According to Young, Michael Sweatman was not only a capitalist but was also a conservationist with a keen interest in promoting private sector involvement in conservation worldwide, particularly in Africa (Young, 2002). The advisory panel of the ICFP included Sweatman and 'representatives of other NGOs, private investment banks and major development agencies (among them two World Bank directors)' (Young, 2002, p51). Sweatman was once a director of WILD, a foundation that was established in the US in 1974 by South African Ian Player with the aim of protecting threatened wilderness areas and wildlife in sub-Saharan Africa (see Chapters 3 and 5 for further details of this particular network in conservation and its links to environmental philanthropy).

Notwithstanding the earlier efforts we referred to above, the creation of the GEF is closely associated with the World Bank. It is said that in September 1989 the Development Committee mandated the World Bank 'to assess requirements for additional funding and the potential interest from donors in supporting actions to address global environmental concerns in developing countries' (World Bank, 1990, pp1–2). Germany and France in particular were at the forefront of this global financing instrument, with France indicating its willingness to contribute FF900 million in the first three years of the facility (World Bank, 1990).[1] The broad parameters within which the GEF was to operate included focusing on country programmes and activities that would yield global environmental benefits. It was envisaged that the GEF would be jointly implemented by UNEP, UNDP and the World Bank, an arrangement that was later viewed as an obstacle to the efficient operation of the Facility (Sharma, 1996).

It follows that, with the support of Western European governments, the World Bank successfully lobbied for the creation of the GEF in November 1990. The GEF rose into prominence at the 1992 Rio Earth Summit where it was adopted as the interim financing instrument for the Convention on Biological Diversity and the Climate Change Convention, and was hailed as 'a unique experiment in the international mobilization and use of funding for global environmental protection and sustainable development' (GEF document cited in Sharma, 1996, p74). It is also viewed as an instrument through which humanity could 'pay a higher "insurance bill" to safeguard the ecological long-term basis of our economic and social wellbeing [and] increased spending on conservation could help fund a worldwide core network of protected areas of biodiversity' (Hillmann and Barkmann, 2009, p37). It was expected that the launching of the GEF would be accompanied by a call for the transfer of funds from the North to the South, which would compensate for the South's willingness to slow down or halt its development projects that were seen by the industrialized countries as a threat to the protection of the environment (Mee et al, 2008).

Meanwhile the creation of the GEF can be looked at from different perspectives. Apart from its concern with environmental and development projects, the GEF is also viewed as a reaction of the World Bank towards criticisms that had been levelled against the Bank. Those criticisms are aimed at development projects such as controversial dams, coal mining and so on that the World Bank had funded (see for example Dorcey, 1997). Critics have used the Bank's bad track record on development projects to argue that it is not an appropriate institution to manage and implement the GEF (McNeely, 1991; Shiva, 1992). Despite these negative views of the Bank, the GEF appealed to governments and other institutions that were under pressure from environmental activists who are fiercely opposed to the global economic model of capitalism. The GEF is also seen as part of the 'Grand Bargain' that took place at the Rio Earth Summit, where rich countries agreed to finance the participation of less developed countries in global environmental projects and programmes.

In environmental circles, the GEF is seen as the world's most important green institution that could 'head-off environmentally-caused conflict', even though its scope is not about conflict resolution (Payne, 1998, p365). The association of the GEF with conflict resolution is based on the view that the Facility will mitigate the scarcity of resources, which is seen by some analysts as a catalyst for wars and conflict, especially in developing countries (see Kaplan, 1994). Thus the GEF is seen as an important actor in financing the protection of the environment and, by extension, the prevention of wars and conflict. Published material supporting the links between environment and conflict/conflict resolution abound (see Maathai, 2006; Ali, 2007). There is, however, a counterview that sees the abundance rather than scarcity of resources as the main contributor of environmentally induced conflict (see Le Billon, 2001).

Of relevance to our discussion here is that the GEF as the multi-donor funding mechanism operating at the global scale has specific areas of focus that limit the scope of participation and access to funding by CBOs and NGOs. At its inception, the GEF was meant to support four activities: biodiversity conservation, reduction of global climate change, protection of international waterways and reduction of ozone-depleting chemicals. In the early years of the GEF biodiversity conservation accounted for 43 per cent of the total costs of the GEF work programme (Mittermeier and Bowles, 1993). These activities were later expanded to the current six areas (see Table 6.1). The reasons for increasing the focal areas were partly an attempt to address weaknesses in the design of the initial focal areas. There was also a need to re-orientate the programme towards environmental challenges of the day that cut across those focal areas. In their assessment of the GEF biodiversity portfolio in its first two years of operation, Mittermeier and Bowles (1993) conclude that the Facility has a poorly articulated mission, its objectives shifted from time to time, and that there was a need for an independent secretariat. Subsequent reviews have shown that the GEF faces four major socio-political challenges. The most recent assessment of the GEF has shown that there is a mismatch between the scales at which drivers of environmental change operate and environmental consequences are addressed; strong public endorsements are not matched by commitments; there

Table 6.1 *GEF focal areas and project funds committed until 2005*

Focal area[a]	Operational programme (OP)	Number of projects (%)[b]	Project funds committed (%)
Biodiversity	OP1 Arid and semi-arid zone ecosystem OP2 Coastal, marine and freshwater ecosystem OP3 Forest ecosystem OP4 Mountain ecosystem OP13 Conservation and sustainable use of biological diversity	52	41
Climate change[c]	OP5 Removal of barriers to energy efficiency and energy conservation OP6 Promoting the adoption of renewable energy by removing barriers and reducing implementing costs OP7 Reducing the long-term costs of low greenhouse gas emitting energy technologies OP11 Promoting environmentally sustainable transport	17	34
International waters	OP8 Waterbody-based operational programme OP9 Integrated land and water multiple focal area operational programme OP10 Contaminant-based operational programme	5	16
Persistent organic pollutants	OP14 Draft Elements of an operational programme for reducing and eliminating releases of persistent organic pollutants	2	*
Land degradation	OP15 Operational programme on sustainable land management	11	*
Multifocal area	OP12 Integrated ecosystem management	12	*

[a] The description of focal areas has changed over time.
[b] 2006 figures.
[c] Including climate change and adaptation (projects on 'climate change' and 'climate change and adaptation' were treated as one category throughout this chapter).
* 9% for all three in total.
Sources: Adapted from Lee et al, 2008; www.sgp.undp.org (accessed 2 July 2010)

is no common currency with which to measure the successes of the projects; and the development of triangular relationships between government, private sector and civil society have created mistrust between the parties involved and have neither improved cooperation among various sectors nor adopted the necessary technology that could enhance the performance of its projects (Miller, 2007; Mee et al, 2008).

Table 6.1 shows that biodiversity conservation and climate change enjoy the lion's share of the Facility. It should be noted that the GEF focal areas are replicated at the local level through the GEF-SGP.

SGP AND THE FLOW OF FUNDING

Since its creation in 1992, the SGP of the GEF has focused on community-level projects in developing countries. As in the GEF in general, the programme supports projects on climate change abatement and adaptation, biodiversity conservation, the protection and management of international waters, reduction of the impact of persistent organic pollutants, and the prevention of land degradation. Grants for projects in biodiversity are meant to support conservation and the management of biodiversity. The projects should ideally be located in areas where ecosystem or constituent species are threatened or at risk, hotspots, sites of endemic species, habitats important for migratory species, and sites falling under treaties or conventions. The conservation and management of biodiversity accounted for 52 per cent of projects by focal area and, by June 2010, $157,288,704 had been spent on 7123 biodiversity-focused projects (GEF-SGP, 2010).

For their part, projects on climate change come second after biodiversity and are meant to ameliorate the impact of climate change on marginal communities in developing countries in accordance with the United Nations Framework Convention on Climate Change (UNFCCC). The objective of the Convention is to stabilize greenhouse gas concentrations in the atmosphere at a level that will prevent dangerous anthropogenic interference with the climate system within a particular timeframe to ensure the adaptation of ecosystems and food production systems to climate change and to maintain sustainable development (United Nations, 1992). The GEF-SGP also supports community projects that promote adaptation to climate change, hence the GEF manages two UNFCCC funds for this purpose: the Least Developed Countries Fund and the Special Climate Change Fund. Like these two funds, the Adaptation Fund,[2] which falls under the Kyoto Protocol, is also meant to finance projects and programmes that promote the resilience of communities to climate change in developing countries. Despite these developments, climate change adaptation remains the least popular focal area (1 per cent) of the GEF-SGP projects. Research has shown the need for differentiated responses to a range of stresses that communities might suffer as a result of climate change (see Ziervogel et al, 2006).

With regard to international waters, the GEF funds SGP projects in which NGOs and CBOs address threats to water systems such as lake basins, groundwater systems, river basins and marine ecosystems that either affect riparian states simultaneously or by means of environmental problems encountered in the neighbouring country. The projects should generally be responsive to the pollution of international waters. By their nature, international waters-related projects are multi-country and therefore require collaboration among NGOs and CBOs across national borders. However, the country-specific nature of funding means that projects are most likely to be confined to the country through which grants are made.

As in the case of funding for projects in biodiversity and climate change and adaptation, financial support for local projects concerned with deforestation and desertification was designed to assist countries to implement the Convention to Combat Desertification. For example, in 2000 the Ad Hoc Committee of the United Nations recommended that the GEF should provide funding for combating desertification[3] (United Nations, 2002). Subsequently, land degradation was included as a GEF focal area in 2002. The GEF-SGP supports projects involving conservation and restoration of arid and semi-arid areas; efficient stoves and biogas to reduce forest loss; integrated watershed management; soil erosion; afforestation; prevention of forest fires; organic farming; policy and barriers to mitigating land degradation, and so on (GEF-SGP: Focal Points, 2006). By June 2010, 1620 land degradation-related projects had been supported by the GEF-SGP to the tune of $34,292,016. These projects were also supported through co-financing mechanisms involving $45,279,811 in cash and $22,031,870 in kind (GEF-SGP: About SGP, 2006)).

The last and one of the least funded GEF-SGP focal areas is the persistent organic pollutants (POPs), which has its roots in decision 19/13 C of 7 February 1997 of the Governing Council of UNEP that sought to initiate international action to protect both the health of the environment and humans by reducing and eliminating discharges and emissions of POPs:

> *POPs are substances that are persistent, bioaccumulative and toxic and can affect generations of humans. Some POPs are also considered to be endocrine disrupters, which, by altering the hormonal system, can damage the reproductive and immune systems of exposed individuals as well as their offspring. POPs can also have developmental and carcinogenic effects.* (UNEP, 2010, p1)

The number of chemicals deemed detrimental to humans and the environment has increased over the years, and so have been controversies over pollutants such as DDT. The Stockholm Convention on Persistent Organic Pollutants was adopted in May 2001 and paved the way for the recognition of POPs as a new focal area of the GEF in 2002 (United Nations, 2001; UNEP, 2010). By June 2010, grants amounting to $5,257,850 had been made to support 241 GEF-SGP projects in POPs.

The five GEF-SGP regions are Africa,[4] Arab states, Asia and the Pacific, Europe and the CIS, and Latin America and the Caribbean. The survey reported here is based on 11,876 projects that are accessible to the public. Since these projects represent 97 per cent of GEF-SGP projects (i.e. 97 per cent of 12,229) and are described in full to gain understanding of the activities involved, they are useful data for understanding and analysing the working of the SGP projects. It should be noted that the number of 11,876 excludes 68 projects that are listed under the Micronesia sub-region in the Asia and the Pacific region. We found country-

Table 6.2 *Comparison of focal areas in five GEF-SGP regions*

Region	Biodiversity	Climate change	International waters	Land degradation	Multifocal	POPs
Africa	1307	510	172	395	385	69
Arab states	322	309	58	123	75	15
Asia and the Pacific	1545	555	201	263	417	52
Europe and the CIS	826	382	69	163	115	38
Latin America and the Caribbean	2682	449	71	327	479	36
Total	6682	2205	571	1271	1471	210

Source: Constructed from http://sgp.undp.org, accessed 1–16 July 2010

specific projects more helpful for the purposes of comparison and discussion than aggregated sub-regional projects. A survey of these projects reveals that most projects focus on biodiversity and affirm the funding priorities of the GEF (see Table 6.2).

There are, however, variations within and between countries and regions. For example, in the Africa region, countries with the highest number of biodiversity projects are predominantly in West and East Africa, with Mali leading the continent with 259 projects (see Table 6.3). Four countries from these two regions, namely, Kenya and Tanzania (East Africa) and Mali and Senegal (West Africa) take up a third of SGP grants in the continent. Niger in West Africa stands out as the country with more land degradation-related projects,[5] while Kenya, which has the highest number of GEF-SGP projects in East Africa, has a significant number of projects that are multifocal in nature and scope. The same trend with high numbers of multifocal projects continues in Botswana, Kenya, Mali, Mozambique and Uganda (see Table 6.3).

The significance of multifocal projects is that they not only cut across the GEF-SGP's six focal areas but also represent innovative local initiatives that negotiate the incompatibility between local relevance and the areas and activities that can be supported through global funds. It should be noted that the average number of projects involved in the reduction and elimination of POPs in the continent was 2.43 per cent, as compared to 46.05 per cent in biodiversity. This means that there are too few projects that are funded to reduce or eliminate organic pollutants in a continent that suffers from domestic and international dumping of toxic wastes. It has recently been reported that 'European states are still using African coasts as dumping ground of toxic waste, even after enactment of legislation aimed at ending the practice by the European Union' (Redfern, 2010, p19).

On average the Arab states have a balance between projects for biodiversity and climate change (35.7 and 34.3 per cent respectively). As Table 6.4 shows, Egypt not only has the highest number of projects in the region but has also an

Table 6.3 *Number of GEF-SGP projects in Africa, January 1990–June 2010*

Countries	Biodiversity	Climate change	International waters	Land degradation	Multifocal	POPs	Total
Benin	9	6	5	3	0	2	25
Botswana	63	15	7	19	38	4	146
Burkina Faso	75	11	0	22	9	4	121
Burundi	4	0	2	0	0	0	6
Cameroon	20	5	1	1	2	3	32
Cape Verde	10	1	0	3	5	0	19
Chad	9	3	0	5	0	2	19
Comoros	15	2	0	2	5	0	24
Cote d'Ivoire	90	85	4	5	5	2	191
Eritrea	2	2	0	2	2	0	8
Ethiopia	35	20	0	13	0	0	68
Gambia	4	3	0	5	0	0	12
Ghana	76	26	5	28	19	9	163
Kenya	99	45	21	20	56	3	244
Lesotho	6	0	1	5	3	2	17
Liberia	10	4	0	1	0	0	15
Madagascar	86	0	0	0	1	0	87
Malawi	2	2	0	4	2	1	11
Mali	136	31	18	12	52	10	259
Mauritania	41	24	5	25	20	1	116
Mauritius	49	18	16	5	25	1	114
Mozambique	38	7	9	19	20	3	96
Namibia	47	26	2	16	7	0	98
Niger	15	22	8	30	13	7	95
Nigeria	2	6	0	1	0	0	9
Rwanda	7	10	4	8	2	1	32
Senegal	129	15	8	24	25	1	202
South Africa	32	19	0	4	7	1	63
Tanzania	82	60	23	47	11	2	225
Togo	4	0	0	7	1	0	12
Uganda	43	22	27	19	43	1	155
Zambia	5	1	0	4	1	0	11
Zimbabwe	62	19	6	36	11	9	143
Total	1307	510	172	395	385	69	2838

Source: constructed from http://sgp.undp.org, accessed 1–16 July 2010)

exceptionally high number of climate change-related projects (74 per cent). The country takes up almost 40 per cent of funding for SGP projects in the Arab states. These projects include converting domestic solid waste into ethanol; the adoption of renewable energy technology; constructing and maintaining biogas units; designing and manufacturing wind turbines; and the distribution of solar heaters. The pattern is the same for Yemen, where there are more projects for climate change than biodiversity. Most climate change-related projects in Yemen involve the use of solar energy for water supply to villages. This way, the projects combine environmental concerns with development imperatives.

Table 6.4 *Number of GEF-SGP projects in Arab states, January 1990– June 2010*

Countries	Biodiversity	Climate change	International waters	Land degradation	Multifocal	POPs	Total
Egypt	39	183	16	0	5	4	247
Jordan	67	18	21	55	8	1	170
Lebanon	18	3	1	6	0	2	30
Morocco	61	28	3	11	26	2	131
Palestinian Authority	54	40	4	8	6	3	115
Syria	18	8	1	6	4	1	38
Tunisia	58	17	9	27	23	2	136
Yemen	7	12	3	10	3	0	35
Total	322	309	58	123	75	15	

Source: constructed from http://sgp.undp.org, accessed 15 July 2010

Thailand has the highest number of projects on international waters compared to the other countries in Asia and the Pacific region (see Table 6.5), or for that matter, in all of the other GEF-SGP regions. This is not surprising because Thailand has been involved in water conflicts with the lower Mekong River basin's riparian states, namely, Cambodia, Lao People's Democratic Republic, and Vietnam (see Sneddon and Fox, 2006). Some of the GEF-SGP projects in the country are directly related to the Mekong River. For example, the GEF supported the Wawi Highland Sustainable Agriculture to stop deforestation and to rehabilitate the watershed of the Mae Suay River, which is one of the tributaries of the Mekong River. Other NGOs and CBOs such as the Non-chemical Agriculture Project, Mun River Flood Plain Recovery Project, Association for Community and Ecology Development, ChiangKhong Concern Group, Photharam Temple, Suan Thai Kaset, Tha Nang Naew Women Cooperatives, Karn Conservation Group, Forest Protection Group (Nakhonratchasima Province), Sustainable Agriculture Development for Self-Reliance Project, Chiang Noi Organization for Development and the Phong River Conservation Group have been involved in various projects that are related to the Mekong River. The tale told by these projects is that though the basin is transboundary, the projects are predominantly bound up with national imperatives.

The GEF-SGP region known as Europe and the CIS deserves a comment concerning how it is delineated in order to clarify the countries involved. Since the SGP is meant for developing countries, countries in Europe proper do not qualify for GEF-SGP grants. The region referred to in the GEF-SGP classification constitutes countries in Eastern Europe, some of which were part of the USSR. It includes the CIS, which was established after the fall of the Soviet Union, through the 1991 Treaty of Minsk. Since its formation, the CIS has assumed the coordinating role for the region and was conceived as a vehicle for facilitating the independence of the former Soviet Republics while at the same time promoting cooperation for mutual benefit (Sakwa and Webber, 1999). The general picture of GEF-SGP projects in

Table 6.5 *Number of GEF-SGP projects in Asia and the Pacific, January 1990–June 2010*

Countries	Biodiversity	Climate change	International waters	Land degradation	Multifocal	POPs	Total
Bhutan	37	18	0	16	6	0	77
Cambodia	28	32	9	8	0	0	77
Fiji	37	5	10	4	3	0	59
India	161	72	4	20	42	12	311
Indonesia	237	32	10	2	45	0	326
Iran	65	28	4	14	54	4	169
Lao	13	3	0	0	1	0	17
Malaysia	63	7	0	0	13	0	83
Marshall Islands	1	0	0	0	0	0	1
Mongolia	123	19	3	58	17	4	224
Nepal	55	35	6	18	11	1	126
Pakistan	80	83	9	15	34	8	229
Papua New Guinea	98	5	2	1	11	0	117
People's Republic of China	9	10	1	1	0	1	22
Philippines	161	35	2	0	50	4	252
Samoa	39	18	8	32	12	2	111
Solomon Islands	2	0	0	0	0	0	2
Sri Lanka	176	41	1	42	63	7	330
Thailand	59	81	126	14	36	8	324
Vanuatu	8	1	0	2	1	0	12
Vietnam	93	30	6	16	18	1	164
Total	1545	555	201	263	417	52	

Source: constructed from http://sgp.undp.org, accessed 1–16 July 2010

this region is the persistent dominance of support for local initiatives in the area of biodiversity, with Poland taking a lead (see Table 6.6). Kazakhstan and Kyrgyzstan have a significant number of projects related to land degradation. Kazakhstan's high number of projects on international waters has very much to do with the hydropolitics of the region where the upstream Kyrgyzstan uses hydropower to meet its high demand for power in winter at the expense of water needed for irrigation (especially cotton) by downstream states such as Kazakhstan and Uzbekistan (see Abbink et al, 2010). Thus, the GEF-SGP sponsored international waters projects in Kazakhstan are responding in part to the need to secure livelihoods downstream and to sustain irrigation schemes in that state.

Compared to other GEF-SGP regions, the region known as Latin America and the Caribbean has the largest concentration of SGP projects (Tables 6.2 and 6.7). It should be noted that Costa Rica and Mexico have the highest concentration of SGP projects in that region.

Table 6.6 *Number of GEF-SGP projects in Europe and the CIS, January 1990–June 2010*

Countries	Biodiversity	Climate change	International waters	Land degradation	Multifocal	POPs	Total
Albania	117	25	5	8	28	4	187
Armenia	3	3	0	3	0	1	10
Belarus	19	30	8	6	0	7	70
Bulgaria	28	37	1	10	2	2	80
Kazakhstan	97	60	24	54	21	9	265
Kyrgyzstan	98	43	4	57	6	9	217
Lithuania	50	21	11	11	11	0	104
Macedonia	19	14	5	2	3	5	48
Poland	251	93	5	0	30	1	380
Slovak Rep	0	12	0	0	0	0	12
Tajikistan	4	1	0	3	0	0	8
Turkey	134	30	6	6	11	0	187
Uzbekistan	6	13	0	3	3	0	25
Total	826	382	69	163	115	38	

Source: constructed from http://sgp.undp.org, accessed 1–16 July 2010

Table 6.7 *Number of GEF-SGP projects in Latin America and the Caribbean, January 1990–June 2010*

Countries	Biodiversity	Climate change	International waters	Land degradation	Multi-focal	POPs	Total
Argentina	41	32	0	27	11	2	113
Barbados	43	12	4	20	19	3	101
Belize	155	7	5	6	0	0	173
Bolivia	166	70	0	9	7	6	258
Brazil	216	1	3	15	4	0	239
Chile	160	30	0	9	59	2	260
Costa Rica	359	21	2	40	67	4	493
Cuba	22	17	0	12	1	2	54
Dominica	36	3	1	5	5	0	50
Dominican Republic	188	93	1	12	36	0	330
Ecuador	173	8	4	31	20	2	238
El Salvador	21	35	0	5	62	0	123
Guatemala	188	44	14	26	68	1	341
Haiti	6	1	1	0	0	0	8
Honduras	95	20	8	14	12	1	150
Jamaica	18	12	0	33	3	0	66
Mexico	402	4	3	0	74	0	483
Nicaragua	65	11	6	20	2	5	109
Panama	26	3	0	12	1	1	43
Peru	198	6	0	1	5	3	213
Suriname	29	7	6	13	9	0	64
Trinidad and Tabago	44	2	7	5	14	3	75
Uruguay	31	10	6	12	0	1	60
TOTAL	2682	449	71	327	479	36	

Source: constructed from http://sgp.undp.org, accessed 1–16 July 2010

The geography of the GEF-SGP suggests that environmental philanthropy brings the South and North together in complex ways (see Chapter 3) and also affirms the critical roles played by NGOs and CBOs in delivering charity on the ground. The fact that the GEF-SGP grants are used by CBOs and NGOs raises questions about whether these organizations are an extension of the arm of the World Bank or whether they are able to negotiate the priorities that are suitable to local circumstances. The question is pertinent especially when large sums of money from big global institutions such as the GEF have to be 'translated' into grassroots initiatives and practices. The theoretical value of the question lies in that it helps us think through philanthropy beyond acts of spending money. As we noted in Chapter 1, giving does not automatically translate into good work; philanthropy should pay attention to why giving takes the form and direction it does. If we were to ask why Africa has been attractive to conservation work we find that there is no single answer to the question, as the following chapter illuminates.

Notes

1 Other interested donors included Australia, Austria, Belgium, Canada, Denmark, Finland, France, Germany, Italy, Japan, the Netherlands, Norway, Spain, Sweden, Switzerland, UK and US. Countries from the global South that participated in discussions about the creation of the GEF included Brazil, China, Cote d'Ivoire, India, Mexico, Morocco and Zimbabwe (World Bank, 1990).
2 The Fund is administered by the Adaptation Fund Board, which is serviced by the GEF. As of 10 February 2010, the 16 board members of the Fund and their alternate members came from the following countries: Senegal, Kenya, South Africa, Egypt, Qatar, Mongolia, Uzbekistan, Poland, Ukraine, Georgia, Moldova, Jamaica, Cuba, Uruguay, Argentina, Norway, Switzerland, Sweden, Finland, Fiji, Maldives, Tanzania, Bangladesh, Japan, Spain, France, UK, Colombia, Lesotho, Pakistan and Ghana (United Nations, 2010).
3 Africa was singled out as a region that urgently needs support in the area of desertification and deforestation.
4 The African region excludes Egypt and Tunisia, which are classified as Arab states in the GEF-SGP classification of regions.
5 This means that local initiatives in Niger deviate from the general concern with biodiversity.

References

Abbink, K., Moller, L. C. and O'Hara, S. (2010) 'Sources of mistrust: An experimental case study of a Central Asian water conflict', *Environmental Resource Economics*, vol 45, no 2, pp283–318
Ali, S. H. (2007) 'Introduction: A natural connection between ecology and peace?', in Ali, S. (ed) *Peace Parks: Conservation and Conflict Resolution*, MIT Press, Cambridge, MA, pp1–18

Clotfelter, C. T. and Ehrlich, T. (1999) 'The world we must build', in Clotfelter, C. T. and Ehrlich, T. (eds) *Philanthropy and the Nonprofit Sector in a Changing America*, Indiana University Press, Bloomington, pp499–516

Dorcey, T. (ed) (1997) *Large Dams: Learning from the Past, Looking at the Future*, Workshop Proceedings, 11–12 April, IUCN, Gland

Gan, L. (1993) 'The making of the Global Environment Facility: An actor's perspective', *Global Environmental Change*, vol 3, no 3, pp256–275

GEF (Global Environment Facility) (2006) *Global Gains through Community-based Approaches. World Bank-Global Environment Facility Operations in Sub-Saharan Africa*, World Bank, Washington DC

GEF (2010) *Behind the Numbers: A Closer Look at GEF Achievements*, World Bank, Washington DC

GEF-SGP (Global Environment Facility Small Grants Programme) (2010) www.sgp.undp.org, accessed 2 July 2010

GEF-SGP: Focal Points (2006) http://sgp.undp.org/index.cfm?module=ActiveWeb&page=WebPage&s=focal_areas, accessed 1–16 July 2010

GEF-SGP: About SGP (2006) http://sgp.undp.org/index.cfm?module=ActiveWeb&page=WebPage&s=focal_areas, accessed 1–16 July 2010

GEF and UNDP (Global Environment Facility and the United Nations Development Programme) (2008) *Small-Grants Programme Report*, World Bank, Washington DC

Hillmann, B. M. and Barkmann, J. (2009) 'Conservation: A small price for long term economic well-being', *Nature*, vol 461, no 3, p37

Kaplan, R. D. (1994) 'The coming anarchy', *The Atlantic Montly*, February

Le Billon, P. (2001) 'The political ecology of war: Natural resources and armed conflict', *Political Geography*, vol 20, no 5, pp561–584

Maathai, W. M. (2006) *Unbowed: One Woman's Story*, London, Heinemann

McNeely, J. A. (1991) 'Global Environment Facility: Cornucopia or kiss of death for biodiversity', *Canadian Biodiversity*, vol 1, no 2, pp5–7

Mee, L. D., Dublin, H. T. and Eberhard, A. A. (2008) 'Evaluating the Global Environment Facility: A goodwill gesture or a serious attempt to deliver global benefits?', *Global Environmental Change*, vol 18, no 4, pp800–810

Miller, A. S. (2007) 'The Global Environment Facility programme to commercialize new energy technologies', *Energy for Sustainable Development*, vol 11, no 1, pp5–12

Mittermeier, R. A. and Bowles, I. A. (1993) 'The Global Environment Facility and biodiversity conservation: Lessons to date and suggestions for future action', *Biodiversity and Conservation*, vol 2, no 6, pp637–655

Payne, R. A. (1998) 'The limits and promise of environmental conflict prevention: The case of the GEF', *Journal of Peace Research*, vol 35, no 3, pp363–380

Redfern, P. (2010) 'EU, US dumping toxic waste in Africa', *East African*, 5–11 July, pp19–20

Sakwa, R. and Webber, M. (1999) 'The Commonwealth of Independent States, 1991–1998: Stagnation and survival', *Europe-Asia Studies*, vol 51, no 3, pp379–415

Salamon, L. M. (1992) *America's Nonprofit Sector: A Primer*, Foundation Center, New York

Sharma, S. D. (1996) 'Building effective international environmental regimes: The case of the Global Environment Facility', *Journal of Environment and Development*, vol 5, no 1, pp73–86

Shiva, V. (1992) *Global Environment Facility: Perpetuating Non-democratic Decision-making*, Third World Network, Penang

Sneddon, C. and Fox, C. (2006) 'Rethinking transboundary waters: A critical hydropolitics of the Mekong Basin', *Political Geography*, vol 25, no 2, pp181–202

UNEP (United Nations Environment Programme) (2010) 'Climate change and POPs: Focus of new study', press release, 12 March, UNEP, Parma

United Nation, (1992) *United Nations Framework Convention on Climate Change*, Geneva

United Nations (2001) *Stockholm Convention on Persistent Organic Pollutants*, UN, New York

United Nations (2002) *Convention to Combat Desertification. ICCD/CRIC(1)/8*, 30 September, UN, New York

United Nations (2010) *Adaptation Fund Board Members and Alternate Board Members*, 10 February, UN, New York

WCED (World Commission on Environment and Development) (1987) *Our Common Future*, Oxford University Press, Oxford

World Bank (1990) *Funding for the Global Environment: The Global Environment Facility*, Discussion Paper, November, World Bank, Washington DC

World Resources Institute (1989) *Natural Endowments: Financing Resource Conservation for Development*, World Resources Institute, New York City

Young, Z. (2002) *A New Green Order? The World Bank and the Politics of the Global Environment Facility*, Pluto, London

Ziervogel, G., Bharwani, S. and Downing, T. E. (2006) 'Adapting to climate change variability: Pumpkins, people and policy', *Natural Resources Forum*, vol 30, no 4, pp294–305

7

Mapping Environmental Philanthropy in Africa

INTRODUCTION

The data presented in the preceding chapter showed that Africa is the recipient of a significant share of GEF-SGP projects – though not the biggest recipient. Chapter 6 furthermore drew attention to the close cooperation between states, NGOs and CBOs. This chapter aims to explore these relations as they have developed over time in Africa. Taking a closer look at the history of nature conservation, including colonial times, may also shed light on the special place Africa seems to occupy in nature conservation, if not always in attracting the majority of environmental philanthropy, then at least in terms of iconography and images of nature and environmental threats. Many of the best known ENGOs actually evolved out of conservation initiatives in Africa, as will be shown below.

The two sides of philanthropy we discussed in Chapter 1 find a clear expression in Africa where the impressive colonial legacy of protected areas and their infrastructure mask the brutalities and the racialization through which these protected areas were established. It is from this historical moment in the creation of protected areas in the continent that this chapter takes its cue. The premise of the chapter is that the history of conservation in the continent provides a platform on which we can understand the roots of environmental philanthropy and its permutations over time. The chapter sheds light on the kinds of environmental threats and wealth that were central to the imaginaries of the continent. In the main the chapter seeks to answer the questions of why and how environmental philanthropy found its way into the continent before it teases out current threads of this philanthropy. It is hoped that the chapter will add to our further understanding of the role of governments in environmental philanthropy, especially when looking at the earlier years of conservation in the continent that were dominated by conferences organized by states to develop rules to govern nature and its (mis) use. Government roles such as these are often missed by research on philanthropy, which overemphasizes philanthropists and foundations.

For European, or more generally philanthropists from the North, the environment and nature conservation in Africa always had a particular appeal. ENGOs as described in Chapter 3 abound and even mushroom on the African continent, and as was shown in Chapters 3, 5 and 6, quite a number of international initiatives were started or inspired by conservationists operating in that continent. An important and perhaps functional reason for that interest could be that the situation in Africa 'demands it' because of its abundance of, and threats to, its rich biodiversity; the limited capacity of the state to implement complex and often expensive conservation plans and management regimes; the overreliance of most governments on foreign aid; and sustained interests in Africa's natural resources. But there is a more complex, and above all a more historically informed picture to paint as the policies and practices pertaining to nature conservation in Africa, as well as the prominent role played by philanthropy in African nature conservation, have quite distinct colonial origins. From the colonial period onwards, prominent members of the elites – in the colonies as well as in the colonizing countries – played an important role in promoting nature conservation in Africa. Initially they interpreted their role mainly as putting pressure on colonial governments, and as the early nature conservation organizations also recruited members that were part of, or had strong ties with, colonial governments, one could argue that nature conservation in Africa was a colonial or imperial project (Prendergast and Adams, 2003; Gissibl, 2006).

After World War II, at the dawn of the independence of many African states, the emphasis shifted to moving beyond colonial ties, towards establishing more transnational ties and the formation of international organizations that could set international standards for nature conservation (Van Dyke, 2008). As the old colonial approach to nature had had quite negative consequences for many Africans – most nature conservation areas were established by evicting African land users – fears were prominent that the newly independent states would de-gazette nature reserves and national parks, and would no longer consider nature conservation a priority (Rangarajan, 2003). These fears were compounded by the high levels of poverty within the countries and their weak financial states. As a result, many environmental organizations started to emphasize fundraising for conservation. To this end, the old elite networks were drawn upon, but also increasingly a wider audience was targeted.

In this chapter, the sometimes contradictory developments that shaped nature conservation on the African continent are presented. It argues that the image of Africa as a 'wild continent' served to justify both the conquering and exploitation of natural resources as well as desires to protect nature that emerged in the second half of the 19th century (see Grove, 1997; Beinart, 2000). Furthermore, the chapter highlights areas of nature conservation that receive a lion's share (how appropriate a phrase in this context) of philanthropy and finally it concludes with an overview of present day trends in nature conservation in Africa, and the impact of philanthropy on these.

Nature Conservation in Africa as an Imperial Project

The important focus on Africa in nature conservation and among ENGOs has its roots in colonial times. Perhaps more than any on other continents, African landscapes and wildlife evoked strong but also contradicting emotions of attraction and fear among Europeans, desires to conquer and tame, and the need to protect (Grove, 1997; Neumann, 1998, 2000). These emotions have had important impacts on visions of and strategies for nature conservation in Africa, and on the relations between African populations and nature conservation.

Explorers and colonialists viewed Africa as a wild place, inhabited by 'wild people', and portrayed it as such in their reports. To some, this wilderness was rather threatening, as can be gleaned from the following quote taken from Joseph Conrad's *Heart of Darkness*, a novel that depicts like no other the feelings of doom and threat experienced by some who ventured into the interior of the continent:

> *At night sometimes the roll of drums behind the curtain of trees would run up the river and remain sustained faintly, as if hovering in the air high over our heads, till the first break of day. Whether it meant war, peace, or prayer we could not tell. The dawns were heralded by the descent of a chill stillness; the wood-cutters slept, their fires burned low; the snapping of a twig would make you start. We were wanderers on prehistoric earth, on an earth that wore the aspect of an unknown planet. We could have fancied ourselves the first of men taking possession of an accursed inheritance, to be subdued at the cost of profound anguish and of excessive toil. But suddenly, as we struggled round a bend, there would be a glimpse of rush walls, of peaked grass-roofs, a burst of yells, a whirl of black limbs, a mass of hands clapping, of feet stamping, of bodies swaying, of eyes rolling, under the drop of heavy and motionless foliage.* (Conrad, 1989 [1902], p68)

In the eyes of many colonial administrators, Africa's wilderness needed to be tamed. Sir Charles Eliot, for instance, who became the Commissioner of the East Africa Protectorate in the late 19th century, thought that the problem with Africa was that its environment required controlling and transforming. As MacKenzie describes, Eliot considered Africa's past as 'uneventful and gloomy' because he presupposed a lack of contact with the outside world resulting from 'natural obstacles', such as deserts, marshes or thick bush that separated the coast from the interior (MacKenzie, 1997, p216). Eliot reported:

> *Nations and races derive their characteristics largely from their surroundings, but on the other hand, man reclaims, disciplines and trains nature. The surface of Europe, Asia and north America has been submitted to this influence and discipline, but it has still to be applied*

to large parts of South America and Africa. (Sir Charles Eliot cited in MacKenzie, 1997, p216)

Missionaries, such as the famous Robert Moffat, often saw it as their duty to discipline local populations to take control over their environment as a first step towards 'civilization' (MacKenzie, 1997). The books and leaflets published by these missionaries popularized the idea of Africa as a 'wild place' among a wider European audience (MacKenzie, 1997). However, these images by no means do justice to Africa's pre-colonial history. The continent was in fact quite well connected globally, with long-distance trade networks stretching out to the Arabic peninsula and Asia, and contacts between North Africa and Europe already existed before Roman times. Yet, this image of isolation and a lack of outside contacts proved to be powerful and persistent, as Eric Wolf (1990) argues in his book *Europe and the People Without History*. Furthermore, recent research indicates that nature itself was much more managed than often thought (cf. Leach and Fairhead, 2000). Nevertheless, colonial administrators and settlers set about 'taming' the wilderness through large-scale agricultural and infrastructural projects.

To others, it was exactly this perceived 'wilderness' that was a main attraction of the continent, a 'lost Eden' (Neumann, 1998) that was coveted by those who felt uneasy with the rapid pace of urbanization and industrialization in Europe and North America. Grove (1995, 1997) argues that the colonial context stimulated the development of an environmentalist critique and conservationist ideology that started in small island settler colonies. It was on these islands – especially on Mauritius – that a 'distinctively French ideology of conservation drew heavily on English desiccation ideas and was strongly tied to social reformism in proto-revolutionary and anti-urban movements' (Grove, 1995, p141). This ideology, according to Grove (1995), influenced forest conservation movements in the British colonies – notably in India and in the US. These movements, he argues, were quite romanticist and anti-establishment.

MacKenzie (1997) notes that eventually the drive to clear large areas of wilderness for development also caused some concern among colonial administrators in Africa. He describes the shift in the writings and career of Sir Harry Johnston, who not only considered himself an administrator, but also a natural history collector, zoologist and artist – creating botanic gardens and small zoos wherever he established a government house. On the one hand he wrote enthusiastically about the economic potential of Africa and its natural attributes, but on the other hand he also expressed mounting alarm at the degradation and decline he perceived.

One of the most critical voices concerning the impact of colonization on the environment was, according to Richard Grove (1997), the Scottish Reverend John Croumbie Brown. Brown was employed by the Cape Colony government from 1862 to 1866 to examine and advise on the biological aspects of colonial settlement. The Reverend's concern was influenced by the Scottish colonial experience. The subjugation of the Scottish landscape and people under 'British' rule resulted in deeply resented changes in land ownership, significant deforestation and population removal. Facilitated by the establishment of Scottish Enlightenment universities, as Grove (1997) claims, and the elaboration of an intellectually rigorous and socially vigorous Calvinist and Congregationalist Protestantism, this influenced much of the modern environmentalism as it has developed in the English speaking world, particularly in the empires and neo-empires. A general lack of opportunities for employment for university-trained Scotsmen in their homeland meant that many sought colonial employ, which is why their ideas became disproportionately significant: 'Some leading Scottish pioneer figures of the early environmental movement are now well-known, John Muir in the US, William Roxburgh, Alexander Gibson, Edward Balfour and Hugh Cleghorn in India' (Grove, 1997, p139; see MacKenzie, 1997, particularly for South Africa).

The environmental movement was strengthened in the mid-19th century by the development in Scotland, as well as in Holland and France, of romantic landscape tastes and by the emergence of a school of landscape painting (Schama, 1995). In France, the writings of Jean-Jacque Rousseau inspired the painters of the l'Ecole de Barbizon to celebrate the Alps and start a movement to protect the forest of Fontainebleau (Selmi, 2009). Evolving landscape and environmental sensibilities were becoming a major vehicle for the expression of nationalism. In Scotland, a Scottish national identity was constructed and asserted against Englishness and English rule (Grove, 1997). This link between landscape and nationalism was projected onto the African landscape, in the case of Scottish nationalists specifically on the South African landscape, as witnessed by the following quote from an article written by the poet Thomas Pringle for *Penny* magazine, a very popular magazine widely read in Scotland in the mid-19th century:

> *The sublimely stern aspect of the country so different from the rich tameness of ordinary English scenery, seemed to strike many of the Southron [English] with a degree of care approaching to consternation. The Scotch, on the contrary, as the stirring recollections of their native land were vividly called up by the rugged peaks and shaggy declivities of this wild coast, were strongly affected, like all true mountaineers on such occasions,* (Grove, 1997, p141)

Penny magazine published a series of articles on (South) Africa by Pringle, which, in conjunction with other popular literature such as the writings of Rider Haggard, by the 1840s 'had massively reinforced the romanticization of Africa in the Scottish mind' (Grove, 1997, p142). Both Pringle and John Croumbie Brown sympathized with local African populations. Pringle explicitly compared the oppression of Africans with the oppression of the Scots, pairing, in his publications, Scots with African populations, and Scots with African landscapes. Grove (1997, p142) claims that 'Since landscape had already been sacralised as a leitmotif of Scots identity, it was but a short step to romanticize and even sacralise the Cape landscape, which

Pringle and his imitators, including John Croumbie Brown, soon did'. In his writings, Brown evoked the Cape colony as a moral landscape that needed reform and development in such a way that the harm done to local populations was undone. He considered deforestation and veld burning – practiced at a large scale by white settlers – as evils that had to be remedied by tree planting, irrigation and measures to combat soil erosion.

Brown's sentiments concerning local populations as victims of environmental degradation caused by European colonization show that colonial employees were not speaking with one voice on the subject of conservation. Brown did, however, come into conflict with the Cape Colony authorities over this, which led to his resignation – this did not prevent him becoming an inspiration to others such as Franklin Benjamin Hough, the founder of the American Forest Service. Nevertheless, MacKenzie (1997, p218) argues that it is a 'characteristic of the apprehensive imperialist: the agency for ecological decline was invariably placed elsewhere'. Many colonial soil erosion and forestry programmes implemented in later years did indeed target African populations as the main culprits who had to adapt their practices (Beinart, 2000).

Around the same time concerns about deforestation and soil erosion started to emerge, alarm bells started to sound about the decline in wildlife populations. In the mid-19th century excessive off-take of ivory and other commercial hunting led to a serious decline in wildlife in many parts of Africa (MacKenzie, 1988; Carruthers 2005; Gissibl, 2006; Selmi, 2009). Colonial administrators, such as Sir Harry Johnston, who was an avid hunter himself, became quite anxious about this decline (MacKenzie, 1997, p217). His fears were shared by a number of African leaders who saw their own hunting practices threatened and tried to impose stricter hunting regulations on white commercial hunters (MacKenzie, 1988; Thomas, 1992; Beinart, 2000). Some of the latter, including for instance Frederick Selous, who had slaughtered hundreds of elephants and other game, equally started to fear the loss of trophy animals and became champions of the protection of wildlife (MacKenzie, 1988). Gradually, hunting for gain and subsistence hunting became frowned upon while sport hunting was elevated to a noble colonial pastime (MacKenzie 1988; Carruthers, 2005). Sport hunting in Africa was described as freedom from a constricting Western lifestyle, 'an escape from a landscape of private property, cities and industrialization' (Carruthers, 2005, p186). During the mid-19th century, western society generally regarded the killing of wild animals for pleasure as morally acceptable, however, it was restricted to 'the refined and elite' (Carruthers, 2005, p186). Colonial settlers, especially in southern Africa, trekking into the interior had to live off the land, which implied hunting for subsistence as well as for trading – very much like local African populations. While the latter were often astounded by the idea of killing animals for pleasure, sport hunting became the norm – propagated through popular literature (Carruthers, 2005). Living off wildlife became considered as unhealthy and uncivilized. Subsistence hunting and hunting for economic gain increasingly were seen as the root cause for declining wildlife populations, and African hunters – despite the fact that some of the earliest proposals for wildlife protection emanated from within African populations – were relabelled as 'poachers' and the main culprits (Neumann, 2000; see also Draper et al, 2004).

Public awareness in Europe of declining numbers of wildlife resulted in new values; issues of cruelty, waste and extinction began to dominate the discourse on hunting (Ritvo, 1987; Carruthers, 2005). Especially in Britain, ideas on imperial masculinity began to include ideas on protecting wildlife and valuing nature. Carruthers argues that the upsurge of British imperialism at the end of the 19th century – when the last phase in the 'scramble for Africa' took place – also encouraged 'a language and ideology related to possession and ownership, and with it came protectionist ideas' (Carruthers, 2005, p188). The increasing importance of mining, industry and agriculture in southern Africa increasingly enclosed wilderness, which then became considered 'a precious inheritance of the Empire to be most jealously safeguarded' (Buxton, 1902, cited in Curruthers, 2005, p188). Hence, the drive to protect wilderness and wildlife in Africa was directed by European – and to some extent American – needs rather than by concerns about the livelihoods of African populations (Anderson and Grove, 1987; Adams and Hutton, 2007). The latter received the main portion of the blame for the destruction of wilderness and wildlife, though again, there were some dissenting voices here, as described below. Nevertheless, as Anderson and Grove argue:

> *Much of the emotional as distinct from the economic investment which Europe made in Africa has manifested itself in a wish to protect the natural environment as a special kind of 'Eden' for the purposes of the European psyche rather than as a complex and changing environment in which people actually have to live ... Africa has been portrayed as offering the opportunity to experience a wild and natural environment which was no longer available in the domesticated landscapes of Europe.*
> (Anderson and Grove, 1987, p4)

The increasing concerns about wildlife and an emergence of a protectionist discourse eventually led to the first international fauna protection convention, drawn up in London in 1900 (Carruthers, 2005). This convention was both the result of and set the stage for the involvement of philanthropists in the protection of nature in Africa (Prendergast and Adams, 2003). While concerns for deforestation and soil erosion were mainly dealt with by colonial governments – except in French colonial territories where a number of tourist associations and scientists working at the Musée Nationale de l'histoire naturelle assisted the Directorate of Water and Forestry (Selmi, 2009) – the protection of wilderness and wildlife from the start involved cooperation between the state and philanthropists, and at a later stage, also the private sector.

Cooperation and Conflicts Between Colonial Governments and Philanthropists in Early Nature Conservation

Fears of the decline of wildlife populations emanated from the circles of hunters in the colonies, and especially in eastern and southern Africa (Prendergast and Adams, 2003; Carruthers, 2005; Gissibl, 2006) – this regional focus is still quite dominant among present day ENGOs (Brockington and Scholfield, 2010). As explained above, between the mid- and late 19th century, hunting for gain gave way to the dominance of sport hunting, and a number of commercial hunters switched to sport hunting, emphasizing their love for nature. The fascination with sport hunting was shared by quite a number of wealthy Americans (Prendergast and Adams, 2003) who were influenced by the near-extinction of the American bison as a result of unbridled hunting. These 'penitent butchers' were highly influential in establishing formal practices of wildlife conservation in Africa. They increasingly started promoting the introduction of game regulations and nature reserves – which indeed became and still are the dominant form of nature conservation in Africa (Adams and Hutton, 2007; Brockington et al, 2008). These conservation strategies were 'borrowed from the world of the English aristocratic rural estates even as the institution died out in England' (Prendergast and Adams, 2003, p251; see also Neumann, 1998). They were also reflected in the establishment of Yellow Stone Park in the US, which in turn inspired nature conservation in Africa, though in locally adapted ways (Beinart and Coates, 1995; Grove, 1995; Selmi, 2009).

Quite early on in the history of nature conservation in Africa, philanthropists started to play an important role, especially in putting pressure on (colonial) governments to implement conservation legislation. One of the most influential philanthropists in nature conservation was Edward North Buxton (Prendergast and Adams, 2003). He was the grandson of Sir Thomas Fowell Buxton, who had been the leader of the anti-slavery movement. Edward N. Buxton and his brother were already involved in nature conservation in the UK, in particular in activities in Epping Forest, where he and his brother sided with local wood-loppers against landowners who wished to enclose the forest. He became a leading figure in the Commons Preservation Society in the UK (Prendergast and Adams, 2003). As will be shown below, this view on the need to prevent exclusion of local populations also influenced his stance on nature conservation in Africa.

Buxton was an avid hunter, who had been on hunting trips to British East Africa and Somaliland – as such he too might have been said to belong to the category of the 'penitent butchers'. He had published accounts of his expeditions in which he expressed his views on the main challenges and actions needed in relation to conservation. Especially through his book *Two African Trips*, he sought engagement with British colonial policy (Prendergast and Adams, 2003). Buxton's attempts were linked to the international conference of African colonial powers –

i.e. Britain, France, Germany, Portugal, Spain, Italy and the Congo Free State that at that time was still the private property of the Belgian King Leopold – held in London between 24 April and 19 May 1900, to discuss the need for environmental protection. In the late 19th and early 20th centuries, concerns about the extinction of wildlife in Africa were well established, and a number of game reserves had been declared, including the Sabie Game Reserve in South Africa that was established in 1892 (Prendergast and Adams, 2003; Carruthers, 2005). The British Foreign Office started working on game regulations in African territories in earnest in 1891, and in 1896 the governor of German East Africa passed a decree establishing game reserves and a licensing system (Prendergast and Adams, 2003; Gissibl, 2006). The conference ultimately resulted in the 1900 Convention for the Preservation of Animals, Birds and Fish in Africa (Carruthers, 2005). The Convention sought to strengthen and standardize game laws across colonial Africa – an endeavour that was fraught with conflicts and contradictions, as is shown below.

The foundation of the Society for the Preservation of the Wild Fauna of the Empire by Buxton and a number of his friends and associates stemmed from a desire to implement the objectives of the Convention, but was, according to Prendergast and Adams (2003, p253) also a 'logical extension of Buxton's view about game preservation in Africa'. Shortly after the Convention had been signed by the parties to the conference, some colonial authorities already proposed the de-gazetting of a number of the newly established game reserves. Furthermore, during the conference, most of the initial objectives had to be toned down, and not all colonial territories were bound equally by the Convention.

The groundwork for the conference had been conducted by German and British colonial administrators, and resulted in a strong German–British alliance (Gissibl, 2006). Some of those engaged in the preparations, however, feared that it would be more difficult to secure adherence of territories such as the Congo Free State and from the Portuguese authorities, and that these would in fact seek to benefit from wildlife protection measures introduced by neighbouring colonial territories. Others disagreed, Wissmann, the retired governor of German East Africa, even proposed Brussels as the venue for the conference, expecting that 'The Congo State will show the utmost readiness to take measures to preserve its natural wealth, ivory. What is true of the Congo State is no less true of the "Congo Français"' (Gissibl, 2006, p131). The British Foreign Office rejected this proposal, and its secretary managed to convince his German counterparts to opt for the organization of the conference in London. Gissibl (2006) argues that the choice of the venue reflected a shift in relations, Britain was now taking the lead, and that this shift also implied that the conference was placed in a much more 'preservationist' context. Had the conference been held in Brussels, the emphasis on the economic aspects of conservation might have been stronger, with representatives of the trading companies active in the Free State trying to gain influence over the proceedings. In London, the conference was dominated by big game hunters, who, together with a few naturalists and zoologists, were consulted as experts (Gissibl, 2006).

The different sizes of delegations sent to the conference probably reflect the varying degrees of interest by the invited parties in the preservation of wildlife. The German and British delegations were the largest and included quite high profile officials and experts. France sent two plenipotentiaries from the London embassy and the French Colonial Department. Portugal, Italy and Spain each only sent one representative from their London embassies; the Congo Free State equally only had one representative present, but this colonial official at least had worked in the Congo (Gissibl, 2006). Hence, the objective of establishing uniform regulations throughout the continent had to be reduced to the much more modest aim of establishing cooperation between the territories of mainland sub-Saharan Africa north of the Zambezi and German South-West Africa. The conference organizers tried to avoid dealing with the self-governing colonies of southern Africa and the Boer republics, but Portugal made ratification dependent on the accession of the British and German territories in southern Africa. Although the African states of Liberia and Abyssinia were excluded from participating in the conference, they were expected to abide by the regulations afterwards, as demanded by France. In the end some agreements were made concerning measures for wildlife protection: the banning of African hunting techniques met with general approval, as did closed hunting seasons and the protection of useful species. Furthermore, the parties to the conference supported the idea of establishing reserves and protected areas. However, restrictions on trade in arms and animal products were subject to fierce debates and dealt with in very vague terms in the Convention (Gissibl, 2006).

These limitations to the Convention and the actions undertaken by a number of colonial administrators to soften the regulations and de-gazette some reserves to allow for hunting by colonial officials and paying visitors were the driving forces behind the foundation of the Society for the Preservation of the Wild Fauna of the Empire. In 1903 Buxton organized a series of meetings at his house with friends and associates to discuss how best to prevent the de-gazetting of the White Nile Reserve in Sudan. A letter was sent to the governor-general of the Sudan, urging him to maintain the protected status of the area. This letter was given extra weight by the signatures of a range of aristocratic and political figures; apart from Buxton these included the Duke and Duchess of Bedford, Sir Edward Grey, Lord Avebury, the Marquis of Hamilton and the Earl of Rosebery. The letter was also signed by businessmen, such as brewery owner Samuel H. Whitbread, leading scientists and naturalists, as well as some of the most renowned colonial administrators, hunters and writers, including Frederick Selous (Prendergast and Adams, 2003). The petition was successful and in December 1903 a circular was sent out announcing the establishment of the Society.

The Society functioned mainly as a pressure group. From the start, as many high profile people as possible were recruited. The Society's strengths, according to Prendergast and Adams (2003) were the personal contacts of its members, its extensive network of overseas correspondents and officials, and its ability to gain the ears of some of the leading government figures. The Society invited senior officials and governors of the African colonies and protectorates, since, as Henry Seton-Karr, a prominent member of the Society expressed it, game preservation could best be done 'by Imperial Government action in the case of the Crown Colonies and Protectorates; by a healthy and active public opinion working through Colonial Governments in the case of self-governing Colonies' (cited in Prendergast and Adams, 2003, p254). While the Society relied mainly on networks established in the Empire (Neumann, 1996; Gissibl, 2006), in later years it extended its network to include prominent figures outside of the Empire such as President Theodore Roosevelt, and others from Canada, Finland and Russia. It also published a journal to inform a wider audience – one of the regular contributors was Colonel Stevenson-Hamilton, who was to become the warden of Kruger National Park in South Africa (Prendergast and Adams, 2003).

The early work of the Society focused mainly on the promotion of game reserves throughout Africa. However, already a few years after its establishment, the Society's scope was broadened to encompass issues such as the relative rights of 'natives', settlers and colonial officials in terms of access to wildlife, poaching and smuggling, the possibilities of tourism and how to deal with the growing threat to wildlife as a result of increasing panic concerning tsetse fly infestation (Prendergast and Adams, 2003). These issues were subject to heated debates, and the interests of the Society did not always coincide with those of colonial administrators – though it must be noted that also within local colonial administrations differences of opinion and interests existed between different departments (Wolmer, 2007; Mavhunga and Spierenburg, 2009). While the Society did take into account economic aspects of wildlife, and certainly recognized the financial benefits from tourism, hunting and the sale of wildlife products, it was against the tendency of many colonial administrators to regard the establishment of reserves and conservation areas as a temporary measure, and to de-gazette these areas when this was considered to be more profitable, or when it was felt that wildlife populations were becoming a threat to agriculture or livestock husbandry – powerful economic sectors especially in settler colonies. Tsetse flies were a danger to cattle and horses, causing the fatal disease trypanosomiasis, and wildlife was considered a vector for these diseases. Many agricultural and veterinary officers therefore considered reserves and conservation areas as reservoirs of tsetse, calling for the abolishment of those located near important agricultural areas and cattle ranches and the extermination of wildlife in those areas. In a number of settler colonies these fears did indeed result in the de-gazetting of reserves and slaughter of wildlife (Mavhunga and Spierenburg, 2007; Wolmer, 2007), and the Society had a hard time convincing authorities that these measures worked (Prendergast and Adams, 2003). Another bone of contention was the widespread practice of allowing colonial officers to hunt, often also in reserves and conservation areas that were off-limits to travelling sports hunters. To Buxton, founder of the Society, 'a sanctuary where people are allowed to shoot is a contradiction in terms' (cited in Prendergast and Adams, 2003, p253). At the follow-up conference held in 1933, this vision of reserves and conservation areas 'matured into the "fortress conservation" of the national park' (Gissibl, 2006, p134). In relation to the 'problem of native hunting', however, Buxton held a much milder opinion, arguing that animals were 'the African's birthright', and that 'from time immemorial the destruction caused by the indigenous inhabitants has not appreciably diminished the stock' (cited in Prendergast and Adams, 2003, p253), though he was against providing them with guns and rifles. Yet, the 1900 Convention had much more negative outcomes for African hunters than for white hunters, and this stance towards 'native hunting' was confirmed in the 1933 conference. Hunting and other forms of access to natural resources by local inhabitants are, nevertheless, issues that in present day conservation circles are still hotly debated (see Hutton et al, 2005) – as many of the issues addressed by the Society still have a contemporary ring to them (Prendergast and Adams, 2003).

Gissibl (2006) also argues that despite the limits of the Convention, it did establish certain standards that not only still influence current debates and practices relating to nature conservation, but also could be claimed by non-governmental actors to be used to exert both intergovernmental and domestic pressure. The Society was an important example, which was soon followed by the establishment of other societies and foundations. In Germany in 1908 the Commission for the Improvement of Wildlife Preservation in German Africa was established; members were mainly recruited from German colonial circles. In France, the Touring Club de France and the Club Alpin Français established in 1913 the Association for National Parks in France and the Colonies (l'Association des Parcs Nationaux de France et des Colonies) (Selmi, 2009). Another influential example was the Movement for the Global Protection of Nature, promoted by the Swiss explorer and member of a prominent banker's family, Paul Sarasin and also established in 1913 (Baer, 1968; Gissibl, 2006). Gissibl (2006, pp135–136) argues that 'this early non-governmental transnationalism thrived on a global awareness fuelled by imperialism and networks of natural scientists and hunters'. Imperialism served as a driving force of international cooperation in environmental matters, though that did not mean that imperial rivalries did not matter (cf. Mavhunga and Spierenburg, 2009).

While the British Society and the French Association mainly 'worked through the Empire', Paul Sarasin, who had established the Swiss League for the Protection of Nature, focused much more on (other) transnational contacts (Gissibl, 2006; Van Dyke, 2008]). Sarasin's main aim was to establish an international body to foster the protection of nature that could propose or create international legislation or treaties concerning the protection of nature. To this end, he put pressure on the Swiss government to organize a conference (Baer, 1968). This conference did indeed take place, with participants from 16 European countries and the US, and as a result, in 1913 the Consultative Commission for the International Protection of Nature was established. However, a year later, World War I broke out, and not much happened. Shortly after the end of the war, Sarasin tried to revive the activities of the Commission, but many of the countries that had been involved faced more urgent problems trying to recover from the devastation of the war. In 1923 the French government organized a conference, entitled 'le Premier Congrès International pour la Protection de la Nature' in which 17 countries participated, but nothing concrete resulted from this conference (Baer, 1968). In 1929 Sarasin died without seeing the realization of his objectives (Van Dyke, 2008).

In the 1930s a number of conferences were organized to promote nature conservation. In 1931, the French government organized a second Congrès International pour la Protection de la Nature, which resulted in the establishment of an International Office for the Protection of Nature in Brussels in 1935 (Baer, 1968). In 1933 Britain organized another Convention for the Preservation of Wild Animals, Birds and Fish in Africa, which was held in London under the auspices of the Society for the Preservation of the Wild Fauna of the Empire. During this convention, as was already mentioned above, the importance of reserves and conservation areas was confirmed (Gissibl, 2006). At the conference, the French Society for Bio-geography and the National Society for Acclimatisation presented the results of an investigation they had conducted under the direction of the French National History Museum into the state of nature reserves around the world. On the basis of these they argued that many present reserves were flawed, and that much stricter controls should be implemented in the form of 'réserves naturelles intégrales', which would preclude any natural resource use or human habitation (Larrère, 2009; Selmi, 2009). Though the conference in general adopted this vision of 'fortress conservation' (Gissibl, 2006), the idea of establishing uniform legislation or the creation of an international body to govern nature protection proved to be still problematic. Rivalries between the participating countries surfaced; in London, for instance, Portugal was taken to task for lagging in the creation of conservation areas, which, in the light of a more general critique on the perceived inability of Portugal to govern its colonies and render them productive, was perceived by the Portuguese authorities as yet another attack on its sovereignty and control over its African colonies (Mavhunga and Spierenburg, 2009). It was not until after the end of World War II that serious steps in the direction of the creation of an international body were taken (Baer, 1968), also as a response to a decline in colonial domination by European powers (Van Dyke, 2008).

A New Scramble for Africa: Conservation from the Dawn of Independence to the Present

Towards the end of World War II, in October 1944, President Roosevelt of the US proposed a meeting of 'the united and associated nations [for] the first step towards conservation and the use of natural resources' (cited in Van Dyke, 2008, p19). Unfortunately, Roosevelt died before his initiative materialized, but his visions contributed to the formation of the United Nations in 1948. With the formation of the UN came the establishment of the United Nations Educational, Scientific, and Cultural Organization (UNESCO). Urged on by the Swiss League for the Protection of Nature, UNESCO's first director, the British biologist Julian Huxley, revived Sarasin's idea concerning the formation of an international non-governmental environmental organization. In 1948, Huxley organized a conference at Fontainebleau together with the Swiss League and the International Council of Scientific Unions (as it was called then), which was attended by 23 governments, 126 national institutions and 8 international organizations (Baer, 1968; Van Dyke, 2008). On 5 October that year most of the delegates signed an act establishing the International Union for the Protection of Nature (IUPN) (in 1956 it was renamed the International Union form the Conservation of Nature and Natural Resources). With the IUPN a new form of organization was introduced: the government-organized non-governmental organization (GONGO). The organization does not allow individual membership, only nations and organizations can become members (Van Dyke, 2008). Starting with only a limited budget the Union organized international conferences and relied on an extensive network of volunteering scientists to draw up reports on the plight of endangered species and nature protection, eventually culminating in the Red Data Books, the authoritative standard as the global 'Endangered Species List' (see Chapter 5). Funding, however, remained a problem for the Union, and Huxley – who had left UNESCO by the end of 1948 – enlisted the help of Sir Peter Scott, Victor Stolan, Max Nicholson and Guy Mountfort to establish the World Wildlife Fund (WWF) (later renamed the World Wide Fund for Nature). In 1961 WWF was set up, initially mainly as a fundraising organization for environmental non-governmental organizations, including the Union.

Despite the fact that within the IUPN and other international forums – such as the League of Nations – a range of concepts for nature protection was discussed, in the end, the national park – as an area where no settlement or natural resource use was permitted – remained the dominant approach, focused on the protection of endangered species (Wöbse, forthcoming). This was a reinforcement of the approach promoted in the 1933 Convention for the Preservation of Wild Animals, Birds and Fish in Africa (Gissibl, 2006), and was adopted as the model approach for Africa, with the exception of North Africa, where the Touring Club de France and the Club Alpin Français were active in promoting the inclusion of communal areas in the reserves, hence including the areas occupied by local agriculturalists and pastoralists (Selmi, 2009). Inspired by orientalism, these organizations considered local populations an important asset for tourism, and urged that no restrictions on natural resource use should be imposed upon them without their consent (Selmi, 2009). However, these organizations were not active in sub-Saharan Africa, where soon Buxton's remarks about Africans' birthright to wildlife were forgotten. As is discussed below, it was not until the late 1980s that local natural resource use appeared on the agenda again.

Due to the domination of the 'fortress' or 'fines and fences' approach to nature conservation, many local African populations developed quite a negative attitude towards conservation. The establishment of many reserves and national parks had resulted in the eviction of local farmers and pastoralists had lost their grazing areas. Trespassers trying to harvest natural resources from reserves and national parks were persecuted and heavily fined when caught, and poachers were treated violently (see Hulme and Murphree, 2001; Brockington, 2002; Hutton et al, 2005; Brockington and Igoe, 2006; Spierenburg and Wels, 2006). Hence, at the dawn of independence of many African states – in the late 1950s and early 1960s – many conservationists were worried that the newly independent African states would accord far less importance to nature conservation and might de-gazette quite a number of reserves and national parks (Bonner, 1994; Rangarajan, 2003; Walley, 2004). Negative local attitudes and pressures on the new governments to economically develop their countries and alleviate poverty were feared could have a negative impact on nature protection. The 'thinly disguised distrust of African abilities to rule themselves [articulated] well with fears that they would devastate their wildlife and landscapes' (Rangarajan, 2003, p83). The famous German zoologists, Bernhard and Michael Grzimek, who co-authored the book *Serengeti Shall not Die* – translated in 18 languages – were quite open about their concerns in their book, and warned about 'the over-hasty conversion of coloured colonies into independent democratic states' (cited in Rangarajan, 2003, p83). In 1961, the IUPN organized a conference in Arusha, Tanganyika (present day Tanzania), to convince the leaders of the newly independent African states of the importance of wildlife conservation (Bonner, 1994). The results were two versions of declarations that the Tanzanian leader, Julius Nyerere, made: one for conservation and the other for his vision for a socialist Tanzania (Noe, 2009).

While some national parks were indeed invaded after independence by groups that had been evicted from these areas (see Wolmer, 2007), such local-level initiatives in general led to new evictions as most post-colonial governments showed a remarkable continuation of colonial conservation policies – also in relation to soil erosion, land use and forestry (Rangarajan, 2003; Spierenburg, 2004; Walley, 2004; Wolmer, 2007; see also Scott, 1998). In fact, providing an overview of evictions for nature conservation, Brockington and Igoe (2006) conclude that in most independent African states evictions to create space for new reserves and national parks continued. Tourism in reserves and national parks was considered an important source of revenue (Walley, 2004). Nevertheless, concerns about the weak financial state of many of the newly independent states led to a flurry of activities by already existing environmental organizations and the establishment of many new ones (Brockington and Scholfield, 2010).

Bonner (1994) also connects the formation of WWF as a fundraising organization to the process of decolonization, to provide the new states with sufficient funding to maintain reserves and national parks and ensure the continuation of wildlife preservation policies. The same applies to the AWF, also established in 1961 as the African Wildlife Leadership Foundation Inc. 'at the height of the African independence movement to help newly independent African nations and people conserve their own wildlife' (see AWF, no date). Some critics, however, interpret this assistance in a different way. Newell (2008) for instance, argues that in this way, these organizations – and hence philanthropy – served as an instrument of neo-colonialism, replacing the retreating empire in its control over natural resources in Africa, providing funding for the creation of wildlife reserves for the enjoyment of the rich (cf. Ramutsindela, 2009). Others argue that the increase in numbers and importance of NGOs reflect an emerging distrust in the state, especially in developing countries (Levine, 2002).

Given the background of the founders and early supporters of these organizations, such remarks are not all that far-fetched. Like their predecessors of the Society for the Preservation of the Wild Fauna of the Empire – the founders and supporters of WWF and AWF were members of a wealthy elite, and many were serious big game hunters (Bonner, 1994; see also Spierenburg and Wels, 2010). This is further evidence of the relevance of elite theory in the analysis of environmental philanthropy (see Chapter 4). The founder of AWF, Russell E. Train, a tax court judge, had for many years been a member of one of the oldest and most exclusive clubs in North America, the Long Point Company, to which the famous Mellon family was also associated. Train was also a member of the 'Hundred Pounder Club', on account of shooting an elephant while on safari in Kenya in 1958, with a left tusk that weighed 105 pounds and a right tusk that weighed 102 pounds (Bonner, 1994). Train was politically conservative – he left the Foundation in 1969 to work for the US government under the Nixon administration – and while the AWF website portrays a positive image of a desire to provide assistance to the newly independent African states, Train's editorials in the Foundation's newsletter had a different tone: 'For better or for worse, the future of most of Africa's game country and the fate of its wildlife resources are in the hands of Africans themselves'; later he wrote: '*In Tanganyika alone, the government recently ordered 100 percent Africanization of the game service by 1966!* ... Replacement of European staff by untrained, unqualified men spells disaster for the game' (cited in Bonner, 1994, p57, emphasis original). Most of the European staff had not had formal training either but apparently this was not considered a problem. The first large grant provided by the Foundation was $47,000 to establish the College of African Wildlife Management in Mweka, Tanzania.

While earlier involvement of members of the political, economical and aristocratic elites in nature conservation in Africa mainly took the form of putting pressure on (colonial) governments and supporting scientists, from the 1960s onwards, more and more emphasis was placed on funding conservation. Huxley and Stolan had enlisted the assistance of Nicholson because they needed someone 'with whom ideas can be developed and speedily directed towards accumulating some millions of pounds without mobilising commissions, committees, etc. As there is no time for Victorian procedure' (Stolan, cited in Bonner, 1994, p62).

Nicholson's efforts to raise funds, however, were not all that fruitful. This all changed when Anton Rupert, a South African businessman, joined the board of trustees in 1968, under the presidency of Prince Bernhard of the Netherlands (Ramutsindela, 2009; Spierenburg and Wels, 2010; see also Chapter 3). Together they developed the idea of the establishment of the 1001 Club (see Chapter 3). The membership list included many of Prince Bernhard's acquaintances (see also Ellis, 1994). On the various lists that circulate, the names of a number of famous businessmen and bankers appear such as David Rockefeller, Henry Ford II, several members of the De Rothschild family and the Agnelli family, to name but a few. South African businessmen were also included in the lists at a time when South Africa was still officially boycotted by the world business community: Anton Rupert's name and that of his son Johann (who presently directs the Rembrandt/Richemont Group), Freddie de Guingand (Founder of the South Africa Foundation, a business lobby organization), Louis Luyt (the 'fertilizer king' of South Africa), but also Rupert's greatest rival Harry F. Oppenheimer, owner of Anglo American and the De Beers company (see Spierenburg and Wels, 2010).

The shifting focus to fundraising also resulted in rivalries among environmental organizations. When the AWF was established, Nicholson of WWF remembered 'this made us realize the full horror that within two years there might be a dozen competing wildlife funds, all going after the same source' (cited in Bonner, 1994, p64). Increasingly, the organizations also started to target the general public – that is, especially in Europe and the US, where levels of income and welfare were rising. This audience was bombarded with 'gloom and doom' messages about the state of wildlife conservation in Africa (Bonner, 1994; see also Escobar, 1998) and the threat posed by humans. Images of the cruelty of poachers were publicized widely and the feeling of crisis urgency elicited (Draper et al, 2004). The strong anti-hunting and anti-resource use message became an effective tool in fundraising, and from the 1970s onwards, donations from the general public started to outweigh contributions by the elite members of the organizations (Bonner 1994; Brockington and Scholfield, 2010; see Chapter 4). However, the messages directed at the general public did not always convey the more nuanced attitudes towards hunting and natural resource use of the organizations' staff and wealthy donors. This sometimes led to conflicting strategies and sudden turnabouts by environmental organizations, as Bonner (1994) describes in relation to the discussions on the ban of ivory trade in 1980s (see Chapter 4).

The battle over the utilization of natural resources is a recurrent theme in nature conservation, as shown above, for instance in relation to Buxton's remarks on hunting by Africans. Huxley, founder of WWF, was in favour of 'proper utilisation', and argued in favour of wildlife utilization – including the controlled hunting of elephants – by or for the benefit of local populations (Bonner, 1994, p98). Nevertheless, until the mid- to late 1980s, most protected areas in Africa had been run in a way that excluded local populations and banned their use of resources in these areas. The messages sent out to the general public were equally uncompromising. In the 1980s, however, many conservation organizations started to realize that this 'fines and fences' or 'fortress' approach was not a sustainable way to manage and protect wildlife (McNeely, 1992). Not only was it too expensive in terms of deploying personnel and equipment, it was also counterproductive, i.e. it did not stop the poaching and further encroachment on wildlife areas. Wildlife managers and policy makers in the field of nature conservation started to proclaim a different approach that emphasized that communities had to become actively involved in wildlife management (Adams, 2004). Instead of an antagonistic party, communities had to become cooperative partners. Several projects were initiated following this logic, and some pioneering efforts that had already started received official political backing and legitimization (see Chapter 4). It was from these circles that calls came to allow the sale of ivory through controlled sales, with a quota set and monitored by the CITES, to allow for greater benefits for local populations, which were believed to result in more local support for the conservation of elephants that were frequently damaging local livelihoods and posed a threat to human lives. WWF initially supported these proposals, however, as the CITES negotiations drew closer, the organization made a 180 degree turn and supported the proposal to ban the ivory trade. Bonner cites from an internal memorandum circulated by WWF-US:

> *Although we support sustainable wildlife utilization projects ... and are committed to an all-out effort to make the CITES quota system work, these concepts are not understood by the vast majority of the 450,000 WWF-US members. Most of these members are more traditionally oriented towards species 'preservation', and there is little understanding of the complexities of conservation in Africa in the 1980s, particularly where wildlife utilization programs are concerned.* (Bonner, 1994, p112)

Meanwhile, the number of ENGOs active in Africa has mushroomed since the 1960s. In a internet search, Brockington and Scholfield (2010) were able to list at least 87 conservation organizations working on the continent. They report that they may have missed organizations originating from or operating in Francophone and Lusophone areas, however, an additional internet search we conducted using keywords in French and Portuguese did not elicit many additional organizations. Many of the smaller, local organizations – and especially in southern Africa there are many such organizations; many national parks for instance have 'friends of...' organizations supporting them – are indeed more difficult to trace through the internet, however, the number of ENGOs that can be traced through the internet is considerable. The survey of the organizations listed by Brockington and Scholfield (2010) reveals that the growth of ENGOs started in the 1960s but really began to flourish in the 1980s, only to increase even more in the 1990s. Of the organizations, 65 have their headquarters in the US and 58 in Europe.

The African-based organizations are based in Kenya, Tanzania and southern Africa. The activities across the continent are not evenly spread, with activity being relatively low in West Africa. However, according to the survey, WWF is the organization with the greatest geographical reach, active in 44 countries. The Wildlife Conservation Society is active in 19 countries, and AWF in 11. The data also show a continued emphasis on funding conservation areas and the protection of charismatic megafauna (Brockington and Scholfield, 2010). The organizations surveyed together spend more than $200 million on conservation in Africa – though this is only a fraction of the money spent on development. Yet, these resources are unevenly distributed, and the field is dominated by a few large organizations. WWF again has most funding to spend, and its expenses are larger than those of the Wildlife Conservation Society and AWF together; 65 per cent of the expenditure is accounted for by the top ten organizations, of which nine are based in the North (Brockington and Scholfield, 2010).

While the total amount of – relatively modest – donations from the general public outweighs the contributions of individual wealthy philanthropists, recently there has been an increasing tendency for ENGOs to work with and seek funding from the corporate sector (Chapin, 2004; Hutton et al, 2005). Chapin (2004) as well as Hutton et al (2005) argue that this is related to a movement 'back to the barriers'. While the involvement of local communities in nature conservation became a popular approach endorsed by ENGOs during the late 1980s and 1990s (Hulme and Murphree, 2001), this approach turned out to be more complicated than expected (Chapin, 2004; see also Spierenburg et al, 2008, 2009). Conservation organizations had little experience of working with local communities and could not deal with the development aspirations of many of these communities. The focus on transfrontier conservation and the creation of large corridors allowing wildlife migrations – also related to ideas of global threats to biodiversity, including those stemming from climate change – is, according to Chapin (2004), a deliberate move away from local communities (see Chapter 4). However, the argument of community benefits through tourism attracted to the new 'megaparks' is still maintained (Ramutsindela, 2004; Spierenburg et al, 2008). Yet, the movement away from local-level involvement coincides with, or may even be the result of, increasingly close relationships between ENGOs and the corporate sector, which also seeks to benefit from biodiversity conservation – either directly (Ramutsindela, 2004) or indirectly through the establishment of a 'green image' that can be of value in PR activities (Newell, 2008). This movement, as Dzingirai (2003) argues, allows the corporate sector to take control over large areas, and may hence represent a next and new scramble for Africa.

At the local level, however, a countermovement against this scramble is occurring. This trend calls for a closer analysis of conservation by CBOs and local NGOs; a subject to which we turn in the next chapter.

References

Adams, W. M. and Hutton, J. (2007) 'Review: People, parks and poverty: political ecology and biodiversity conservation', *Conservation & Society*, vol 5, no 2, pp147–183.

Adams, W. M. (2004) *Against Extinction: The Story of Conservation*, London, Earthscan

Anderson, D. and Grove, R. (1987) 'The scramble for Eden: Past, present and future in African conservation', in Anderson, D. and Grove, R. (eds) *Conservation in Africa. People, Policies and Practice*, Cambridge University Press, Cambridge, pp1–12

AWF (African Wildlife Foundation) (no date) 'About AWF'. www.awf.org, accessed 10 September 2010

Baer, J. G. (1968) 'Aperçu historique de la protection de la nature', *Biological Conservation*, vol 1, no 1, pp7–11

Beinart, W. (2000) 'African history and environmental history', *African Affairs*, vol 99, pp269–302

Beinart, W. and Coates, P. (1995) *Environment and History: The Taming of Nature in the USA and South Africa*, Routledge, London

Bonner, R. (1994) *At the Hand of Man: Peril and Hope for Africa's Wildlife*, Vintage Books, New York

Brockington, D. (2002) *Fortress Conservation: The Preservation of the Mkomazi Game Reserve, Tanzania*, Indiana University Press, Indiana

Brockington, D. and Igoe, J. (2006) 'Eviction for conservation: A global overview', *Conservation and Society*, vol 4, no 3, pp424–470

Brockington, D., Duffy, R. and Igoe, J. (2008) *Nature Unbound: Conservation, Capitalism and the Future of Protected Areas*, Earthscan, London

Brockington, D. and Scholfield, K. (2010) 'The work of conservation organisations in sub-Saharan Africa', *Journal of Modern African Studies*, vol 48, no 1, pp1–33

Carruthers, J. (2005) 'Changing perspectives on wildlife in southern Africa, c. 1840 to c. 1914', *Society and Animals*, vol 13, no 3, pp183–199

Chapin, M. (2004) 'A challenge to conservationists', *World Watch Magazine*, November/December, pp17–31

Conrad, J. (1989) [1902] *Heart of Darkness*, Penguin Books, London

Draper, M., Spierenburg, M. and Wels, H. (2004) 'African dreams of cohesion: The mythology of community development in transfrontier conservation areas in southern Africa', *Culture and Organization*, vol 10, no 4, pp341–353

Dzingirai, V. (2003) 'The new scramble for the African countryside', *Development and Change*, vol 34, no 2, pp243–263

Ellis, S. (1994) 'Of elephants and men: Politics and nature conservation in South Africa', *Journal of Southern African Studies*, vol 20, no 1, pp53–69

Escobar, A. (1998) 'Whose knowledge, whose nature? Biodiversity, conservation, and the political ecology of social movements', *Journal of Political Ecology*, vol 5, pp53–82

Gissibl, B. (2006) 'German colonialism and the beginnings of international wildlife preservation in Africa', *GHI Bulletin Supplement*, vol 3, pp121–143

Grove, R. (1995) *Green Imperialism: Colonial Expansion, Tropical Island Edens and the Origins of Environmentalism, 1600–1860*, Cambridge University Press, Cambridge

Grove, R. (1997) 'Scotland in South Africa: John Croumbie Brown and the roots of settler environmentalism', in Griffiths, T. and Robin, L. (eds) *Ecology and Empire:*

Environmental History of Settler Societies, University of Natal Press, Pietermaritzburg, pp139–153

Hulme, D. and Murphree, M. (2001) 'Community conservation in Africa, an introduction', in Hulme, D. and Murphree, M. (eds) *African Wildlife and Livelihoods, The Promise and Performance of Community Conservation*, James Currey, Oxford, pp1–8

Hutton, J., Adams, W. M. and Murombedzi, J. (2005) 'Back to the barriers? Changing narratives in biodiversity conservation', *Forum for Development Studies*, vol 2, pp341–370

Larrère, R. (2009) 'Histoire(s) et mémoires des parcs nationaux', in Larrère, R., Lizet, B. and Berlan-Darqué, M. (eds) *Histoire des Parcs Nationaux. Comment Prendre soin de la Nature?*, Editions Quae, Paris, pp23–42

Leach, M. and Fairhead, J. (2000) 'Fashioned forest pasts, occluded histories? International environmental analysis in West African locales', *Development and Change*, vol 31, no 1, pp35–39

Levine, A. (2002) 'Convergence or convenience? International conservation NGOs and development assistance in Tanzania', *World Development*, vol 30, no 6, pp1043–1055

MacKenzie, J. M. (1988) *The Empire of Nature: Hunting, Conservation and British Imperialism*, Manchester University Press, Manchester

MacKenzie, J. M. (1997) 'Empire and the ecological apocalypse: The historiography of the imperial environment', in Griffiths, T. and Robin, L. (eds) *Ecology and Empire: Environmental History of Settler Societies*, University of Natal Press, Pietermaritzburg, pp215–228

Mavhunga, C. and Spierenburg. M. (2007) 'A finger on the pulse of the fly: Hidden voices of colonial anti-tsetse science on the Rhodesian and Mozambican borderlands, 1945–1956', *South African Historical Journal*, vol 58, pp117–141

Mavhunga, C. and Spierenburg, M. (2009) 'Transfrontier talk, cordon politics: The early history of the Great Limpopo Transfrontier Park in southern Africa, 1925–1940', *Journal of Southern African Studies*, vol 35, no 3, pp715–735

McNeely, J. A. (ed) (1992) *Parks for Life. Report of the IVth World Congress on National Parks and Protected Areas*, IUCN, Gland

Neumann, R. P. (1996) 'Dukes, earls and ersatz Edens: Aristocratic nature preservationists in colonial Africa', *Environment and Planning D: Society and Space*, vol 14, pp79–98

Neumann, R. P. (1998) *Imposing Wilderness: Struggles over Livelihood and Nature Preservation in Africa*, University of California Press, Los Angeles

Neumann, R. P. (2000) 'Primitive ideas: Protected area buffer zones and the politics of land in Africa', in Broch-Due, V. and Schroeder, R. A. (eds) *Producing Nature and Poverty in Africa*, Nordisk Afrikainstitutet, Stockholm, pp220–242

Newell, P. (2008) 'CSR and the limits to capital', *Development and Change*, vol 39, no 6, pp1063–1078

Noe, C. (2009) 'Bioregional planning in southeastern Tanzania: The Selous–Niassa corridor as a prism for transfrontier conservation areas', unpublished PhD thesis, University of Cape Town, Cape Town

Prendergast, D. K. and Adams, W. M. (2003) 'Colonial wildlife conservation and the origins of the Society for the Preservation of the Wild Fauna of the Empire', *Oryx*, vol 37, no 2, pp251–260

Ramutsindela, M. (2004) 'Globalisation and nature conservation strategies in 21st-century southern Africa', *Tijdschrift voor Economische en Sociale Geografie*, vol 95, no 1, pp61–72

Ramutsindela, M. (2009) 'The interconnections between environmental philanthropy and business: Insights from the southern African nature foundation', *Transformation*, vol 70, pp54–69

Rangarajan, M. (2003) 'Parks, politics and history: Conservation dilemmas in Africa', *Conservation and Society*, vol 1, no 1, pp77–98

Ritvo, H. (1987) *The Animal State: The English and other Creatures in the Victorian Age*, Harvard University Press, Cambridge

Schama, S. (1995) *Landscape and Memory*, Harper Collins, London and New York

Scott, J. (1998) *Seeing Like a State. How Certain Schemes to Improve the Human Condition have Failed*, Yale University Press, New Haven, CT

Selmi, A. (2009) 'L'émergence de l'idée de parc national en France. De la protection des paysages à l'expérimentation coloniale', in Larrère, R., Lizet, B. and Berlan-Darqué, M (eds) *Histoire des Parcs Nationaux. Comment Prendre soin de la Nature?*, Editions Quae, Paris, pp43–57

Spierenburg, M. (2004) *Strangers, Spirits and Land Reforms: Conflicts about Land in Dande, Northern Zimbabwe*, Brill, Leiden

Spierenburg, M. and Wels, H. (2006) '"Securing space": Mapping and fencing in transfrontier conservation in southern Africa', *Space and Culture*, vol 6, no 3, pp294–312

Spierenburg, M. and Wels, H. (2010) 'Conservative philanthropists, royalty and business elites in nature conservation in southern Africa', *Antipode*, vol 42, no 3, pp647–670

Spierenburg, M., Steenkamp, C. and Wels, H. (2008) 'Promises of economic development in the Great Limpopo, southern Africa: Networks and partnerships in transfrontier conservation', in Rutten, M., Leliveld, A. and Foeken, D. (eds) *Africa's Poor: Policy Aims and Impact*, Brill, Leiden, pp144–168

Spierenburg, M., Wels, H., van der Waal, K. and Robins, S. (2009) 'Transfrontier tourism, relations between local communities and the private sector in the Great Limpopo transfrontier park', in Hottola, P. (ed) *Tourism Strategies and Local Responses in Southern Africa*, CABI, Wallingford, pp167–182

Thomas, S. J. (1992) *The Legacy of Dualism and Decision-making: The Prospects for Local Institutional Development in CAMPFIRE*, Centre for Applied Social Sciences/Branch of Terrestrial Ecology, Department of National Parks and Wildlife, Harare

Van Dyke, F. (2008) *Conservation Biology: Foundations, Concepts, Applications*, Springer, Berlin/New York

Walley, C. J. (2004) *Rough Waters: Nature and Development in an East African Marine Park*, Princeton University Press, Princeton, NJ

Wöbse, A. (forthcoming) 'Framing the heritage of mankind: National parks on the international agenda, 1913–1972', in Gissibl, B., Hoehler, S. and Kupper, P (eds) *Civilizing Nature: A Global History of National Parks*

Wolf, E. R. (1990) *Europe and the People Without History*, University of California Press, Berkeley, CA

Wolmer, W. (2007) *From Wilderness Vision to Farm Invasions: Conservation and Development in Zimbabwe's South-east Lowveld*, James Currey, London

8

Rising to Local Challenges: Grassroots Conservation Initiatives

INTRODUCTION

Implicit in the global funding of local initiatives (see Chapters 3, 5 and 6) and the dense network of philanthropists and local organizations in Africa (see Chapter 7) is the view that local conservation initiatives rely on external sources and are often a product of top-down approaches. In reality, this is not always the case as specific local situations could spur environmental protection measures and the mobilization of assets (such as financial and social capital). Chapter 8 is intended to show the various ways in which local CBOs and NGOs have attempted to drive environmental initiatives that are relevant to their contexts, in contrast to the view that international donors dictate the direction of NGO and CBO activities. In this chapter we focus on CBC from the perspective of community aspirations and initiatives rather than the involvement of communities as stakeholders in co-management frameworks. We see co-management as more of an imposed management regime, rather than a grassroots initiative, which often misses out the intricate relationships between the community and the resources. Also, we do not intend to discuss CBC as a paradigm shift in ecology and applied ecology as to do so would limit our understanding of grassroots environmental initiatives. To be sure, as a paradigm shift, CBC seeks to embrace ecosystems approaches and participatory ecosystem management in which the inclusion of humans in both conservation and ecosystem management is crucial (Berkes, 2004). Such approaches presume that grassroots initiatives cannot exist on their own – they are always or should be part of a 'scientifically' defined human response to environmental challenges. Thus, the conceptualization of CBC as a link between development imperatives and conservation objectives is not the preserve of a scientific community but should also be seen as a result of local responses to the unfolding reality, as this chapter attempts to show. We are also conscious that CBC can be a neo-populist approach to conservation, development and the relationship between society and the state. Nevertheless, we see value in thinking about CBC as conservation activities emerging from within the community. In fact CBC is true to its name if it is not imposed onto the local community by outside forces. CBC 'must be embedded in local communities if it is to flourish as a voluntary rather than a coercive effort' (Western, 1994, p499) and should exhibit a clear link between conservation and community interests. Understanding CBC from this perspective implies that donors should explore new relationships with local communities rather than rely on the usual top-down approach.

The chapter draws examples from Asia, specifically Sri Lanka and Indonesia. According to the GEF-SGP (see Chapter 6), these two countries have the highest number of locally initiated environmental projects in Asia. Rather than focusing on external grants, this chapter is concerned with local initiatives and the extent to which local resources are mobilized towards an environmental cause and developmental needs of the locals. These initiatives are, in our view, important for understanding the possibilities for environmental philanthropy in the global South. The first step towards understanding the possibilities for such philanthropy is to appreciate environmental conditions and challenges and the ways in which local communities tackle them. It is from those community responses that we might be able to understand avenues for local philanthropy. The premise here is that philanthropy cannot be mobilized in a vacuum as it requires agency. Some lessons on CBOs and local NGOs and their contribution to an environmental cause can be gleaned from the Equator Initiative (EI), which is briefly introduced and explained below.

CBOs and the Equator Initiative

It should be stated upfront that our reference to the EI is not intended to evaluate the EI. Rather, we use the Initiative as an example of the critical roles that locally initiated NGOs and CBOs play in the conservation of biodiversity and local developmental needs. The Initiative was founded by Tim Wirth (President of the UN Foundation) and Mark Mallooch Brown (UNDP administrator) and was launched in 2002 (Timmer and Juma, 2005). The manager of the EI, Sean Southey describes the EI as:

> *a partnership of the United Nations Development Programme (UNDP) with the government of Canada, Conservation International, Fordham University, the German Federal Ministry of Economic Development and Cooperation, the Convention on Biological Biodiversity, the International Development Research Centre, the World Conservation Union (IUCN), The Nature Conservancy, the Television Trust for the Environment and the United Nations Foundation, in collaboration with the United Nations Fund for International Partnerships.* (Southey, 2005, p53)

Its main goal is to identify and support local community endeavours toward developing a synergy between poverty alleviation and biodiversity conservation in the equatorial region – which lies between 23.5 degrees south and north of the equator. It should be emphasized that the focus of EI is on home-grown local initiatives.

The EI is based on the conception of the equatorial region as the locus of the 'greatest concentrations of both human poverty and biological wealth' (Southey, 2005, p53). This way, the EI is different from the Equator Principles that were adopted in 2003 by ten leading banks from seven countries as a series of guidelines on the voluntary management of social and environmental risks by these banks (see Amalric, 2005). The EI operates on four pillars:

- The Equator Prize – the Prize is considered 'a prestigious international award that recognizes and honours outstanding local efforts and community initiatives to effectively reduce poverty through the conservation and sustainable use of resources' (Southey, 2005, p53). It is intended to profile the efforts of local and indigenous groups along the equatorial belt on an international stage. For example, the EI supported the Zimbabwean-based Chibememe Earth Healing Association (Zimbabwe) to present its concerns to the World Parks Congress that was held in Durban in 2003 (Southey, 2005). It is anticipated that once a community initiative has been endorsed by the EI, such an initiative is more likely to gain support from other lobby groups and sponsors. The first Prize was awarded in Johannesburg in 2002 at the World Summit on Sustainable Development. The finalists of the Equator Prize since its inception are shown in Tables 8.1, 8.2 and 8.3.
- Equator dialogues – the dialogues are designed as a forum through which ideas and experiences could be shared and exchanged, and the meetings to facilitate these are sponsored by the partners we referred to above. The ultimate goal of these meetings is to bring community initiatives and experiences into the policy making domain and to broaden the benefits from these initiatives to society as a whole – scaling up (Hooper et al, 2004). Thus, the EI supports the dissemination of lessons from local innovations as a way of advancing global biodiversity and development goals (Timmer and Juma, 2005). The extent to which CBC initiatives can be replicated at different scales in various contexts is debatable. There is a view that CBCs are local responses with minimal chances of transferability. The opposing view is that successful CBCs have the potential to offer important lessons on how to achieve global biodiversity goals through local actions (Shukla and Sinclair, 2010).
- Equator knowledge – the third pillar of the EI on knowledge refers to 'a comprehensive research and learning initiative dedicated to synthesizing lessons from local conservation and poverty reduction practices' (Southey, 2005, p53). It seeks to support the documentation of local best practices.
- Equator ventures – while the EI recognizes achievements by the local NGOs and CBOs, it nonetheless seeks to expand biodiversity enterprises through an investment programme.

Table 8.1 *Africa region finalists for the Equator Prize, 2002–2010*

Countries	CBO/NGO initiatives	No. of projects
Benin	Réseau de Développement de Réserves Naturelles Communautaires (REDERC ONG)	1
Burkina Faso	Association Songtaab-Yalgré	1
Cameroon	Support Group for Conservation and Sustainable Development Initiative (CACID); ITOH Community Graziers Common Initiative Group; RIBA Agroforestry Resource Center (RARC)	3
Comoros	Mohéli Marine Park	1
Cape Verde	Associção Communitária Nova Experiência Marítima da Cruzinha da Garça (ACNEMC)	1
Democratic Republic of the Congo	Pole Pole Foundation/Kahuzi-Biega National Park; Centre d'Appul au Développement Intégral/Mbankana (CADIM)	2
Ethiopia	Guassa-Menz Natural Resource Management Initiative	1
Ghana	Wechiau Community Hippo Sanctuary	1
Kenya	Honey Care Africa Ltd; Il Ngwesi Group Ranch; Pastoralist Integrated Support Programme; Kipsaina Crane and Wetland Conservation Group; Shompole Community Trust; Kibale Environmental Volunteers (KENVO); Kwetu Training Centre for Sustainable Development; Mara River Water User's Association; Muliru Farmers Conservation Group (MFCG)	9
Madagascar	Association of Manambolo Natives (FITEMA); The Village of Andavadoaka; Association ADIDY Maitso	3
Mali	Pole des actions d'integration des droits humains en Afrique (PACINDHA);	1
Namibia	Torra Conservancy; N≠a Jaqna Conservancy	2
Niger	Ecole Instrument de Paix-Niger	1
Nigeria	Ekuri Initiative; Small Holders Foundation	2
Senegal	Collectif des Groupements d'interests Economiques des Femmes pour la Protection de la Nature (COPRONATI); Fédération Régionale des Groupements de Promotion Féminine Ziguinchor; La Fédération Locale des GIE de Niodior (FELOGIE)	3
South Africa	Makuleke Community: Pafuri Camp	1
Tanzania	HASHI Soil Conservation Project; Suledo Forest Community; Rufiji Environmental Management Project (REMP-MUMARU); Amani Nature Reserve; Ujamaa Community Resource Trust	5
Uganda	Kibale Association for Rural and Environmental Development (KAFRED) (twice finalist).	1
Zimbabwe	Chibememe Earth Healing Association (CHIEHA)	1

Source: constructed from www.equatorinitiative.org, accessed 21 July 2010

Table 8.2 *Asia and Pacific region finalists for the Equator Prize, 2002–2010*

Countries	CBO/NGO initiatives	No. of Projects
Bangladesh	Shidhulai Swanirvar Sangstha	1
Cambodia	Tmatboey Community Protected Area Committee; Monks Community Forestry	2
Federated States of Micronesia	Conservation Society of Pohnpei	1
Fiji	Fiji Locally Managed Marine Area Network	1
India	Medicinal Plants Conservation Centre; Kerala Kani Samudaya Kshema Trust; Tribal Communities of the Jeypore Tract of Orissa; Genetic Resources, Energy, Ecology and Nutrition (GREEN) Foundation; Aharam Traditional Crops Producers' Company (ATCPC); Samudran Women's Federation, Orissa	6
Indonesia	Ngata Toro Community; Bunaken National Park Management Advisory Board (BNPMAB) and Bunaken Concerned Citizen's Forum (FMPTNB); The Indonesian Community-based Marine Management Foundation; Tonia Fishermen Community; Yayasan Mitra Tani Mandiri	5
Lao People's Democratic Republic	Nam Ha Ecoguide Service	1
Malaysia	Uma Bawang Resident's Association (UBRA); Batu Puteh Community of Lower Kinabatangan (MESCOT);	1
Papua New Guinea	Conservation Melanesia; Sepik Wetlands Management Initiative (SWMI);	2
Philippines	Kalinga Mission for Indigenous Children and Youth Development, Inc (KAMICYDI); Pederaysyon sa Nagkahiusang mga Mag-uuma nga Namalipud ug Nagpasig-uli sa Kinalayahan Inc; Center for Empowerment and Resource Development; Camalandaan Agroforest Farmers Association; Association for Rural Upliftment; Trowel Development Foundation, Inc	6
Solomon Islands	Arnavon Community Marine Conservation Area Management Committee	1
Sri Lanka	Rush and Reed Conservation and Diversification Program of the Podujana Himikan Kamituwa (Committee for People's Rights); Community Development Centre; Sri Lanka Wildlife Conservation Society	3
Thailand	CBIRD Center, Sub Tai; Pred Nai Community Forestry Group	2
Vanuatu	Crab Bay Community Resource Management Initiative; Nguna-Pele Marine Protected Area	2
Vietnam	Phu My Leporina Wetland Conservation Project; Bambou Village de Phu An	2
Yemen	Rosh Protected Area Community	1

Source: constructed from www.equatorinitiative.org, accessed 21 July 2010

Table 8.3 *Latin America and the Caribbean region finalists for the Equator Prize, 2002–2010*

Countries	CBO/NGO initiatives	No. of Projects
Belize	Toledo Institute for Development and Environment (TIDE)	1
Bolivia	Capitania del Alto y Bajo Izozog (CABI); Asociación de Apicultores de la Reserva de Tariquía (AART); Chalalan Albergue Ecológico; Consejo Regional Tsimané Mosetene Pilon Lajas (CRTM PL)	4
Brazil	Green Life Association of Amazonia (AVIVE); Bolsa Amazonia; Cananela Oyster Producers Association (COOPEROSTRA); Couro Vegetal da Amazónia Project; Sociedade Civil Mamirau; Cooperative Agro-extratovista Yawanawa (CCPYAWA); Polo de Proteção da Biodiversidade e Uso Sustentável dos Recursos Naturais; Associação dos Pequenhos Agrossilvicultores do Projecto Reca; Carnaúba viva	9
Colombia	Inter-institutional Consortium for Sustainable Agriculture on Hillside/River Cabuyal Watershed Users Association (CIPASLA-ASOBESURCA); Red de Mujeres Productoras y Comercializadores de Plantas Medicinales y Aromaticas; Proyecto Nasa; FrutaSă, Industria e Comércio Exportacíon Ltda; Asociación de Productores Indigenas y Campesinos de Riosucio Caldas Asproinca; Corporación Serraniagua	6
Costa Rica	Fundación Pro Reserva Forestal Monte Alto; CoopeTárcoles R.L – Cooperativa de Pescadores Artesanales de Tárcoles	2
Cuba	Empresa Forestal Integral de Bayamo	1
Ecuador	Junta de Manejo Participativo Pesquero de Puerto Cayo; Associación de Trabajadores Autónomos San Rafael – Tres Cruces-Yunac Rumi (ASRATY); Asociación de Mujeres de Isabela 'Pescado Azul'; Federación Plurinacionál de Turismo Comunitário del Ecuador (FEPTCE); Unión de Organizaciones Campesinas e Indigenas de Cotacachi; Complejo Ecoturístico Kapawi S.A.	6
Guatemala	Organización Manejo y Conservación, s.c./WCS-Guatemala; AlimentosNutri-Naturales; Asociación para la Conservación de la Reserva Indigena BIOITZA	3
Honduras	Garifuna Emergency Committee	1
Mexico	Café de la Selva; Comunidad Indigena de Nuevo San Juan Parangaricutiro; Community Tours Sian Ka'am (CTSK); Sociedad Cooperativa de Producción Pesquera 'Pescadores de Vigia Chico y Cozumel'; Fundación San Crisanto A.C.; Red Indígena de Turismo de México A.C.	6
Nicaragua	Programa de Campesino a Campesino, Siuna (PCaC)	1
Peru	Ese'eja Native Community of Infierno; Asociación para la Investigación y el Desarrollo Integral (AIDER); Asociación de Artesanas de Arbolsol y Huaca de Barro del Distrito de Mórrope; Asociación de Pobladores por el Progreso y Desarrollo de Campo Amor Zarumilla	4
Venezuela	Fundación para la Agricultura Tropical Alternativa y el Desarrollo Integral (FUNDATADI)	1

Source: constructed from www.equatorinitiative.org, accessed 21 July 2010

Research on the CBOs and NGOs referred to in Tables 8.1, 8.2 and 8.3 offers conclusions that are worthy of consideration. These are summarized below:

- CBC is not necessarily a waste of resources that should otherwise be channelled to professional and well-established international organizations – a line of thinking that is hardly ever publicly or explicitly expressed by conservationists and environmentalists alike, but often silently adhered to and acted upon (cf. Draper et al, 2004). Locally initiated biodiversity conservation projects can be well organized and administered to achieve biodiversity conservation, hence some of them have been recognized through the Equator Prize. The Prize is an indicator of local best practices.
- Studies on the 2002 and 2004 Equator Prize finalists show that most CBC projects were initiated by CBOs or local NGOs and required certain forms of triggers (Seixas and Davy, 2008; Shukla and Sinclair, 2010). For example, it was found that 27 CBC initiatives in the equatorial region were triggered by, among other things, unsustainable resource extraction practices, legal and political conflicts, environmental disasters and deteriorating welfare conditions (Shukla and Sinclair, 2010). The over-extraction of teak wood was a catalytic event for the Baripada Forest Reserve Initiative in early 1990. It became a focus of local NGOs such as the Vanwasi Klyan Ashram and the Janserva Foundation (Shukla and Sinclair, 2010).
- In contrast to the view that CBOs pursue agendas set by donors, community conservation projects do not always require funding to get off the ground. Most self-organized CBC initiatives require operational funding at a later stage. 'Funding seems a less important element to start an initiative when environmental awareness and livelihood threats trigger immediate community action' (Seixas and Davy, 2008, p110). In fact the initial funding for the Baripada Forest Reserve Initiative came from the community.

These conclusions are significant for our analysis in that they emphasize the grassroots nature of CBOs and many local NGOs and how these organizations emerged largely as a response to local environmental circumstances. This statement should not be construed as meaning that the organizations participating in EI are insulated from external influences, far from it. The point here is that most of them are a product of self-organizing efforts. These local initiatives imply that the EI has, to borrow from Seymour (1994), 'discovered'[1] rather than 'designed'[2] conservation activities that are worth supporting in response and as an answer to external influences (see Chapter 9). This begs the question of how CBC projects originate, evolve, survive or disappear. In answering these questions, Seixas and Davy (2008) list six elements (what they call 'ingredients of a great meal') that are necessary for a successful CBC: involvement and commitment of key players; funding; strong leadership; capacity building; partnership with supportive organizations and government; and economic incentives. In this chapter we seek to understand CBOs and local NGOs in terms of triggers at the local level in parts of Asia.

We are mindful that Asia as a region is not a monolithic entity or geographical space but is instead diverse in terms of religion, modes of governance and so on. Its variations in environmental conditions and challenges facing societies make any generalization a difficult undertaking. There are nonetheless some aspects of the region and sub-regions that can be tied together into common threads for analytical purposes. South Asia (Bangladesh, Bhutan, India, Maldives, Nepal, Pakistan and Sri Lanka), for example, is culturally and politically diverse but shares common points of commonality such as the colonial past, biodiversity and natural resource management regimes (Kothari, 2003). By way of another example, the increase in NGO activities in Southeast Asia is partly ascribed to regionalization in that part of the sub-continent, especially the Association of South East Asia Nations (ASEAN) that was formed in 1967. NGOs in Southeast Asia can be formally affiliated with the ASEAN Secretariat provided they are 'A non-profit-making association of ASEAN persons, natural or juridical, organized to promote, strengthen and help realize the aims and objectives of ASEAN cooperation and specifically in the social, [cultural], economic and scientific fields' (Aviel, 1999, p79).

These qualifications imply that the ASEAN Secretariat would ideally support and work with organizations originating from member countries. NGOs in the region have explored these conditions to form regional associations and to formulate regional projects.

It follows that there are common attributes of NGOs in the South Asian region that could be explored to understand the activities of CBOs and local NGOs at various scales. The focus of our discussion is on these organizations within specific countries and, more importantly, the local communities they serve and from which they originate. We draw examples from Sri Lanka and Indonesia but also recognize that these countries are quite different and that the CBOs and NGOs operating in these countries face different challenges. However, certain elements of CBOs in these two countries could be woven together into a common narrative of grassroots approaches to environmental challenges. Both countries have CBOs/NGOs that have been recognized and supported by the Equator Initiative. We refer to CBOs and local NGOs in these countries in order to demonstrate that these organizations respond to local circumstances on their terms. This is indeed the case with the Rush and Reed Conservation and Diversification Programme in Sri Lanka. Our intention is not to give full details of NGOs in the region as much of this information is available in the literature and websites.

THE SRI LANKAN CASE

As in other developing countries, the Sri Lankan government did not give due recognition to the involvement of communities in environmental conservation and protection in the formulation of its environmental policies. In fact, nature conservation was a preserve of the state – a practice inherited from the Westphalian state and its totalizing control. These tendencies also played out in the colonial state in the region as a whole. In Southeast Asia, local monarchs or colonial administrators used ad hoc processes to preserve the wilderness, create sanctuaries and forest reserves (McNeely et al, 1994). The result was the creation of the first generation of national parks in the sub-region, including Wilpattu National Park in Sri Lanka in 1938 (McNeely et al, 1994). Before attaining its national park status on 25 February 1938, the British colonial administration had already declared Wilpattu a game sanctuary in 1905 (see de Soyza, 2005, for a detailed discussion).

This state-centric approach gave way to co-management approaches to natural resources for a number of reasons that we refer to in Chapters 4 and 7. It suffices to mention that the evolution of CBNRM globally, the social and political dynamics in Sri Lanka, the influential role of international NGOs, and the threats to community livelihoods created conditions for the switch towards involving communities in the management and use of natural resources. For example, Amarasinghe and de Silva (1999) advocated an approach in which resource users and the government of Sri Lanka would have equal responsibilities in the management of fisheries. Furthermore, a joint project of the United States Agency for International Development (USAID) and the government of Sri Lanka concluded that co-management is a necessary approach towards the management of environmental resources in Sri Lanka and that the government in that country cannot achieve these objectives alone (DeCosse and Jayawickrama, 1997). The ascendancy of co-management approaches in Sri Lanka is in line with the general view that collaborative management 'offers a route to sustainable management' and governance of common resources' (Pretty, 2003, p1912). As we have intimated above, we do not think that co-management approaches fully explain responses to environmental challenges by groups at the grassroots. Thus, CBC and local NGOs have a genesis that should be understood in contexts other than co-management schemes.

According to Goodhand and Lewer, local NGOs in Sri Lanka can be divided into first and second generations; with the first generation coming from 'a church-based, welfare and charity background' (Goodhand and Lewer, 1999, p74) most of which predate the outbreak of political conflict in that country in 1983. The second generation of local NGOs is a product of the increase in funding which became available in the 1980s and 1990s at the height of the conflict in that country. In the context of natural resource management, these CBOs and local NGOs offer what Pretty calls, the third way between centralized regulation and enclosures:

> *These groups are indicating that, given good knowledge about local resource; appropriate institutional, social, and economic conditions; and processes that encourage careful deliberation, communities can work together to use natural resources sustainably over the long term.*
> (Pretty, 2003, p1913)

There is of course a debate on whether communities can manage resources on their own without harmful consequences, and whether we are expecting too much from the community given the complexity of the biophysical environment, contemporary environmental challenges and social dynamics within communities. For the purpose of our discussion, we pay attention to how local NGOs and CBOs have self-organized to respond to their environmental and socio-economic circumstances. According to Arjun Guneratne, the early local NGOs in Sri Lanka were established by Sri Lanka's Anglophone middle-class who modelled their organizations on those in Europe and the US (Guneratne, 2008, 2010). One of Sri Lanka's leading ENGOs, the Environmental Foundation Ltd (EFL), which was modelled on the Natural Resources Defense Council:

> *sought to position itself to fill a void in the NGO landscape by being the first public-interest law firm in Sri Lanka, one focused on seeing to it that the law with regard to environmental matters was implemented and that government departments entrusted with environmental responsibilities carried out their statutory duties.* (Guneratne, 2008, p108)

Other NGOs such as The Rush and Reed Conservation and Diversification Programme in Sri Lanka were more concerned with livelihoods issues as the brief discussion below illustrates.

Committee for People's Rights and the Rush and Reed Conservation and Diversification Programme

> *We stand by the credo that if we only study the salient points in our rural traditions and pattern of life, we should be able to find solutions to the degradation brought about by development ... our vision goes beyond weaving to embrace an entire cult of living ... we have added value to the lives of these village folk and given them recognition as valuable individuals in society.* (Piyasoma Benthota, cited in *Sunday Observer online*, 2003])

These words by the coordinating secretary of the Committee for People's Rights, Benthota, capture the claim we make in this chapter, namely, that locals have the propensity to link environmental conditions to their livelihoods and to proceed with self-initiated conservation actions. The story of the Rush and Reed Conservation Programme is that it was initiated by the Committee for People's Rights (CPR) in the early 1990s. The CPR is classified as a CBO in both the EI and the GEF-SGP on the grounds that it is a community organization championing community needs and aspirations. The CPR works in partnership with GEF-SGP, the National Crafts Council, the Department of Agrarian Services, the National

Handicrafts Board, the National Design Centre, Green Movement of Sri Lanka and the Movement for National Land and Agricultural Reform (Equator Initiative, 2004)).

The catalysts for the Rush and Reed Conservation Programme include the destruction of the environment by chemical input from green revolution technologies, threats to indigenous knowledge and value systems, marginalization, etc. The community lamented that the reed plots in the paddy fields from which its members sustained their livelihoods had been lost, as is evident from Angeline Noma's comments:

> *What a lot of household vessels I wove from my own reeds then! ... For my husband, I wove 'magal' mats for drying paddy and large boxes for bringing paddy to the threshing floor. I took 'ambula' (meals) to him in 'rice boxes' that I made. My family slept on the mats I made. My children went to school carrying books in the bags I wove. On our 'atuwa' (kitchen shelves), we had big 'kuruni' boxes to keep paddy. We also had 'duppis' (dust bins) and 'hendi alu' (ladle holders) which I made of rush and hung in my kitchen* (cited in *Sunday Observer online*, 2003).

Though these comments sound nostalgic, they do point to the ways in which the environment and farming practices were tied to cycles of rural life hence the CPR stepped forward to revive the culture of weaving as a livelihood strategy and to create the market for crafts that had been destroyed by the dumping of foreign material and products. For this to happen, traditional cultivation, especially paddy cultivation, is encouraged, supported and made attractive. The highlight of the revival of interest in rush and reed is the Design Fair in which outstanding weavers can scoop prizes. For example, Somawaithie Achchiego from the village of Dambara won the Designer Award in 2003 (*Daily News online*, 2004).

The programme is also important in that the community contributes to the conservation of its environment, especially wetlands from which community members get the supply of rush and reed. It has rehabilitated ecological processes, conserved rush and reed varieties, and led to the increase in species diversity (Equator Initiative, Podujana Himikam Kamituwa, 2004). The programme has been listed on the Best Practices Data Base in Improving the Living Environment, which is a testimony to the significant role CBC plays (UN-Habitiat, 2010). The relevance of CBOs and local NGOs in nature conservation is further corroborated by examples in Indonesia.

The Case of Indonesia

The history of NGOs and CBOs in Indonesia is inextricably linked to the political environment in that country, especially the emergence of state-sponsored NGOs and the rise of the resistance movement in the rural sector. The government sought to create state-sponsored grassroots organizations such as the village people's defence council, family welfare guidance, neighbourhood associations and village youth associations (Nugroho, 2010). The Suharto regime supported organizations such as these during its experimentation with the green revolution in the 1960s through to the 1980s, when government sought to intervene to alleviate the problem of food security – which is often ascribed to a poor political economy and population explosion. This explains why the NGOs had a national reach with a strong focus on development in rural areas. As in other parts of Asia, the green revolution was short lived and its successes were replaced with concerns over the deterioration of the quality and fertility of soil. The negative consequences of the green revolution on agricultural production were compounded by the oil boom that reoriented the workforce and its activities away from agriculture to industry.

Not all rural-focused NGOs were a product of state intervention. As early as the 1970s rural NGOs focused on issues such as community development and self-management, though they had to appear 'friendly' under Suharto's repressive regime because 'the military often assumed rural NGO activities at village level (as well as labour NGOs at the regional or factory level) were aimed at organizing local grassroots movements and thus masked political agitation (Billah, cited in Nugroho, 2010, p91).

The aim of these self-organized NGOs was broad and therefore went beyond the government's initial orientation towards food security to encompass a suite of rights that rural communities were entitled to and for which they were to strive to secure. They were critical of the government's rural development policy while at the same time providing alternative views, plans and practices of rural and sustainable development – pursuing the role of advocacy and development simultaneously. The end of the Suharto regime in 1998 gave NGOs the political space to grow. The regime change was accompanied by the promotion of local autonomy, which in turn presented local NGOs and CBOs with an opportunity to pursue their goals, including the preservation and use of biodiversity (see Suharno and Friedberg, 2003).

A distinction should be drawn between self-organized NGOs and those that emerged as part of the common strategy to bring local communities into externally designed conservation and natural resources management strategies and plans. For example, the USAID-supported initiatives in Indonesia's coastal areas had two main goals, namely, community-based coastal resource management and small-scale community-based marine protected areas (Crawford et al, 2006).

It was understood that the realization of these goals depended on harnessing existing local conditions. Accordingly, Derek Armitage (2003) suggests that conservation in the Banawa-Marawola region in Central Sulawesi could be enhanced by (1) maintaining traditional agro-ecological systems and associated adaptive resource management strategies used by locals; and (2) building upon the region-wide Kamalise movement – whose vision is to reinstate traditional rules and systems by which social relations and society–environment interactions could be governed, especially in territories that historically belonged to traditional groups – to forge conservation alliances among communities, government and non-governmental organizations (Armitage, 2003; see also Baker and Butchart, 2000). In writing about sacred forests in West Kalimantan (Indonesia) Wadley and Colfer (2004) observe that the social and religious foundation of sacred sites could be harnessed to promote global biodiversity goals. The point here is that externally driven conservation efforts seek to align existing cultural practices with conservation imperatives, where this is possible. And, calls for collaborative networks between international NGOs, Indonesian conservationists, government departments and local communities in order to protect birds, forests, marine resources and so on should be understood in the context of the significance of locally situated cultural assets to conservation imperatives. These efforts do not suggest that communities are unable to self-organize and to attend to their environmental circumstances. To the contrary, there are locally driven conservation projects such as in the Ngata Toro Community.

The Ngata Toro example

> *Lore Lindu Biosphere Reserve and National Park comprises one of the largest remaining mountainous rain forests of Sulawesi. It is of high importance from a biodiversity, cultural as well as archaeological point of view. Approximately 90% of the area is montane forest above 1,000 meters altitude, representing most of Sulawesi's unique mountain flora and fauna. The valleys of Lore-Besoa, Napu and Bada contain perhaps the finest group of megalithic stone relics in Indonesia, although all but a few lie outside the biosphere reserve boundary.* (UNESCO, MAB Biosphere Reserves Directory, 2007)

The Lore Lindu described above is one of the seven biosphere reserves established in Indonesia. The first generation of these reserves (Cibodas, Komodo, Lore Lindu and Tanjung Putting) was established in 1977. Of significance to our discussion is the Lore Lindu National Park which not only provides habitats for endangered mammal species and 77 bird species that The Nature Conservancy in Indonesia claims 'are found nowhere else on earth', but is also home to the indigenous peoples of Ngata Toro village whose 18,000 hectares of land lie inside the 217,000 hectare national park (The Nature Conservancy, 2010).

The environmental and socio-political challenges facing the Ngata Toro community are related to their struggles to survive in protected areas from which thousands of people have been turned into conservation refugees. Living in an enclave within a national park demands that the Ngata Toro community should find ways of 'living with and in nature', and that their ways of living should be seen to be in line with contemporary ideas of conservation (cf. Newmann's, 2000, distinction between 'good' and 'bad' natives). The community is therefore required to be self-organized to sustain harvesting and production of non-timber products; promote low external impact agricultural activities, including fish farming; and to be involved in eco-tourism. Methods to achieve these objectives include:

> *identification of special areas for resource extraction and for protection through participatory land use mapping and spatial planning; traditional fines and social sanctions to discourage illegal activities; a system of customary law; collaboration with Park Authority; and traditional forest rangers controlling sustainable extraction of natural resources.* (Adhikari, 2007, pp64–65)

The Ngata Toro community was nominated for the Equator Prize in 2002 because it had revitalized traditional laws and institutions that are supportive of the goals of conservation. In fact, the nomination dossier reads the objectives of the community initiatives as being to:

- *preserve the tropical forest ecosystem, particularly Lore Lindu National Park, through revitalizing indigenous knowledge and traditional laws for access, control and sustainable use of natural resources, and*
- *obtain maximum benefit from the preservation/conservation of the tropical forest ecosystem in which they live in order to ensure sustainable natural resource-based development [in accordance with] Toro philosophy 'Mahintuwu mampanimpu katuwua toiboli Topehoi' (To protect and preserve together our life and environment as bestowed by God).* (Equator Initiative, Ngata Toro Community/Village 2004)

Institutions such as the Institute for Indigenous People of Ngata Toro Village and the Organization for the Indigenous Women of Ngata Toro Village have emerged to champion community values and aspirations in the context of nature conservation and socio-economic imperatives (Equator Initiative, Ngata Toro Community/Village, 2004). Nonetheless, the story of the Ngata Toro Village raises questions about the extent to which local needs and aspirations are negotiated in the environment characterized by conflict of interests. International and national partners of the Ngata Toro community are concerned about the population growth in the community and the negative implications the growth might have on biodiversity (The Nature Conservancy, 2010; UNESCO, MAB Biosphere Reserves Directory, 2007). These concerns, together with the Indonesian government's interest in protecting the forests, will probably influence activities by the Ngata Toro community in and outside the park. In whose interest will community organizations in the area act? Who is likely to sponsor such organizations? Answers to these questions can be attempted once we understand the nature and properties of the boundaries and connections between local actions and external influences. Perhaps one of the external influences on CBC is that of the state itself. While we know much of the external conditionalities that come with funding from institutions such as the World Bank, this knowledge is not matched by the literature on how the national environment contributes to or hinders the efforts of CBOs. In Chapter 9 we pay attention to the national context, the goal being to understand how the state acts as a channel for funding local conservation activities and how this type of funding impacts on CBC.

Notes

1 Conservation projects are said to be discovered when such activities are initiated by local communities but can be identified and supported by outside agencies.
2 Designed projects refer to 'externally catalyzed initiatives focused on particular project sites' (Seymour, 1994, p473).

References

Adhikari, T. (2007) 'Partnerships in conservation and development: Institutional linkages in the Equator Initiative program cases', unpublished masters thesis, University of Manitoba, Winnipeg, MB

Amalric, F. (2005) *The Equator Principles: A Step Towards Sustainability*, CCRS Working Paper No 01/05, Centre for Corporate Responsibility and Sustainability, University of Zurich, Zurich

Amarasinghe, U. S. and de Silva, S. S. (1999) 'Sri Lankan reservoir fishery: A case for introduction of a co-management strategy', *Fisheries Management and Ecology*, vol 6, pp387–399

Armitage, D. R. (2003) 'Traditional agroecological knowledge, management and the sociopolitics of conservation in Central Sulawesi, Indonesia', *Environmental Conservation*, vol 30, no 1, pp79–80

Aviel, J. F. (1999) 'The growing role of NGOs in ASEAN', *Asia-Pacific Review*, vol 6, no 2, pp79–92

Baker, G. and Butchart, S. (2000) 'Threats to the Maleo Macrocephalom Malao and recommendations for its conservation', *Oryx*, vol 34, no 4, pp255–261

Berkes, F. (2004) 'Rethinking community-based conservation', *Conservation Biology Papers*, vol 18, no 3, pp621–630

Crawford, B., Kasimidi, M., Korompis, F. and Pollnac, R. B. (2006) 'Factors influencing progress in establishing community-based marine protected areas in Indonesia', *Coastal Management*, vol 34, pp39–64

Daily News online (2004) www.dailynews.lk, accessed 11 September 2010

DeCosse, P. J. and Jayawickrama, S. S. (1997) *Comanagement of Resources in Sri Lanka: Status, Issues and Opportunities*, USAID and Government of Sri Lanka, Colombo

de Soyza, M. A. (2005) 'Reconciling stakeholder perceptions that inform conservation management options for Wilpattu National Park, Sri Lanka, against colonial conservation legacy, nation building and civil war', unpublished MPhil thesis, University of Cape Town, Cape Town

Draper, M., Spierenburg, M. and Wels, H. (2004) 'African dreams of cohesion: Elite pacting and community development in transfrontier conservation areas in southern Africa', *Culture and Organization*, vol 10, no 4, pp341–353

Equator Initiative (2004) http://sgp.undp.org/downloads/Biodiversity%20-%20 srilanka%20Ea.pdf, accessed 10 September 2010

Equator Initiative, Podujana Himikam Kamituwa (Committee for People's Rights) (2004) www.equatorinitiative.org/images/stories/nominations/Nom2004/2004-0026_nom_ podujanahimikamkamituwa_srilanka.pdf, accessed 21 July 2010

Equator Initiative, Ngata Toro Community/Village (2004) www.equatorinitiative.org/ images/stories/nominations/Nom2004/2004-0136_nom_ngatatorocommunity_ indonesia.pdf , accessed 10 September 2010

Goodhand, J. and Lewer, N. (1999) 'Sri Lanka, NGOs and peace-building in complex political emergencies', *Third World Quarterly*, vol 20, no 1, pp69–87

Guneratne, A. (2008) 'The cosmopolitanism of environmental activists in Sri Lanka', *Nature and Culture*, vol 3, no 1, pp98–114

Guneratne, A. (2010) 'From big game to biodiversity: Middle-class environmental activists and wildlife conservation in Sri Lanka', in Gellner, D. N. (ed) *Varieties of Activist Experience: Civil Society in South Asia*, Sage, Los Angeles and New Delhi, pp217–249

Hooper, M., Jafry, R., Marolla, M. and Phan, J. (2004) *The Role of Community Scaling-up in Achieving the MDGs: An Assessment of Experience from the Equator Prize*, www.equatorinitiative.org, accessed 21 July 2010

Kothari, A. (2003) 'Protected areas and social justice: The view from South Asia', *The George Wright Forum*, vol 20, no 1, pp4–17

McNeely, J. A., Harrison, J. and Dingwall, P. (1994) *Protecting Nature: Regional Reviews of Protected Areas*, IUCN, Gland

The Nature Conservancy (2010) 'Lore Lindu National Park', www.nature.org/ wherewework/asiapacific/indonesia/work/art6215.html, accessed 11 September 2010

Newmann, R. P. (2000) 'Land, justice and the politics of conservation in Tanzania', in Zerner, C. (ed) *People, Plants and Justice: The Politics of Nature Conservation*, New Columbia University Press, New York

Nugroho, Y. (2010) 'NGOs, the internet and sustainable rural development: The case of Indonesia', *Information, Communication and Society*, vol 13, no 1, pp88–120

Pretty, J. (2003) 'Social capital and the collective management of resources', *Science*, vol 302, pp1912–1914

Seixas, C. M. and Davy, B. (2008) 'Self-organization in the integrated conservation and development initiatives', *International Journal of the Commons*, vol 2, no 1, pp99–125

Seymour, F. J. (1994) 'Are successful community-based conservation projects designed or discovered?' in Western, D., Wright, R. M. and Strum, S. C. (eds) *Natural Connections: Perspectives in Community-based Conservation*, Island Press, Washington DC, pp472–496

Shukla, R. and Sinclair, A. J. (2010) 'Strategies for self-organization: Learning from a village-level community-based conservation initiative in India', *Human Ecology*, vol 38, pp205–215

Southey, S. (2005) 'Partnering to scale-up community-based conservation', *UN Chronicle*, no 4, pp53–54, 58

Suharno, D. M. W. and Friedberg, C. (2003) 'Resource management issues: NGOs relate to the new legal framework for local autonomy in Indonesia', *International Social Science Journal*, vol 55, no 178, pp573–575

Sunday Observer online (2003) www.sundayobserver.lk, , accessed 11 September 2010

Timmer, V. and Juma, C. (2005) 'Biodiversity conservation and poverty reduction come together in the tropics: Lessons learned from the Equator Initiative', *Environment*, vol 47, no 4, pp24–44

UNESCO, MAB Biosphere Reserves Directory (2007) www.unesco.org/mabdb/br/brdir/directory/biores.asp?mode=all&code=INS+03, accessed 3 October 2010

UN-Habitat (2010) '2010 Best Practices Database', www.unhabitat.org/bestpractices/2010/bplist.asp, accessed 12 September 2010

Wadley, R. L. and Colfer, C. J. P. (2004) 'Sacred forest, hunting, and conservation in West Kalimantan, Indonesia', *Human Ecology*, vol 32, no 3, pp313–338

Western, D. (1994) 'Linking conservation and community aspirations', in Western, D., Wright, R. M. and Strum, S. C. (eds) *Natural Connections: Perspectives in Community-based Conservation*, Island Press, Washington DC, pp499–511

9

State-Sponsored Community Conservation

In the previous chapter we highlighted the ways in which grassroots organizations have emerged to address environmental conditions affecting their livelihoods and well-being. A question that arises from local responses is whether those responses are local manifestations of wider processes. In other words, are local communities responding to local environmental conditions as a result of their own understanding of these conditions or are they doing so because of external influences, especially the availability of donor funds meant to protect biodiversity – as part of the global goal of conservation? Questions of this nature have been central to the study of scale and the localness of the local has generated much heated debate among social scientists, mainly as a result of the evidence that most local activities and agendas of all sorts *are* related to, or flow from, processes taking place at other scales (i.e. national, regional and global) (see Marston, 2000; Swyngedouw, 2004; Legg, 2009). We have been cautioned not to essentialize the local as discrete places nor overemphasize particular scales as this could lead to a scalar trap (meaning the failure to look beyond activities taking place at a particular scale) (Mohan and Stokke, 2000; Brown and Purcell, 2005). The implications of a scalar trap in CBOs and local NGOs are that focusing on the activities of organizations operating at the local level could obstruct the understanding of the multiple ways in which these organizations are connected to different actors for various reasons (see Chapter 3). Those connections help clarify what we mean by local NGOs and CBOs in the context of conservation action and funding mechanisms and procedures. Any meaningful discussion about local NGOs should grapple with the question of 'the local' as a level or location or scale – depending on the context in which it is used. In other words we need to know and understand the extent to which local conservation activities are driven by local communities or how those communities act as a conduit for external donations meant to shape national conservation outcomes.

It follows that conceptions of scale, and the complexities and interrelatedness between scales, are important for understanding how activities taking place at local levels are integral to different kinds of internal and external processes. Rather than simple horizontal and vertical hierarchies, scales constitute complex networks through which ideas and practices flow (Legg, 2009). For our purpose, the notion of networked scales implies that nature conservation plans in different localities are potentially linked to national plans, which have a global relevance. Writing on scales, Engel-Di Mauro (2009) has argued that our understanding of activities on the ground could be enhanced by adopting approaches similar to that of world systems that capture multiple scales simultaneously (see Chapter 3). The point here is that, 'if one wishes to define and explain the interaction of social and nonhuman systems, understanding the scale of interaction and the scale of different environmental and social processes is of paramount importance' (Engel-Di Mauro, 2009, p117).

In the context of this chapter and the book as a whole, community conservation might appear localized but the effects of community activities have a wider reach. Those effects could be positive as when community conservation contributes to global conservation goals, hence there is talk of scaling up local initiatives among conservationists and related professionals. Scaling up community initiatives at the intersection of poverty alleviation and biodiversity means 'to bring more quality benefits to more people over a wider geographical area more quickly, more equitably, and more lastingly' (International Institute of Rural Reconstruction, cited in Hooper et al, 2004). Following the same logic, local conservation efforts are supported in order to mitigate the effects of local action on wider geographical areas and society as a whole. The activities of local groups could also be supported because they fit into national discourses of the time or are integral to processes of legitimation. The example of Australia's National Landcare Programme (NLP) is useful for reflecting on the connections between local environmental actions and state sponsorship and national politics. Expressed differently, the relevance of the Landcare Programme to our discussion lies in that the programme makes the links between local conservation activities and national environmental programmes explicit. Furthermore, the programme is publicly funded, which means the activities are not hidden under the veil of secrecy we have seen in the case of clandestine networks of the elites (see Chapters 3 and 5). The Programme has been described as 'an Australian success story [and] an important international example of the potential of state-sponsored community participation to contribute to rural development' (Curtis et al, 1999, p5). We pay attention to details of this Programme below.

The Local–National Nexus in the National Landcare Programme

Meanings of landcare differ from place to place and the genesis of those meanings can best be understood through the lens of society–environment relationships and interactions, because the lens highlights the need for people to care for the environment on which they depend. Landcare in Australia has become associated with responses to environmental challenges, especially the formation of groups that share concerns over environmental issues in rural areas. John Cary and Trevor Webb have attempted to distinguish between three types of landcare activities in Australia, namely, the NLP, community landcare and the landcare movement (Cary and Webb, 2001). They consider the NLP as a bureaucratic or government-managed programme. For them, the community landcare constitutes networks of voluntary community groups. They see the landcare movement as a broad action group encompassing landcare groups, individuals, governments, scientists and so on, who are all concerned with land degradation (Cary and Webb, 2001). Whereas it is important to recognize the diversity of landcare groups, the boundaries between them are not easy to draw. This is more so because of the common concerns of these groups with environmental issues.

Australia's NLP emerged in the state of Victoria in 1986 and subsequently spread nationwide in the 1990s (Lockie, 2000). It is acknowledged that both the National Farmers Federation (NFF) and the Australian Conservation Foundation (ACF) were instrumental in the creation of the NLP, especially in successfully lobbying the Commonwealth Government to fund the programme. These two organizations:

> *argued the need to establish a programme [i.e. National Land Management Programme] that recognized the importance of self-help approach, which relied heavily upon local community groups, within a framework which recognized the responsibilities of Local, State and Federal Governments.* (Lockie, 2000, p47)

The involvement of the ACF and the NFF in the NLP should be understood in the context of the histories, goals and visions of these two organizations.

The contexts of the ACF and NFF

The history of the ACF provides further evidence of the connections between ENGOs and the elite (see Chapter 3). The Foundation emerged during the period (i.e. 1965–1975) that is considered the beginning of modern interest groups in Australia (Offe, 1985). The period was characterized by professionalizing and consolidating interest groups and the adoption of innovative approaches such as developing strategic relationships between these groups, government and business in pursuit of the interests of a group. As in the case of Prince Bernhard and the formation of Southern African Nature Foundation (Ramutsindela, 2009; see Chapter 3), the catalyst for the formation of the ACF was Prince Philip (Duke of Edinburgh), who, in his visit to Australia in February 1963, sought to and succeeded in creating the ACF as a branch of the WWF (Warhurst,

1994). According to Warhurst, 'Prince Philip ... was extremely important to the ACF in raising its profile, gaining access to government leaders, and assisting in fund-raising in elite circles' (Warhurst, 1994, p77). These are the same roles that Prince Bernhard played with regard to conservation in southern Africa (see Chapter 3) and confirms our argument on the importance of elite philanthropy in conservation. In the case of the ACF in Australia, the Foundation not only gained political clout through its association with high profile individuals, but it also had a close relationship with the government from its formative year in 1965. For example, its first president in 1967–1971, Sir Garfield Barwick, was the chief justice of the Supreme Court; its senior staff took positions in government departments dealing with conservation and environmental matters; and 'after first making a small establishment grant, the federal government approved annual grants of AU$20,000, rising to AU$50,000 and finally, in August 1972, [to] AU$150,000' (Warhurst, 1994, p77). Throughout its history, the ACF has had a close relationship with government, notwithstanding its switch from its initial alliance with the conservatives to Labour and the democrats.

This brief sketch of the formative history of the ACF supports our argument that the flagship of ENGOs is neither pre-given nor a definite product of leadership and management qualities, as argued by Delfin and Tang (2007). Rather we see the attainment of such a status as also largely shaped by the connections that these organizations have with the elites (Brulle, 2000; Ellison, 2003; Ramutsindela, 2009). To give merit to the theme of this book, the flow of philanthropy and other forms of financial support to environmental projects through ENGOs should be understood as an important factor in the making of ENGOs. The relationships between ENGOs and philanthropists are not only mediated by concerns over the environment but also include considerations of benefits and influence. As we shall see below, the ACF and NFF were influential in the creation of the NLP, which relied on government grants (Simpson and Clifton, 2010).

The ACF was created in 1965 as a non-profit organization committed to an environmental cause. It describes itself as 'a professional, collaborative and courageous ... national, community-based environmental organization ... [which] campaigns to protect, restore and sustain the environment' (ACF, 'About ACF', ACFonline, accessed 3 September 2010). Although the ACF lobbied government to obtain support for the NLP as we noted above, it has since become critical of farmers in the Landcare Programme. In its view, the first ten years of the NLP has yielded nebulous results for biodiversity, partly because of the lack of scientific input into the programme (ACF, 1999). Its current focus has also shifted towards food and farming systems in the global capitalist world as evident in its objectives for 2020 for the state of Victoria where the seeds for the NLP were first sown. These objectives are to:

- *position the Victorian food system as a whole, and Melbourne as a city, as world-leading exemplars of how to produce and market*

healthy, sustainable foods in a highly variable, warming and drying climate;
- *ensure that all Victorians have access to safe, healthy, affordable fresh foods;*
- *decrease average consumption of dietary fat in Victoria by 20% by 2020, and treble average consumption of fresh fruit and vegetables (increasing it radically in areas currently identified as 'food deserts', which should have all but disappeared by 2020);*
- *halve the overall rate of obesity in the Victorian population and reduce it by a factor of four among children, by 2020 (working with other sectors including health, education and sport);*
- *achieve energy use targets of 50/50 by 2020 – 50% reduction in energy consumption and 50% of energy derived from renewable sources – across the Victorian food and farming system;*
- *achieve water use targets of 'factor 4' by 2020 – halving water consumption and doubling total production – equating to a fourfold increase in productivity from the water used;*
- *achieve water recycling targets of 'factor 4' by 2020 – doubling the proportion of water that is recycled, and doubling the use of recycled water – especially in urban food production and in the processing sector;*
- *achieve waste reduction targets of 'factor 4' by 2020 – halving Victorian food waste (and waste along the food chain) and doubling the proportion of food waste that is recycled or used for bio-energy production;*
- *halve greenhouse gas emissions from Victorian food transport by 2020;*
- *ensure that the Victorian livestock sector is carbon-neutral (on-farm) by 2020 and has access to operating pilot schemes producing energy from biomass, biogas, solar and wind;*
- *ensure that all new residential developments in Victorian cities incorporate Food Sensitive Urban Design principles as well as Water Sensitive Urban Design principles; and*
- *develop several new cohorts of leaders across the food system and along the food chain, providing intensive leadership training for 1,000 people by 2020.* (Campbell, 2009, p6)

For its part, the NFF was established in July 1979 as a national voice for farmers, and formed part of the trend towards amalgamation that characterized the era of modern Australian interest groups (Warhurst, 1994). Its formation is also ascribed to shifts in Australian agricultural policy, as the discussion below illustrates. Until the 1970s Australian farmers lacked common unifying objectives, and the government's highly interventionist and ad hoc approaches led to the lack of a clear rural policy. Such a policy vacuum existed despite the Curtin Labour government's Rural Reconstruction Commission that was established in the 1940s to advise the government on the reorganization and rehabilitation of the country's rural economy (Whitford and Boadle, 2008). The attempt by the Country Party to woo rural constituencies by emphasizing the need to give voice to farmers who produce, own and sell the product did nothing to engender policy shifts in agriculture (see perspectives on this in Makeham and Bird, 1969; Warhurst, 1982; Hefford, 1985; Smith, 1989). However, the election of the Whitlam Labour government in 1972 is seen as a catalyst for policy change in agriculture. The newly established Industries Assistance Commission (IAC) and the 1974 Rural Policy Green Paper infused 'a much more economically rational approach to agricultural policy' (Botterill, 2005, p213). Though the Labour government lost power to the Coalition government after introducing these changes, the principles of deregulation in agriculture that had been set in motion were maintained: farmers had to reorganize themselves under a new deregulated agricultural environment. Botterill summarizes the 1970s as a catalyst for the NFF in these words:

> *the events of the 1970s and the formation of the IAC had two important implications for the farm lobby: first, the battle of ideas had been won by the proponents of deregulation and, second, when farmers were seeking support they needed to be much more professional in their approach.* (Botterill, 2005, p215)

Thus, from its inception, the NFF subscribed to the free-market economy and therefore shared the government's broad goals for agriculture: free trade, deregulation and structural adjustment (Botterill, 2005).

After more than 30 years of existence, the NFF still describes itself as a voluntary body dedicated to:

> *proactively generating greater understanding and better-informed awareness of farming's modern role, contribution and value to the entire community ... [and committed to] presenting innovative and forward-looking solutions to the issues affecting agriculture, striving to meet current and emerging challenges, and advancing Australia's vital agricultural production base.* (NFF, no date a)

Its specific aims are to:

- *ensure that Australians are provided with food and fibre of the highest quality, while maintaining affordability for consumers;*
- *champion the cause of Australian agriculture in embracing the very latest in technologies to deliver the very best products for domestic and, increasingly, international customers;*

- *promote the interests of Australian farmers and to proactively interact with members to ensure Australian agriculture continues to be dynamic in meeting the ever-changing needs and expectations of the Australian community;*
- *strive in achieving acceptance by governments of the major role Australian agriculture plays in the economic, environmental and social fabric of the nation, as well as farmers' commitment to adequate self-regulation and review - thus ensuring the highest standards across all facets of farm practice; and*
- *adopt all measures necessary to emphasise rightful recognition of Australian agriculture as the 'backbone' of the nation.* (NFF, no date b, emphasis added)

These aims are captured in the NFF's new logo that was launched in 2006 and that emphasizes, among other things, the farmers' interest in land and the connectedness of the farmer and the community. Of significance to the discussion in this chapter is the recognition that NFF enjoys as an environmental campaigner. For example, it won the Public Relations Institute of Australia (PRIA) Award in 2007 for its campaign for environmental stewardship for which the judges of the Award are reported to have said that it was a 'highly successful campaign to reposition farmers as environmental stewards. This was clearly a well targeted, well planned and well executed strategy which used research to good effect' (NFF, no date a).

We refer briefly to these two organizations in order to shed light on the NLP. The alliance between the ACF and NFF has been explained in terms of the need by these organizations to get the Commonwealth Government to commit to substantial funding of conservation-related activities (Lockie, 2000). According to Botterill, 'the NFF's first major involvement with environmental issues came in a joint submission with the Australian Conservation Foundation ... in the late 1980s calling for government action to promote soil conservation' (Botterill, 2005, p216). The NFF in particular incorporated environmental issues in the 1980s in its efforts to respond to the environmental impact of agricultural practices. Around the same time (i.e. mid-1980s) the philanthropic sector also made attempts to support farmers. For example, The Ian Potter Foundation collaborated with farmers and the Victoria government through its Potter Farmland Plan (Youl et al, 2006). Both the ACF and the NFF had access to the Commonwealth Government and also shared similar sentiments regarding the market-based economy (Lockie, 2000; Botterill, 2005).

The NLP and its activities

Allan Curtis and his colleagues have argued that though most landcare groups operate independently of the government they are not grassroots organizations (Curtis et al, 1999). Instead, they can be seen as 'local organizations which act on behalf of and are accountable to their membership and ... are involved in development' (Esman and Uphoff, cited in Curtis et al, 1999, p7). Landcare groups are predominantly farm-based organizations made up of land users, who mostly operate on private or leased land (Curtis, 2000). The groups have specifically formed to improve land management practices and the rehabilitation of degraded land. Studies have shown that the most dominant activity among landcare groups is revegetation and the protection of remnant vegetation, while issues related to community development and indigenous vegetation remain at the bottom of the activities of these groups (Simpson and Clifton, 2010). They constitute a communitarian approach in which private land users must be willing to consider their own interests while at the same time paying attention to the ecological and economic interests of the entire community. This way landcare groups combine resource management and stewardship.

There are different views on why landcare groups and landcare network groups were formed in the first place. Lockie cautions that the emergence of landcare groups should not be understood through the lens of environmental determinism – meaning that environmental deterioration did not lead to the formation of landcare groups (Lockie, 2000). Rather they should be understood in the context of how farmers, state agencies and agribusiness houses construct and negotiate the political economic environment (Lockie, 2000). Viewed from this perspective, the NLP is partly a product of the neo-liberalization of the Australian state, a view which is aptly captured by the following quotation:

> *state deregulation [in Australia] has not abandoned farmers to the ravages of international markets or transnational agribusiness ... but it has created an environment in which responsibility to monitor and manage risk has been transferred from collective organizations to individuals.* (Lockie, 1998; p25)

For instance, following the downsizing of the Departments of Agriculture and Natural Resources, and the abolishment of statutory marketing boards, farmers had to reorganize themselves to take on off-farm tasks that were previously performed by government agencies and statutory bodies. In the process, state policy constructed farmers as 'economically rational actors' (Lockie, 1998, p27). In response, farmers formed landcare group networks as a platform on which they could speak with one voice and to improve communication among themselves and between themselves and the government. These networks secure resources through lobbying, grant submission and from donations from local businesses.

The NLP in Australian politics

In 1989 Prime Minister Robert Hawke embraced the NLP as part of his government policy on the environment and designated 1990 as the 'Year of Land

Care' as a statement to highlight soil erosion as the most serious environmental problem facing Australia at the time (The Bob Hawke Prime Ministerial Library Online, no date). He pledged AU$320 million to finance the NLP; $100 million towards the development of the Murray-Darling basin; $50 million towards sustainable development with environmental sensitivity; $20 million towards saving endangered wildlife species; and $8 million for research on the greenhouse effect (The Bob Hawke Prime Ministerial Library Online, no date). Hawke's successor, Paul Keating continued to use the NLP as an articulation of the Labour Party's environmental policy. For example, in launching the Labour Party's election campaign in Melbourne on 14 February 1996, former Prime Minister Keating reminded his audience that the NLP was launched by the Labour Party in 1989 to demonstrate the Party's commitment to the protection of the environment (Keating, 1996). This is clear from the following lines from his speech on the same day:

> *Three years ago ... I sought a mandate to protect our environment; ...[in 1993] We asked that we be entrusted with the care of the Australian environment, and we have taken that responsibility very seriously. In 1996 our natural environment has a better future than it has had at any time in the past 200 years ... Landcare, which Labor started in 1989, has been given support to match the great enthusiasm with which Australian farming communities have adopted it. Major community participation programs like Save the Bush and Coastcare are flourishing. We have put aside six million hectares of forest for potential inclusion in a world class system of forest reserves. Last month we delivered an environment statement which contained the biggest commitment in our history for the protection of our land, its productive capacity and its biodiversity. That environment statement takes the programs we have conceived and nurtured over the past five to ten years to a new level. And the statement is fully funded. It is not contingent upon the sale of Telstra. We have delivered on the environment in the past and we will deliver in the future – and we will deliver policy, not political blackmail.* (Keating, 1996)

In July 2008 the NLP formed part of a broad natural resource management initiative, Caring for our Country, which brought together the Natural Heritage Trust, the National Action Plan for Salinity and Water Quality, the NLP, the Environmental Stewardship Programme and the Working on Country Indigenous Land and Environment (Department of Sustainability, Environment, Water, Population and Communities, 'What is caring for our country?', Australian Government, Land and Coasts website, 2010). More recently, the NLP has re-emerged as an important element of electioneering. For example, the leader of the Nationals, Mr Truss, has accused the Labour Party of assaulting the NLP as an iconic community-based programme by means of budget cuts (Truss, 2010). In response, former Prime Minister Bob Hawke participated in launching the new vision for NLP on 12 September 2010 and urged Australians to commit themselves to the environment by saying 'as distinct from putting your coin in the tin we want you to put yourself in the tin – contribute yourself' (*The Land* website, 12 September 2010).

The NLP is also understood as a strategy for reintegrating rural and remote areas that were largely characterized by a sense of alienation and frustration into the Australian body politic. According to Pritchard and McManus (2000), it was this sense of being forgotten by governments that led to the development of various political movements in rural Australia. Others have argued that the government paid attention to environmental problems in order to maintain legitimacy. That is to say, the NLP is seen as part of the government's strategy for legitimation. The Programme is also consistent with existing government political discourses and its neo-liberal policies (Lockie, 2000).

Funding the NLP

> *The key assumptions underlying the community landcare program[me] were that with limited government funding of a self-help program[me], landcare group action will facilitate a process of community participation that will mobilize a large proportion of the rural population and produce more aware, informed, skilled, and adaptive resource managers with a stronger stewardship or land ethic and thereby results in the adoption of improved management practices and assist the move to more sustainable resource use.* (Curtis and De Lacy, 1996, p21)

As we have intimated above, organizations that pushed for the establishment of a landcare programme anticipated that the programme would receive government funding. This expectation became a reality when the government adopted the NLP as a national project. The Commonwealth Government committed more than AU$300 million to the 'Decade of Landcare' (i.e. 1990–2000) (Curtis and De Lacy, 1996). On 22 May 1997 Prime Minister John Howard officially launched the Natural Heritage Trust (NHT) as the government's main channel for funding landcare projects. The Australian government defined the goals of the NHT as including:

- *improving the condition of land resources that underpin the sustainability and productivity of resource based industries;*
- *securing access to land resources for productive purposes;*
- *encouraging the development of sustainable and profitable land management systems for application by land-holders and other natural resource managers and users; and*

- *preventing or controlling the introduction and spread of feral animals, weeds and other biological threats to productivity.* (Government of Australia, no date a)

The Prime Minister considered the $1.25 billion Trust as the Coalition government's 'biggest injection of funds for the environment in the nation's history' (Howard, 1998, p5). As Table 9.1 shows, the government committed substantial amounts of funding in the first two financial years (i.e. 1997/1998 and 1998/1999). This financial boost resulted from the government's sale of Telstra – the national telecommunication organization – during these first years of NHT. Subsequently there was a decline in government support for the NLP. The decline suggests that 'the National Landcare Program's initial intention that government support could be used to initiate groups with groups quickly becoming independent organizations was unrealistic' (Simpson and Clifton, 2010, p420).

Halfway through the first Decade of Landcare (i.e. 1995), the government acknowledged problems pertaining to the funding of the NLP and proposed, among other things, that the programme should adopt an integrated approach in which land, water, vegetation and nature conservation should be managed together (Government of Australia, 1995). More importantly, the government also sought to define its role as being to stimulate private investment in landcare actions and to facilitate public investment and community action off-farm (Government of Australia, 1995).

The Australian government also created a local action arm of the NHT in the form of the Envirofund that was established in 2002. Individuals, legal entities and sponsoring organizations (for example local, state or territory government, regional natural resource management bodies or incorporated community groups) could apply for grants up to $50,000 for activities that had a high public benefit (Government of Australia, no date b).

Table 9.1 *NHT government revenues, 1997–2007*

Financial Year	Amount AU$
1997/1998	1,286,978*
1998/1999	1,286,978*
1999/2000	188,000
2000/2001	114,908
2001/2002	301,872
2002/2003	82,850
2003/2004	130,169
2004/2005	326,355
2005/2006	328,631
2006/2007	319,274

Note: * Receipts from Telstra sale amounted to $1,100,000.
Source: Compiled from annual reports of the Government of Australia

The NHT was abandoned on 30 June 2008 and was replaced by 'Caring for our Country', which was announced as a one-stop shop in a joint press release by Peter Garrett (Minister for the Environment, Heritage and the Arts) and Tony Burke (Minister for Agriculture, Fisheries and Forestry) on 14 March 2008 (Government of Australia, 2008). This new programme received an injection of $2.25 billion over five years and covered the NHT, NLP, Environmental Stewardship and Working on Country programmes, and its six focal points are Australia's national reserve systems; biodiversity and natural icons; coasts and aquatic habitats; sustainable farm practices and landcare; natural resource management in remote and northern Australia; and community skills, knowledge and engagement (Government of Australia, 2008). As could be expected, the new programme was touted as evidence of delivering election commitments by the Rudd government.

Since 2008, the government has used Caring for our Country as a channel for funding the activities of communities and farmers that contribute to protecting and managing Australia's natural environment. In the 2008/2009 fiscal year, Caring for our Country provided $22.8 million for 138 Open Grants projects; $4.9 million for environmental stewardship bids; $30 million for Reef Rescue and $17.2 million for landcare grants (Government of Australia, 2009). In the 2009/2010 budget, the government invested $33.6 million to be used to support the National Landcare Facilitators Initiative over four years (Government of Australia, 2010). It is envisaged that 56 landcare facilitator positions would be created to support local communities and landcare groups throughout the country (Government of Australia, 2010).

Concluding Remarks

The foregoing discussion highlights the links between community conservation groups and national government plans, as well as external (elite) influence triggering national initiatives. It confirms our argument that local actions should be understood in broad contexts of scale because these actions are often integral to processes that are not (entirely) controlled by the locals. In the case of Australia, changes in agricultural policies, especially the injection of free-market principles into the agricultural sector, created a new environment for farmers, hence the emergence of the NFF. The reliance of farmers on government funding meant that landcare groups were bound to operate within the parameters set by government. The government, rather than landcare groups, largely defined the conservation agendas, especially through the restructuring of funding instruments. The close connections between local groups and the state raise questions of power in CBC and the role of sponsorships in shaping that power. It pinpoints some of the very reasons why this book was written in the first place: to follow and understand the flows of (philanthropic) capital working in and for the environment; to analyse the worldviews, paradigms and ideologies that come with the money; and how these agendas are pursued across and through the various levels of networked and interlinked scales across the globe.

REFERENCES

ACF (Australian Conservation Foundation) (1999) *Response to Draft National Framework for Management & Monitoring of Australia's Native Vegetation* (September), ACF, Melbourne

ACF (2011) 'About ACF', www.acfonline.org.au/default.asp?section_id=231, accessed 9 February 2011

The Bob Hawke Prime Ministerial Library online (no date) 'Hawke government 1989', www.library.unisa.edu.au, accessed 25 September 2010

Botterill, L. C. (2005) 'Policy change and network termination: The role of farm groups in agricultural policy making in Australia', *Australian Journal of Political Science*, vol 40, no 1, pp207–219

Brown, C. and Purcell, M. (2005) 'There is nothing inherent about scale: Political ecology, the local trap, and the politics of development in Brazilian Amazon', *Geoforum*, vol 36, no 5, pp607–624

Brulle, R. J. (2000) *Agency, Democracy, and Nature: The US Environmental Movement from a Critical Theory Perspective*, MIT Press, Cambridge MA

Campbell, A. (2009) *Paddock to Plate: Policy Propositions for Sustaining Food and Farming Systems,* The future food and farm project propositions paper, Australian Conservation Foundation, Melbourne

Cary, J. and Webb, T. (2001) 'Landcare in Australia: community participation and land management', *Journal of Soil and Water Conservation,* vol 56, no 4, pp274–278

Curtis, A. (2000) 'Landcare: approaching the limits of voluntary action', *Australian Journal of Environmental Management*, vol 7, no 1, pp19–27

Curtis, A. and De Lacy, T. (1996) 'Landcare in Australia: Beyond the expert farmer', *Agriculture and Human Values*, vol 13, no 1, pp20–55

Curtis, A., Britton, A. and Sobels, J. (1999) 'Landcare networks in Australia: State-sponsored participation through local organizations', *Journal of Environmental Planning and Management*, vol 42, no 1, pp5–21

Delfin, F. G. and Tang, S. (2007) 'Elitism, pluralism, or resource dependency: patterns of environmental philanthropy among private foundations in California', *Environment and Planning A*, vol 39, no 9, pp2167–2186

Department of Sustainability, Environment, Water, Population and Communities (2010) 'What is caring for our country?', Australian Government, Land and Coasts website, http://www.nrm.gov.au/about/caring/index.html, accessed 3 October 2010

Ellison, K. (2003) 'The business of eco-philanthropy', *Frontiers in Ecology and the Environment*, vol 1, no 7, p396

Engel-Di Mauro, S. (2009) 'Seeing the local in the global: Political ecologies, world systems, and the question of scale', *Geoforum*, vol 40, no 1, pp116–125

Government of Australia (no date a) *Landcare (brochure),*www.nht.gov.au/nht/index.html#what, accessed 15 September 2010.

Government of Australia (no date b) *Australian Government Envirofund*, www.nht.gov.au/envirofund/index.html accessed 15 September 2010

Government of Australia (1995) *Decade of Landcare Plan: National Overview*, Government of Australia, Canberra

Government of Australia (2008) *Annual Report*, Government of Australia, Canberra

Government of Australia (2009) *Annual Report*, Government of Australia, Canberra

Government of Australia (2010) *Annual Report*, Government of Australia, Canberra

Hefford, R. (1985) *Farm Policy in Australia*, University of Queensland Press, St Lucia

Hooper, M., Jafry, R., Marolla, M. and Phan, J, (2004) *The Role of Community Scaling-Up in Achieving the MDGs: An Assessment of Experience from the Equator Initiative*, New York

Howard, J. (1998) 'The Natural Heritage Trust: Action for the future', *Natural Heritage*, vol 1, no 1, p5

Keating, P. (1996) 'Speech at the 1996 ALP Campaign Launch', 14 February, Melbourne

The Land website (2010) 'Hawke helps landcare launch new vision', http://theland.farmonline.com.au/news/nationalrural/agribusiness-and-general/general/hawke-helps-landcare-launch-new-vision/1939299.aspx, posted on 12 September 2010

Legg, S. (2009) 'Of scales, networks and assemblages: The league of nations apparatus and the scalar sovereignty of the Government of India', *Transactions of the Institute of British Geographers*, vol 34, no 2, pp234-253.

Lockie, S. (1998) 'Landcare in Australia: cultural transformation in the management of rural environments', *Culture and Agriculture*, vol 20, no 1, pp21–29

Lockie, S. (2000) 'Environmental governance and legitimation: State–community interactions and agricultural land degradation in Australia', *Capitalism Nature Socialism*, vol 11, no 2, pp41–58

Makeham, J. P. and Bird, J. D. (eds) (1969) *Problems of Change in Australian Agriculture*, University of New England, Armidale

Marston, S. A. (2000) 'The social construction of scale', *Progress in Human Geography*, vol 24, pp219–242

Mohan, G. and Stokke, K. (2000) 'Participatory development and empowerment: The dangers of localism', *Third World Quarterly* vol 21, no 2, pp247–268

NFF (National Farmers Federation) (no date a) 'About NFF', www.nff.org.au/aboutus.html, accessed 10 September 2010

NFF (no date b) 'Aims & objectives', www.nff.org.au/objectives.html, accessed 10 September 2010

Offe, C. (1985) 'New social movements: Challenging the boundaries of institutional politics', *Social Research*, vol 52, no 4, pp817–868

Pritchard, B. and McManus, P. (eds) (2000) *The Dynamics of Change in Rural and Regional Australia*, University of New South Wales, Sydney

Ramutsindela, M. (2009) 'The interconnections between environmental philanthropy and business: Insights from the Southern African Nature Foundation', *Transformation*, vol 70, pp54–69

Simpson, G. and Clifton, J. (2010) 'Funding and facilitation: Implications of changing government policy for the future of voluntary landcare groups in Western Australia', *Australian Geographer*, vol 41, no 1, pp403–423

Smith, M. J. (1989) 'Changing agendas and policy communities: Agricultural issues in the 1930s and the 1980s', *Public Administration*, vol 67, pp149–165

Swyngedouw, E. (2004) 'Globalisation or "glocalisation"? Networks, territories and rescaling', *Cambridge Review of International Affairs*, vol 17, no 1, pp25–48

Truss, W. (2010) 'House of Representatives – Budget Response Speech', 24 May, Canberra

Warhurst, J. (1982) 'The Industries Assistance Commission and the making of primary industry policy', *Australian Journal of Public Policy*, vol 41, pp15–32

Warhurst, J. (1994) 'The Australian Conservation Foundation: The development of a modern environmental interest group', *Environmental Politics*, vol 3, no 1, pp68–90

Whitford, T. and Boadle, D. (2008) 'Australia's Rural Reconstruction Commission, 1943–46: A reassessment', *Australian Journal of Politics and History*, vol 54, no 4, pp525–544

Youl, R., Marriot, S. and Nabben, T. (2006) *Landcare in Australia: Founded on Local Action*, Secretariat for International Landcare and Rob Youl Consulting, Melbourne

10

Power Relations, Priorities and the Future of Environmental Philanthropy

Much of private welfare work of organized philanthropy in the last half of [the 19th] century was aimed less at the relief of misery than the preservation of social order and the organization of political power. (Katz, cited in Clotfelter and Ehrlich, 1999, p50)

What common traits tend to characterize people engaged in wildlands philanthropy? Regardless of background, it seems many are attuned to wild beauty. Besides having a deep aesthetic connection to natural landscapes, they share a desire to be socially useful in a way that transcends a brief human life span. (Butler et al, 2010, pxxv)

Philanthropy can often be the most cost-effective way for a company to improve its competitive context, enabling companies to leverage the efforts and infrastructure of nonprofits and other institutions. (Porter and Kramer, 2002, p61)

The contrasting perspectives on philanthropy captured in the three quotations above are instructive in that they reveal different perspectives on philanthropy as a concept. In this book we have tried to show that environmental philanthropy is often a double-edged sword, being able to do both good and harm to the environment and human well-being, although quite often in unpredictable, unanticipated and unintended ways. The positive and negative impacts of environmental philanthropy are inherent in the nature of philanthropy that, in the words of Damon, 'conducts its affairs without reference to common codes' (Damon, 2006, p2). The question that comes to mind regarding environmental philanthropy is first and foremost whether such common codes are necessary. We might be tempted to answer affirmatively, given the history of environmental philanthropy that we have referred to in the various chapters of this book. The entrenched Cartesian idea of nature that has been sponsored over the years has led to massive resettlements and removals and these processes continue to take place in the 21st century (Milgroom and Spierenburg, 2008; Dowie, 2009). In the absence of a code of conduct, the negative impact of conservation on local communities is likely to work against efforts to improve the values of conservation. However, codes of conduct are no simple, straightforward answer to these problems, given that existing guidelines such as, for instance, the World Bank guidelines on resettlement have not been entirely successful (Milgroom and Spierenburg, 2008; see Chapter 6). Discussions about codes of conduct require not only confronting the difficult question about donors' intentions, but also about common conceptualizations of nature and the environment.

In this chapter we reinforce the message of our book by proceeding as follows. First, we point to the need for integrating environmental philanthropy into the main debate concerning impacts of philanthropy. More communication and exchange between different fields of philanthropy could benefit our understanding of philanthropy in general and environmental philanthropy in particular. We are of the view that the sponsorship of nature stands to benefit from experiences in philanthropy as a whole. In turn, there are also lessons from the environmental domain that could benefit our thinking about philanthropy in general. These lessons include understanding the ways in which problems are framed in order to spur philanthropic actions as well as the need to pay attention to the geography of philanthropy. Second, we reiterate the need to understand context and how it shapes meanings of philanthropy. Critiques of philanthropy will benefit from contextualizing sponsorship and by being attentive to the complex nature of philanthropy and the various contexts in which it is embedded. As we have shown in this book, philanthropy also has a temporal component that could aid our understanding of its trajectories and the actions that flow from it. In the last section we paint a picture of philanthropy with a broad brush and also suggest lines of inquiry into environmental philanthropy and its futures.

ENVIRONMENTAL PHILANTHROPY AS PHILANTHROPY

We see no reason why environmental philanthropy should not be concerned with the impact that sponsored conservation projects have on both nature and society. Has environmental philanthropy been used to support the preservation of critical habitats, species and so forth? Has it been directed to the most pressing environmental challenges of our time? And, if so, what have the impacts been? With regard to the impact of environmental philanthropy on society the following questions could be asked: do donors want to know and are they made aware of the consequences of conservation projects for the most marginalized segments of society? If they do, what sorts of moral questions do they ask themselves? To benefit the theme of this book, we argue that these types of questions cannot be ignored if environmental philanthropy is to achieve its intended goals.

Given that 2010 was the United Nations International Year of Biodiversity in which new biodiversity targets were set, it is logical to assume that these targets will be considered the focal point for conservation as well as funding. At the time of writing (i.e. October 2010), moves were underway in Nagoya, Japan, to get the Tenth Meeting of the Conference of Parties of the Convention on Biological Diversity to deliberate and agree on the following draft strategic goals for 2011–2020:

- Addressing the underlying causes of biodiversity loss by mainstreaming biodiversity across government and society. To meet this goal, there should be, among other things, the spread of universal knowledge about the values of biodiversity; the values of biodiversity should be integrated into national and local development and poverty reduction strategies and planning processes; and incentives harmful to biodiversity eliminated or minimized;
- Reducing the direct pressures on biodiversity and promoting sustainable use (i.e. of biodiversity). The target here is to reduce the rate of biodiversity loss and degradation and fragmentation of natural habitats by half or close to zero;
- Improving the status of biodiversity by safeguarding ecosystems, species and genetic diversity;
- Enhancing the benefits to all from biodiversity and ecosystem services;
- Enhancing implementation through participatory planning, knowledge management and capacity-building (United Nations, 2010a).

These goals are certainly not new in conservation circles but they nevertheless represent a sustained effort that requires substantial funding. We comment on what these objectives mean for the future of philanthropy below. For the moment we concentrate on the moral compass of philanthropy. Of significance to the theme of this book are the kinds of questions that sponsors should ask themselves when they make a contribution towards these targets. Public and private funds have been and are being mobilized towards meeting the strategic conservation goals of the Conference of the Parties (COP) of the Convention on Biological Diversity (CBD). For example, at a high-profile dinner hosted under the LifeWeb Initiative on 24 October 2010 in Nagoya (i.e. during the COP 10 Meeting), the US government committed over US$50 million to Costa Rica through the Tropical Forest Conservation Act. Private foundations, such as the Gordon and Betty Moore Foundation, the Linden Trust, the Walton Family Foundation, and The Nature Conservancy also pledged funding. A total of about $30 million ($7 million from the Netherlands and $20 million from the US) was earmarked for biodiversity and sustainable landscapes in Colombia; and another $5 million was promised by the French government to assist Mozambique with the conservation of its biodiversity (United Nations, 2010b). We anticipate that other governments, foundations and philanthropists are most likely to make contributions to activities marking the International Year of Biodiversity. While this flow of money is positive and should be encouraged, it does not automatically translate into 'doing good', as we have argued in this book. Our caution about the flow of money should not be misconstrued as suggesting that there is no urgent need to fund conservation work. To make such a suggestion would be grossly irresponsible. On the contrary, we think that the energy and zeal to raise funds for biodiversity protection should be matched by the quest to understand the impact those funds might have on nature and society.

There is a need to understand philanthropists and their interests. After all, philanthropy is driven by particular interests and these interests are not static. This book has attempted to capture some of these interests from historical and geographical perspectives in the hope that research will build on the trajectories we have sketched. We noted the ways in which cultural processes of identity construction in the occidental world have influenced and still influence how philanthropists think about the broad concept of 'nature' and how (local) people (and communities) are considered as either inside or outside this imagined 'natural sublime'. Yet, such conceptualizations and the ways in which they impact on environmental philanthropy are not static, as our discussions of sustainable use, community-based initiatives and CSR have shown, hence our analysis and evaluation of philanthropy also needs to be adapted. The book nevertheless provides some indications of certain processes and factors that continue to be important in studying and understanding (environmental) philanthropy. These concern the way philanthropists relate to each other, as well as to states and NGOs. We anticipate some continuity in philanthropists' behaviour due to elite networking (see Chapters 3, 5 and 7) that is manifested in contemporary elite environmentalism and the relationships between celebrities and conservation (Brockington, 2009).

Placing (Environmental) Philanthropy in Context

Throughout the book we argued that the complexities of environmental philanthropy lie in the various contexts in which it operates ranging from the geo-political domain, elite formations, local-state (South–South) and South–North relations, to broader socio-economic, socio-political dynamics and historical pathways. We see environmental philanthropy as constantly being invented and reinvented, shaped and reshaped by waves of shifting dynamics of and inter-linkages between various contexts. Our view is that environmental philanthropy is always situational in time and space and therefore every period 'produces' its own varieties of environmental philanthropy. Even big foundations that have already been in the field of philanthropy for a long time have shifted their focus over time, responding to new challenges and realities, coining new catchwords, adapting and inventing new strategies and priorities to respond to funding opportunities.

The threat of communism for instance, once a major influence on thinking about environmental philanthropy (see Chapter 3) is now gone but threats of climate change are the order of the day; furthermore, the economic world order seems to be shifting with the emergence of the so-called BRIC countries and other emerging economies, creating other spheres of influence worldwide.

Flows of funding through environmental philanthropy are not equally distributed across the globe; certain regions are deemed more critical for protecting the environment than others and tend to have a high concentration of conservation activities. The question of why Africa seems to have such an appeal to environmental philanthropists is crucial for understanding conceptualizations of nature and why philanthropy remains important in the region. As we have noted, there are other concentrations of conservation activities in Latin America and Asia, which are highly supported by funding agencies such as the GEF (see Chapter 6). Historical trajectories are important in understanding these concentrations. However, the self-organizing strengths of local residents and how they understand and respond to surrounding environmental problems and challenges are also crucial. Such local initiatives and the increased mobilization of 'ordinary' members of the public – facilitated also by new communication technologies – could provide a new context in which environmentalism will no longer be the domain of the elite class. The 'environmentalism of the poor', which focuses on grassroots needs such as poverty alleviation, solutions to local environmental problems, social justice and so forth, is a reality in most developing countries. In contrast to the received wisdom that sees community conservation as a waste of financial resources, CBC has proven worthy of recognition as examples of the Equator Prize finalists have shown. The question that scholars of philanthropy should grapple with is why these local initiatives appear less attractive to environmental philanthropists. Our view is that CBC provides a new avenue through which power relations in philanthropy could be debated.

Our analysis confirms that the boundaries between environmental philanthropy and other interests have always been blurred, and that, often implicitly and between the lines, political and economic interests seem to take precedence over strictly environmental concerns. In times of a shifting economic world order in combination with a global economic crisis, environmental philanthropy might be especially prone to becoming 'hijacked' for other interests and purposes. Especially when the economic crisis affects the availability of funds, this may lead to a stricter prioritization of practices that fit closely with donors' own interests. So far, it is expected that the effects of the crisis will take some time to register in the domain of philanthropy – though some foundations experienced a marked decrease in funds as a result of the depreciation of stock portfolios (Centre for Philanthropical Studies, no date; cf. Pergams et al, 2004). However, other options might also be possible. We reason that in this particular day and age, environmental philanthropy is standing at yet another crossroads to decide which adaptations to make to be able to continue to play on the global environmental chessboard. It remains questionable, though, whether we can actually speak of 'conscious decisions' in this regard, or whether environmental philanthropy is unintentionally pushed in a certain direction. Nevertheless, based on our analysis in this book, in the following section we would like to 'dream' our way into a future for environmental philanthropy and imagine possible ways that environmental philanthropy could take from here.

INTO THE FUTURE

The first road for environmental philanthropy into the future we would like to briefly explore here is the possibility that the particular 'Western' way of conceptualizing nature – with quite a marked distinction between nature and culture – that has dominated environmental philanthropy for such a long time, as shown throughout the book, is slowly but surely influenced or even replaced by a more holistic vision of nature that pays attention to human well-being. There are strong indications in the field of environmental sciences that such a vision is increasingly gaining currency. The fact that Elinor Ostrom, who introduced the concept of social-ecological systems, won the Nobel Prize for Economy in 2009 may serve as an important boost to that development. In its assessment of biodiversity conservation strategies, the Millennium Ecosystem Assessment – a UN initiative – linked biodiversity and human well-being, and paid explicit attention to what were referred to as cultural services derived from ecosystems (Bhattacharya et al, 2005). Social and natural scientists are increasingly cooperating and developing new research models for the study of social-ecological systems, as for instance through the Programme on Ecosystem Change and Society initiated by the International Council for Science (ICSU, 2010). Furthermore, in the field of conservation, there is increasing attention to the conservation of cultural landscapes (for example Gimona and Van der Horst, 2007; Satoyama Initiative, 2010). We hope that the development of these different conceptualizations of nature and environmental action will influence environmental philanthropy and reverse the current trend of a 'back to the barriers' movement (see Chapter 4).

Shifts in global economic relations and the entrance of new players in the field of environmental philanthropy may also stimulate changes in the conceptualization of nature. Although it should also be noted that economic growth in the South has equally led to a scramble for raw materials and is fuelling a spate of large-scale land acquisitions for industrial agriculture – including the production of biofuels – mining and timber harvesting (International Land Coalition, 2010). As noted in Chapter 4, some of the CSR activities initiated by Asian companies to off-set the emission of carbon have also had negative impacts on local communities. However, certain high-profile environmental initiatives, such as the Satoyama Initiative, which was initiated by the Japanese government with the aim of conserving socio-ecological production landscapes (Satoyama Initiative, 2010) may indeed stimulate a different approach among environmental philanthropists – both inside and outside Asia. The Satoyama Initiative received official recognition and support from the COP to the CBD in Nagoya, and links are now established with organizations in Latin America. Hence, it may be worthwhile to briefly explore different conceptualizations of nature that can be encountered in Asia, to provide counter-examples to a concept that entails a strong separation of culture and nature.

We do realize that by doing so, we are treading on the dangerous grounds of essentialist interpretations and risk falling into the traps of Orientalism and Occidentalism (cf. resp. Said, 1978; Carrier, 1995). We are careful not to idealize these different conceptualizations or the effects these in turn could have – or not – on environmental philanthropy, as our critical remarks about land grabbing and carbon offsetting projects indicate. Yet, the possibilities of a new direction of environmental philanthropy coming from the East are intriguing if we assume that there might be a link between the size of the economy and the flow of philanthropy (see Chapter 1; Pergams et al, 2004). Will the growing economies of China and India bring with them new forms of sponsorships for nature? The question is pertinent to the discussion of this book, which points to how the western idea of nature has been entrenched and sponsored over the years. What are the chances for China and India to push for other ideas of nature that are embedded in the cultures of these countries?

All around the globe, examples can be found of concepts of nature that are much more inclusive – and it must be noted that the 'western' idea of nature conservation focusing on 'the pristine' and eliminating human influence, though now quite dominant, also has a relatively short history (Bhattacharya et al, 2005). One example pertains to how the word nature is expressed in the Mandarin language in China. The Chinese word *Zi Ran* is probably coming closest to what we generally understand by the concept of nature, but never to be understood as 'an embracing category', as in the English language (Chen, 2005, p95). *Zi Ran* is used 'as a verb, to follow the course of nature or the spontaneous inclination; as an adjective, describing attributes neither cultivated nor supernatural, and as a noun, which refers sometimes to the cosmic nature and sometimes to the human instinct or desire' (Chen, 2005, p95). Its main intellectual sources are from Taoism; Chen argues that Tao 'models itself after nature' (Chen, 2005, p96). It refers to all kinds of natural phenomena such as wind, water, valleys, colours and odours. Taking the example of water, Chen posits that in Taoism it is suggested that man should be like water as 'it benefits all things and does not compete with them … It dwells in lowly places that all disdain' (Lao Zi quoted in Chen, 2005, p97). It suggests a road of 'non-action' (*Wu Wei*), not so much as in inactivity, but meaning '"taking no action that is contrary to nature"' (Chen, 2005, p97). In this way, *Zi Ran* refers more to a particular lifestyle than to a philosophical conception; it refers to concepts of nature that include humans, instead of excluding them in sanitized notions of nature and wilderness. While Girardot et al think that Chinese concepts of nature could be revived to confront some of the critical environmental problems such as high pollution in China, they also caution that these concepts could easily be 'corrupted' by 'Western' environmentalism (Girardot et al, 2001). This is a danger that is present in any attempt to utilize local concepts in an instrumental way to foster nature conservation without carefully studying them, as has occasionally happened for instance in using areas that are locally considered as sacred as a basis for nature conservation (Bhattacharya et al, 2005).

As another example of dealing with nature in a more holistic way, it may be worth pondering on the following description of the Indian[1] idea of nature:

> *For Indians, nature is not something outside them. Both the words* prakarti *and* kudrat *mean the entire creation, which includes the human species as well. Not only are human beings part of nature, it is also within them. They are as much an embodiment of nature as are the other things, living or nonliving, moving or stationary.* (Srivastava, 2005, p158)

Therefore it is said that '(t)he notion of community should not just be confined to human beings; rather, it should include all animals and plants. The notion of *vasudhā kutumbakam* – "the entire earth is my family" – is fundamental to the Indian notion of nature' (Srivastva, 2005, p182).

Both 'Asian' conceptions of nature presented above seem to be far removed from the Cartesian types of dualisms that European notions of nature have ingrained over time in environmental conservation activities around the world. Dualisms that are also key to understanding the criteria that philanthropists from the North formulated for their financial support and initiation of environmental projects all over the world. According to those criteria, humans are not allowed to interfere with or 'pollute' the natural sublime. The alternative concepts of nature referred to above suggest in contrast to these occidental notions, that humans are themselves part and parcel of the natural sublime. If these classical and perhaps essentialized and romanticized 'Asian' notions of nature would become more dominant in environmental philanthropy, it could mean that those people and communities that have to live with (often dangerous) nature, literally on their doorstep, would finally be accepted as serious partners in environmental management. This would imply taking local residents' development aspirations seriously, and not only focusing on those that coincide with the interests of conservationists, as is happening often under the guise of various 'people and parks' projects. The challenge, of course, is that current conventions and legislative regimes are predominantly western in outlook; they are both universalized and globalized. This outlook continues to underpin contemporary conventions, treaties and protocols that govern nature conservation policies around the world.

Another route for environmental philanthropy into the future would be that it will become even more entangled with or even inseparable from the global politics of research and protocols concerning the processes of climate change. This scenario is already starting to play out and it is very much in line with and similar to the earlier and current discourses in environmental philanthropy on the constant threat of the extinction of flora and fauna. It would further consolidate the course of environmental philanthropy into the domain of advocacy and intertwine environmental philanthropy even more to policies of multilateral institutions and of nation states around the world. The recent UN CBD in Nagoya, Japan, can be read as proof of exactly this process. As we have shown throughout the book, environmental philanthropy is and has historically been very much involved with saving particular endangered species around the globe. At the summit in Nagoya and on the CBD website, it is explicitly stated that climate change is 'the *new* great threat to biodiversity' (CBD, 2010a, emphasis added). In a press release of 18 October 2010 it is stated that 'Climate change, biodiversity loss, deforestation and land degradation addressed as a single challenge at the Aichi Nagoya Biodiversity Summit' and issues can therefore not 'be addressed in a compartmentalized approach' (CBD, 2010b). In a related magazine, it is unambiguously stated that 'biodiversity management can be an important means for helping slow down climate change and its impacts' (Countdown 2010, no date). At the same time, the CBD is heavily criticised 'that its work has been dominated by a tendency to generate text rather than action' (CESAGEN website, accessed 26 October 2010), a sentiment shared by many as Monbiot and Chapron (2010) argue in *The Guardian* '[i]n fact, as a study in *Science* earlier this year suggested, the commitment governments made in 2002 appears to have had no significant impact at all'. To counter the possibility that environmental philanthropists are also considered to be lacking in impact, it is probably necessary for them to particularly stress their advocacy role. This positioning of environmental philanthropists can range from the more militant line of advocacy, such as that demonstrated by Paul Watson of the Sea Shepherd Conservation Society,[2] to the sheer business approach to lobbying as practiced by The Nature Conservancy.[3]

Many ordinary people around the world have become rather weary of all the 'philanthro-capitalists'[4] such as Warren Buffet or Bill Gates, big organizations and institutions such as the Ford or Carnegie Foundation, trying to make this world a better place. This weariness has led to a tendency that people of modest means have started to take more personal initiatives and for instance tie their particular donations to one or more small environmental projects they know and they trust. In terms of 'dream work' it is possible that this individualization of environmental philanthropic donations will grow alongside the 'big spenders' in the industry. Recent research in South Africa has shown that most giving is done within the close circles of the extended family and friends (Habib and Maharaj, 2008). It is where giving becomes synonymous with solidarity. As a result of the downfall of the Madoff empire, the Wall Street Journal featured an article by Lucette Lagnado who asked herself the questions 'How could one man [Madoff] deceive so many? And what does the affair say about American Jewish values? The pain is being felt *especially intensely* in philanthropic circles, which may never fully recover' (Lagnado, 2008, emphasis added). Lagnado suggests that 'Thanks to Mr. Madoff, Jewish charity may have to return to its roots, becoming once again a widespread *communal effort*, instead of being concentrated in a few powerful hands' (emphasis added). Lagnado writes particularly about the Jewish community in the US here, but we think it is representative of a broader longing in philanthropic thinking: 'I would like to see the comeback of the pushke – the little collection box that was once in every Jewish home ... [I]t is simply that in our post-Madoff universe I find myself longing for the kind of more humble, more individual tzedakah, or personal charity' (Lagnado, 2008), in other words, a philanthropy built on personal solidarity, instead of other strategic considerations. Many more people around the world would all of a sudden become labelled as (environmental) philanthropists. Like the individuals, communities or neighbourhoods that start nature conservancies in South Africa, both in the rural and urban environment.[5] Small may become beautiful again (cf. Schumacher, 1973). And, when it does, it could change power relations that are often cemented through wealthy philanthropists while at the same time promoting equality as a principle of philanthropy. It is an ideal that runs counter to current strands of formalized environmental philanthropy.

Though the future directions of environmental philanthropy are open-ended, they are impacted upon by the recent global economic decline. The global economic climate has forced foundations to rethink their role in changing times, which became a focus of the *EGA Journal* in the Spring of 2009. The following comments by the Rockefeller Philanthropic advisors, Douglas Bauer and Lauren Russell Geskos, offer some insights into possible futures:

> *Environmental grantmakers have never been as challenged to do more with fewer resources, but rather than taking a cautious route, funders need to be more creative, organized, and bold than ever before. With Beldon Fund, Pew Charitable Trusts, and Rockefeller Brothers Fund as models, we need to think about* public policy *even more now that Washington is listening, and also about being brave* enough to dip into our reserves *or even to spend down.* (Bauer and Geskos, 2009, p3, emphasis added)

The call to focus on public policy and to spend more indicates that the focus of the big foundations might not be drastically changed by current economic conditions. Our book suggests avoiding being obsessed with spending and instead asking questions about what the spending does to both the environment and society.

NOTES

1 Srivastava is careful not to pretend that Indian culture is the same as the Indian nation state, but is nevertheless arguing that although 'India is enormously diverse ... [a]t the same time, there is a subterranean unity [in thinking about nature]' (Srivastava, 2005, p143).

2   See www.seashepherd.org
3   See www.nature.org
4   A term coined by Alan Marston in 2007, http://exittheratrace.blogspot.com/, visited 26 October 2010.
5   For example the National Association of Conservancies and Stewardship South Africa. See for details www.nacsa.co.za/, particularly look at what kind of conservancies were initiated in the various provinces of South Africa. See also www.conservancies.co.za/

REFERENCES

Bauer, D. and Geskos, L. R. (2009) 'Turn crisis into opportunity', *EGA Journal*, Spring, pp3–4

Bhattacharya, D. K., Brondizio, S. E., Spierenburg, M., Ghosh, A., Traverse, M., de Castro, F., Morsello, C., Siqueira, A. (2005) 'Cultural services', in Chopra, K., Leemans, R., Kumar, P. and Simons, H. (eds) *Ecosystems and Human Well-being, Policy Responses, Volume 3 of the Findings of the Responses Working Group of the Millennium Ecosystem Assessment*, Island Press, Washington DC, pp401–422

Brockington, D. (2009) *Celebrity and the Environment: Fame, Wealth and Power in Conservation*, Zed Books, London

Butler, T., Vizcaíno, A. and Brokaw, T. (2010) *Wildlands Philanthropy: the Great American Tradition*, Earth Aware, San Rafael, CA

Carrier, J. G. (ed) (1995) *Occidentalism: Images of the West*, Oxford University Press, Oxford

CBD (Convention on Biological Diversity) (2010a) 'Introduction', www.cbd.int/climate/intro.shtml, visited 26 October 2010

CBD (2010b) 'Press release', www.cbd.int/doc/press/2010/pr-2010-10-18-pavilion-en.pdf, visited 26 October 2010

Centre for Philanthropical Studies, VU University (no date) 'Geefgedrag en werving van vermogende donateurs [giving by and recruiting of wealthy donors]', www.geveninnederland.nl/SYM-5.2.1-vermogen-om-te-geven.html, last accessed 5 February 2011

CESAGEN website (Centre for Economic and Social Aspects of Genomics) (2010) 'Introduction', www.cesagen.lancs.ac.uk/virtual/biodiversity/section3/intro.htm, accessed 26 October 2010

Chen, S.M. (2005) '"Zi Ran" (nature): A word that (re)structures thought and life', in Tazi, N. (ed) *Keywords: Nature*, Juta, Cape Town

Clotfelter, C. T. and Ehrlich, T. (1999) 'The world we must build', in Clotfelter, C. T. and Ehrlich, T. (eds) *Philanthropy and the Nonprofit Sector in a Changing America*, Indiana University Press, Bloomington, pp499–516

Countdown 2010 (no date) 'Biodiversity and climate change', Countdown 2010, Brussels, www.countdown2010.net/2010/wp-content/uploads/FS6Climate_small.PDF, accessed 26 October 2010

Damon, W. (2006) 'Introduction: Taking philanthropy seriously', in Damon, W. and Verducei, S. (eds) *Taking Philanthropy Seriously*, Indiana University Press, Bloomington, pp1–11

Dowie, M. (2009) *Conservation Refugees: The Hundred-Year Conflict between Global Conservation and Native Peoples*, MIT Press, Boston, MA

Gimona, A. and van der Horst, D. (2007) Mapping hotspots of multiple landscape functions: a case study on farmland afforestation in Scotland, *Landscape Ecology*, vol 22, no 8, pp1255–1264

Girardot, N. J., Miller, J. and Xiaogan, L. (eds) (2001) *Daoism and Ecology: Ways within a Cosmic Landscape*, Harvard University Press, Boston, MA

Habib, A. and Maharaj, B. (eds) (2008) *Giving and Solidarity: Resource Flows for Poverty Alleviation and Development in South Africa*, Human Sciences Research Council Press, Pretoria

ICSU (International Council for Science) (2010) Programme on Ecosystem Change and Society, www.icsu.org/1_icsuinscience/ENVI_PECS_1.html, accessed 5 February 2011

International Land Coalition (2010) *Annual Report 2009*, downloaded from www.landcoalition.org/publications/2009-annual-report, accessed 5 February 2011

Lagnado, L. (2008) 'When the big spenders fail, who will save Jewish charity?', *The Wall Street Journal* online, 26 December, http://online.wsj.com/article/SB123024310766834039.html, accessed 26 October 2010

Milgroom, J. and Spierenburg, M. (2008) 'Induced volition: resettlement from the Limpopo National Park, Mozambique', *Journal of Contemporary African Studies*, vol 26, no 4, pp435–448

Monbiot, G. and Chapron, C. (2010) 'Back biodiversity 100, save our wildlife', *The Guardian*, 4 October, www.guardian.co.uk/environment/2010/oct/04/back-biodiversity-100-save-wildlife, accessed 26 October 2010

Pergams, O. R. W., Czech, B., Haney, J. C., and Nyberg, C. (2004) 'Linkage to conservation activity to trends in the US economy', *Conservation Biology*, vol 18, no 6, pp1617–1623

Porter, M. E. and Kramer, M. R. (2002) 'The competitive advantage of corporate philanthropy', *Harvard Business Review*, December, pp56–68

Said, E. (1978) *Orientalism*, Vintage, New York

Satoyama Initiative, (2010) http://satoyama-initiative.org/en/, accessed 5 February 2011

Schumacher, E. F. (1973) *Small is Beautiful: A Study of Economics as if People Mattered*, Harper & Row, London

Srivastava, V. K. (2005) 'On the concept of nature', in Tazi, N. (ed) *Keywords: Nature*, Juta, Cape Town, pp141–185

United Nations (2010a) 'Revised and updated strategic plan, technical rationale and suggested milestones and indicators', UNEP/CBD/COP/10/9, 18 July, Geneva

United Nations (2010b) 'From commitment to action: Over US$120 million announced for biodiversity and protected areas', press release, 24 October, Nagoya

Selected Further Reading

Books

Aalders, G. (2007) *De Bilderberg Conferenties: Organisatie en Werkwijze van een Geheim Trans-atlantisch Netwerk*, Uitgeverij Van Praag, Amsterdam

Aalders, G. (2009) *De Prins kan mij nog meer Vertellen: Prins Bernhard – Feit en Fictie*, Uitgeverij Elmar, Rijswijk

Aaronovitch, D. (2009) *Voodoo Histories: The Role of the Conspiracy Theory in Shaping Modern History*, Jonathan Cape, London

Adam, T. (ed) (2004) *Philanthropy, Patronage and Civil Society: Experiences from Germany, Great Britain, and North America*, Indiana University Press, Bloomington

Adams, J. S. and McShane, T. O. (1992) *The Myth of Wild Africa: Conservation Without Illusion*, University of California Press, London/Berkeley

Adams, W. M. (2001) *Green Development: Environment and Sustainability in the Third World*, Routledge, London

Adams, W. M. (2004) *Against Extinction: The Story of Conservation*, Earthscan, London

Anderson, D. and Grove, R. (eds) (1987) *Conservation in Africa. People, Policies and Practice*, Cambridge University Press, Cambridge

Anheier, H. K. and Leat, D. (2006) *Creative Philanthropy*, Routledge, London and New York

Arnold, R. (1999) *Under Influence: Wealthy Foundations: Grant-driven Environmental Groups and Zealous Bureaucrats that Control your Future*, Free Enterprise Press, Bellevue, WA

Barnard, R. (2007) *Apartheid and Beyond: South African Writers and the Politics of Place*, Oxford University Press, Oxford

Beinart, W. and Coates, P. (1995) *Environment and History: The Taming of Nature in the USA and South Africa*, Routledge, London

Bekoff, M. and Pierce, J. (2009) *Wild Justice: The Moral Lives of Animals*, University of Chicago Press, Chicago

Berman, E. H. (1983) *The Ideology of Philanthropy: The Influence of the Carnegie, Ford and Rockefeller Foundations on American Foreign Policy*, State University of New York, Albany, NY

Blanc, J. J., Barnes, R. F. W., Craig, G. C., Dublin, H. T., Thouless, C. R., Douglas-Hamilton, I. and Hart, J. A. (2007) *African Elephant Status Report: An Update from the African Elephant Database*, IUCN, Gland

Bond, P. (2000) *Elite Transition: From Apartheid to Neoliberalism in South Africa*, Pluto Press, London

Bonner, R. (1994) *At the Hand of Man: Peril and Hope for Africa's Wildlife*, Vintage Books, New York

Brantlinger, P. (2003) *Dark Vanishings: Discourse on the Extinction of Primitive Races, 1800–1930*, Cornell University Press, Ithaca

Bremner, R. H. (1980) [1960] *American Philanthropy*, Second Edition, University of Chicago Press, Chicago

Broch-Due, V. and Schroeder, R. A. (eds) (2000) *Producing Nature and Poverty in Africa*, Nordisk Afrikainstitutet, Stockholm

Brockington, D. (2009) *Celebrity and the Environment: Fame, Wealth and Power in Conservation*, Zed Books, London

Brockington, D., Duffy, R. and Igoe, J. (2008) Nature Unbound. Conservation, Capitalism and the Future of Protected Areas, Earthscan, London

Bruggemeier, F. J., Ciok, M. and Zeller, Th. (2005) *How Green were the Nazis? Nature, Environment, and Nation in the Third Reich*, Ohio University Press, Ohio

Brulle, R. J. (2000*) Agency, Democracy, and Nature: The US Environmental Movement from a Critical Theory Perspective*, MIT Press, Cambridge, MA

Budiansky, S. (1995) *Nature's Keepers. The New Science of Nature Management*, Phoenix Giant, London

Buell, L. (1995) *The Environmental Imagination. Thoreau, Nature Writing, and the Formation of American Culture*, Harvard University Press, Cambridge, MA

Butler, T., Vizcaíno, A. and Brokaw, T. (2010) *Wildlands Philanthropy: The Great American Tradition*, Earth Aware, San Rafael, CA

Carnegie, A. (2006) *The 'Gospel of Wealth' Essays and Other Writings*, Penguin, London

Carruthers, J. (2001) *Wildlife and Warfare: The Life of James Stevenson-Hamilton*, University of Natal Press, Pietermaritzburg

Chapstick, P. H. (1992) *The African Adventurers: A Return to the Silent Places*, St. Martin's Press, New York

Chhatre, A. and Saberwal, V. (2006) *Democratizing Nature: Politics, Conservation, and Development in India*, Oxford University Press, New Delhi

Clotfelter, C. T. and Ehrlich, T. (eds) (1999) *Philanthropy and the Nonprofit Sector in a Changing America*, Indiana University Press, Bloomington

Coetzee, J. M. (1988) *White Writing: On the Culture of Letters in South Africa*, Yale University Press, New Haven

Conrad, J. (1989) [1902] *Heart of Darkness*, Penguin Books, London

Crais, C. and Scully, P. (2009) *Sara Baartman and the Hottentot Venus: A Ghost Story and a Biography*, Princeton University Press, Princeton

Damon, W. (2004) *The Moral Advantage: How to Succeed in Business by Doing the Right Thing*, Berrett-Koehler, San Francisco

Damon, W. and Verducei, S. (eds) (2006) *Taking Philanthropy Seriously*, Indiana University Press, Bloomington

Domisse, E. (in cooperation with Esterhuyze, W.) (2005) *Anton Rupert: A Biography*, Tafelberg Publishers, Cape Town

Dowie, M. (1996) *Losing Ground: American Environmentalism at the Close of the Twentieth Century*, MIT Press, Cambridge, MA

Dowie, M. (2001) *American Foundations: An Investigative History*, MIT Press, Cambridge, MA

Dowie, M. (2009) *Conservation Refugees: The Hundred-year Conflict between Global Conservation and Native Peoples*, MIT Press, Cambridge, MA
Duffy, R. (2000) *Killing for Conservation: Wildlife Policy in Zimbabwe*, James Currey, Oxford
Edwards, M. (2008) *Just Another Emperor? The Myths and Realities of Philanthrocapitalism*, Demos, London
Enright, K. (2008) *Rhinoceros*, Reaktion Books, London
Estulin, D. (2007) *De ware geschiedenis van de Bilderberg-conferentie*, Kosmos-Z&K Uitgevers, Utrecht, Antwerpen
Friedman, L. J. and McGarvie, M. D. (eds) (2003) *Charity, Philanthropy and Civility in American History*, Cambridge University Press, Cambridge
Gibson, C. C. (1999) *Politicians and Poachers: The Political Economy of Wildlife in Africa*, Cambridge University Press, Cambridge
Girardot, N. J., Miller, J. and Xiaogan, L. (eds) (2001) *Daoism and Ecology: Ways within a Cosmic Landscape*, Harvard University Press, Boston, MA
Goodall, J. (with Berman, Ph.) (1999) *Reason for Hope: A Spiritual Journey*, Thorsons, London
Goodall, J. (2009) *Hope for Animals and their World: How Endangered Species are being Rescued from the Brink*, Icon Books, Cambridge
Grainger, A. (1990) *The Threatening Desert: Controlling Desertification*, Earthscan, London
Griffiths, T. and Robin, L. (eds) (1997) *Ecology and Empire: Environmental History of Settler Societies*, University of Natal Press, Pietermaritzburg, pp125–138
Gottlieb, R. (1993) *Forcing the Spring: The Transformation of the American Environmental Movement*, Island Press, Washington DC
Grove, R. (1995) *Green Imperialism: Colonial Expansion, Tropical Island Edens and the Origins of Environmentalism, 1600–1860*, Cambridge University Press, Cambridge
Grove, R. H., Vinita Damodoran and Satpal Sangwan (1998) (eds.) *Nature and the orient: the environmental history of South and Southeast Asia*, Oxford University Press, Oxford, Delhi, Calcutta, Chennai, Mumbai
Habib, A. and Maharaj, B. (eds) (2008) *Resource Flows for Poverty Alleviation and Development in South Africa*, Human Sciences Research Council Press, Pretoria
Haraway, D (1989) *Primate Visions: Gender, Race and Nature in the World of Modern Science*, Routledge, London
Heynen, N., McCarthy, J., Prudham, S. and Robbins, P. (eds) (2007) *Neoliberal Environments: False Promises and Unnatural Consequences*, Routledge, London
Hilty, J., Lidicker, W. and Merenlender, A. (2006) *Corridors Ecology: The Science and Practice of Linking Landscapes for Biodiversity Conservation*, Island Press, Washington DC.
Hobson, J. (2005) *Venus in the Dark: Blackness and Beauty in Popular Culture*, Routledge, London
Holmes, R. (2007) *The Hottentot Venus. The Life and Death of Saartjie Baartman, Born 1789 – Buried 2002*, Jonathan Ball, Johannesburg
Huggett, R. (1997) *Catastrophism: Asteroids, and other Dynamic Events in Earth History*, Verso, London
Hulme, D. and Edwards, M. (eds) (1997) *NGOs, States and Donors: Too Close for Comfort?* McMillan Press, London.

Hulme, D. and Murphree, M. (eds) (2001) *African Wildlife and Livelihoods. The Promise and Performance of Community Conservation*, James Currey, Oxford

Ilchman, W. F., Katz, S. N. and Queen II, E. L. (eds) (1998) *Philanthropy in the World's Traditions*, Indiana University Press, Bloomington

Kiss, A. (ed) (1990). *Living with Wildlife: Wildlife Resource Management with Local Participation in Africa*, World Bank, Washington DC

Klinkenberg, W. (1979) *Prins Bernhard: een politieke biografie, 1911–1979*, Onze Tijd, Amsterdam

Larrère, R., Lizet, B. and Berlan-Darqué, M. (eds) (2009) *Histoire des parcs Nationaux. Comment prendre soin de la Nature?*, Editions Quae, Paris

Leaky, R. and Morrell, V. (2001) *Wildlife Wars: My Fight to Save Africa's National Treasures*, St. Martin's Press, Gordonsville

MacKenzie, J. M. (1988) *The Empire of Nature: Hunting, Conservation and British Imperialism*, Manchester University Press, Manchester

MacKenzie, J. M. and Dalziel, N. R. (2007) *The Scots in South Africa: Ethnicity, Identity, Gender and Race, 1772–1914*, Manchester University Press, Manchester

Magubane, B. M. (2007) *Race and the Construction of the Dispensable Other*, UNISA Press, Pretoria

Mauss, M. (1924) *The Gift*, translated by Cunnison, I., Free Press, New York

Maxwell, A. (1999) *Colonial Photography and Exhibitions. Representations of the 'Native' and the Making of European Identities*, Leicester University Press, London

Meyers, N. (1992) *The Primary Source: Tropical Forests and our Future*, Norton, London

Mudimbe, V. Y. (1994) *The Invention of Africa. Gnosis, Philosophy, and the Order of Knowledge*, Indiana University Press, Bloomington

Nash, R. F. (2001) *Wilderness and the American mind*, 4th edition, Yale University Press, Yale

Neumann, R. P. (1998) *Imposing Wilderness: Struggles over Livelihood and Nature Preservation in Africa*, University of California Press, Los Angeles

Panitch, L. and Leys, C. (ed) (2007) *Coming to Terms with Nature: Socialist Register 2007*, New Monthly Review, New York

Pfeffer, J. and Salancik, G. R. (1978) *The External Control of Organizations: A Resource Dependence Perspective*, Stanford University Press, Stanford, CA

Player, I. (1972) *The White Rhino Saga*, Collins, London

Putnam, R. D. (1976) *The Comparative Study of Political Elites*, Prentice Hall, Englewood Cliffs

Ramutsindela, M. (2004) *Parks and People in Postcolonial Societies: Experiences in Southern Africa*, Kluwer and Springer, Dordrecht

Ramutsindela, M. (2007) *Transfrontier Conservation in Africa: At the Confluence of Capital, Politics and Nature*, CABI, Wallingford

Reid, D. R. (as told to Peter Stiff) (1982) *Selous Scouts Top Secret War*, Galago, Johannesburg

Ribot, J. C. (2004) *Waiting for Democracy: The Politics of Choice in Natural Resource Decentralization*, World Resource Institute, Washington DC

Roelofs, J. (2003) *Foundations and Public Policy: The Mask of Pluralism*, State University of New York Press, Albany, NY

Rootes, C. (2003) *Environmental Protest in Western Europe*, Oxford University Press, Oxford

Ryan, J. R. (1997) *Picturing Empire: Photography and the Visualization of the British Empire*, University of Chicago Press, Chicago

Salamon, L. M. (1992) *America's Nonprofit Sector: A Primer*, Foundation Center, New York

Schama, S. (1995) *Landscape and Memory*, Harper Collins, London and New York

Schenkel, A. F. (1995) *The Rich Man and the Kingdom: John D Rockefeller, Jr, and the Protestant Establishment*, Fortress Press, Minneapolis

Schrift, A. D. (1997) *The Logic of the Gift: Toward an Ethic of Generosity*, Routledge, New York

Shiva, V. (1992) *Global Environment Facility: Perpetuating Non-democratic Decision-making*, Third World Network, Penang

Shneewind, J. B. (ed) (1996) *Giving: Western Ideas of Philanthropy*, Indiana University Press, Bloomington

Snow, D. P. (1992) *Inside the Environmental Movement: Meeting the Leadership Challenge*, Island Press, Washington DC

Steele, N. (1992) *Poachers from the Hills: Norman Deane's Life in Hluhluwe Game Reserve*, Nick Steele, Melmoth

Stiff, P. (2004) *The Covert War: Koevoet Operations in Namibia, 1979–1989*, Galago, Johannesburg

Suich, H., Child, B. and Spenceley, A. (eds) (2009) *Evolution and Innovation in Wildlife Conservation: From Parks and Game Ranches to Transfrontier Conservation Areas*, Earthscan, London

Thompson, J. H. (2006) *An Unpopular War: From Afkak to Bosbefok: Voices of South African Servicemen*, Zebra Press, Cape Town

Wallerstein, I. (1974) *The Modern World System*, Academic Press, New York

Wels, H. (2003) *Private Wildlife Conservation in Zimbabwe: Joint Ventures and Reciprocity*, Brill, Leiden

Western, D., Wright, R. M. and Strum, S. C. (eds) (1994) *Natural Connections: Perspectives in Community-based Conservation*, Island Press, Washington DC

Wolch, J. R. (1990) *The Shadow State: Government and Voluntary Sector in Transition*, Foundation Centre, New York

Wolf, E. R. (1990) *Europe and the People without History*, University of California Press, Berkeley, CA

Wolmer, W. (2007) *From Wilderness Vision to Farm Invasions: Conservation and Development in Zimbabwe's South-east Lowveld*, James Currey, Oxford

Worster, D. (2008) *A Passion for Nature: The Life of John Muir*, Oxford University Press, Oxford

Wright Mills, C. (1956) *The Power Elite*, Oxford University Press, Oxford

Wylie, J. (2007) *Landscape*, Routledge, London

Young, Z. (2002) *A New Green Order? The World Bank and the Politics of the Global Environment Facility*, London, Pluto

Journal Articles

Alon, I., Lattemann, L., Fetscherin, M., Li, S. and Schneider, A. (2010) 'Use of public corporate communications of social responsibility in Brazil, Russia, India and China (BRIC)', *International Journal of Emerging Markets*, vol 5, no 1, pp6–22

Arts, B. (2002) '"Green alliances" of business and NGOs. New styles of self-regulation or "dead-end roads"?', *Corporate Social Responsibility and Environmental Management*, vol 9, pp26–36

Ball, S. J. (2008) 'New philanthropy, new networks and new governance in education', *Political Studies*, vol 56, no 4, pp747–765

Beinart, W. (2000) 'African history and environmental history', *African Affairs*, vol 99, pp269–302

Berkes, F. (2004) 'Rethinking community-based conservation', *Conservation Biology Papers*, vol 18, no 3, pp621–630

Brockington, D. and Scholfield, K. (2010) 'The work of conservation organisations in sub-Saharan Africa', *Journal of Modern African Studies*, vol 48, no 1, pp1–33

Bryant, R. L. (2009) 'Born to be wild? Non-governmental organisations, politics and the environment', *Geography Compass*, vol 3/4, pp1540–1558

Burchell, J. (2006) 'Confronting the "corporate citizen"', *International Journal of Sociology and Social Policy*, vol 26, no 3, pp121–137

Büscher, B. (2010) 'Anti-politics as political strategy: Neoliberalism and transfrontier conservation in southern Africa', *Development and Change*, vol 41, no 1, pp29–51

Castree, N. (2008a) 'Neoliberalising nature: Processes, outcomes and effects', *Environment and Planning A*, vol 40, no 1, pp153–173

Castree, N. (2008b) Neoliberalising nature: The logics of deregulation and reregulation', *Environment and Planning A*, vol 40, no 1, pp1–22

Cernea, M. M. and Schmidt-Soltau, K. (2006) 'Poverty risks and national parks: Policy issues in conservation and resettlement', *World Development*, vol 34, vol 10, pp808–1830

Chapin, M. (2004) 'A challenge to conservationists', *World Watch*, December, pp17–31

Cobb, N. K. (2002) 'The new philanthropy: Its impact on funding arts and culture', *Journal of Arts Management, Law, and Society*, vol 32, no 2, pp125–143

Curtis, A., Britton, A. and Sobels, J. (1999) 'Landcare networks in Australia: State-sponsored participation through local organizations', *Journal of Environmental Planning and Management*, vol 42, no 1, pp5–21

Dahlsrud, A. (2008) 'How corporate social responsibility is defined: An analysis of 37 definitions', *Corporate Social Responsibility and Environmental Management*, vol 15, no 1, pp1–13

Delfin, F. G. and Tang, S. (2007) 'Elitism, pluralism, or resource dependency: patterns of environmental philanthropy among private foundations in California', *Environment and Planning A*, vol 39, no 9, pp2167–2186

Draper, M. (1998) 'Zen and the art of garden maintenance: The soft intimacy of hard men in the wilderness of KwaZulu-Natal, South Africa, 1952–1997', *Journal of Southern African Studies*, vol 24, no 4, pp801–828

Draper, M., Spierenburg, M. and Wels, H. (2004) 'African dreams of cohesion: Elite pacting and community development in transfrontier conservation areas in southern Africa', *Culture and Organization*, vol 10, no 4, pp341–351

Dryzek, J. S. (1996) 'Political inclusion and the dynamics of democratization', *American Political Science Review*, vol 90, pp474–487

Duffy, R. (2006) 'The potential and pitfalls of global environmental governance: The politics of transfrontier conservation areas in southern Africa', *Political Geography*, vol 25, pp89–112

Dzingirai, V. (2003) 'The new scramble for the African countryside', *Development and Change*, vol 34, no 2, pp243–263

Ellis, S. (1994) 'Of elephants and men: Politics and nature conservation in South Africa', *Journal of Southern African Studies*, vol 20, no 1, pp53–69

Ellis, S. (1998) 'The historical significance of South Africa's Third Force', *Journal of Southern African Studies*, vol 24, no 2, pp261–299

Enderle, G., (2004) 'Global competition and corporate responsibilities of small and medium-sized enterprises', *Business Ethics: A European Review*, vol 13, no 1, pp51–63

Escobar, A. (1998) 'Whose knowledge, whose nature? Biodiversity, conservation, and the political ecology of social movements', *Journal of Political Ecology*, vol 5, pp53–82

Ferguson, B. (2009) 'REDD comes into fashion in Madagascar', *Madagascar Conservation and Development*, vol 4, no 2, pp132–137

Ferris, J. M. and Sharp, M. K. (2000) 'California foundations: Trends and patterns', *The Center on Philanthropy and Public Policy*, vol 2, no 1, University of Southern California, Los Angeles

Gan, L. (1993) 'The making of the Global Environment Facility: An actor's perspective', *Global Environmental Change*, vol 3, no 3, pp256–275

Garriga, E. and Melé, D. (2004) 'Corporate social responsibility theories: Mapping the territory', *Journal of Business Ethics*, vol 53, pp51–71

Gissibl, B. (2006) 'German colonialism and the beginnings of international wildlife preservation in Africa', *GHI Bulletin Supplement*, vol 3, pp121–143

Glick-Schiller, N. (2006) 'Introduction: What can transnational studies offer the analysis of localized conflict and protest?', *Focaal, European Journal of Anthropology*, vol 47, pp3–17

Gonzalez III, J. L. (2005) 'Is there room for more social responsibility in Asia's business and economic turn around?', *Asia Pacific Perspectives*, vol V, no 2, pp1–15

Goodhand, J. and Lewer, N. (1999) 'Sri Lanka, NGOs and peace-building in complex political emergencies', *Third World Quarterly*, vol 20, no 1, pp69–87

Guneratne, A. (2008) 'The cosmopolitanism of environmental activists in Sri Lanka', *Nature and Culture*, vol 3, no 1, pp98–114

Herva, V. P (2006) 'Flower lovers, after all? Rethinking religion and human–environment relations in Minoan Crete', *World Archaeology*, vol 38, no 4, pp586–598

Hutton, J., Adams, W. M. and Murombedzi, J. (2005) 'Back to the barriers? Changing narratives in biodiversity conservation', *Forum for Development Studies*, vol 2, pp341–370

Jamali, D. and Mirshak, R. (2007) 'Corporate social responsibility (CSR): Theory and practice in a developing country context', *Journal of Business Ethics*, vol 72, pp243–262

Karppi, I. and Haveri, A. (2009) '"Publicity": Policy push in the age of privatisation', *The Service Industries Journal*, vol 29, no 4, pp491–502

Lambert, D. and Lester, A. (2004) 'Geographies of colonial philanthropy', *Progress in Human Geography*, vol 28, no 3, pp320–341

Leach, M. and Fairhead, J. (2000) 'Fashioned forest pasts, occluded histories? International environmental analysis in West African locales', *Development and Change*, vol 31, no 1, pp35–39

Letts, C., Ryan, W., and Grossman, A. (1997) 'Virtuous capital: What foundations can learn from venture capitalists', *Harvard Business Review*, vol 75, March–April, pp2–16

Levine, A. (2002) 'Convergence or convenience? International conservation NGOs and development assistance in Tanzania', *World Development*, vol 30, no 6, pp1043–1055

Lockie, S. (2000) 'Environmental governance and legitimation: State–community interactions and agricultural land degradation in Australia', *Capitalism Nature Socialism*, vol 11, no 2, pp41–58

Marinetto, M. (1999) 'The historical development of business philanthropy: Social responsibility in the new corporate economy', *Business History*, vol 41, no 4, pp1–20

Mavhunga, C. and Spierenburg, M. (2009) 'Transfrontier talk, cordon politics: The early history of the Great Limpopo Transfrontier Park in Southern Africa, 1925–1940', *Journal of Southern African Studies*, vol 35, no 3, pp715–735

McCarthy, D. (2004) 'Environmental justice grant making: Elites and activists collaborate to transform philanthropy', *Sociological Inquiry*, vol 74, no 2, pp250–270.

McCarthy, J. and Prudham, S. (2004) 'Neo-liberal nature and the nature of neo-liberalism', *Geoforum*, vol 35, pp275–283

Mee, L. D., Dublin, H. T. and Eberhard, A. A. (2008) 'Evaluating the Global Environment Facility: A goodwill gesture or a serious attempt to deliver global benefits?', *Global Environmental Change*, vol 18, no 4, pp800–810

Meijer, M., de Bakker, F. G. A., Smit, J. H. and Schuyt, T. (2006) 'Corporate giving in The Netherlands 1995–2003: Exploring the amounts involved and the motivations for donating', *International Journal of Nonprofit and Voluntary Sector Marketing*, vol 11, pp13–28

Miller, A. S. (2007) 'The Global Environment Facility programme to commercialize new energy technologies', *Energy for Sustainable Development*, vol 11, no 1, pp5–12

Mittermeier, R. A. and Bowles, I. A. (1993) 'The Global Environment Facility and biodiversity conservation: Lessons to date and suggestions for future action', *Biodiversity and Conservation*, vol 2, no 6, pp637–655

Morrison, D. E. and Dunlap, R. E. (1986) 'Environmentalism and elitism: A conceptual and empirical analysis', *Environmental Management*, vol 10, pp581–598

Muukonen, M. (2009) 'Framing the field: Civil society and related concepts', *Non-Profit and Voluntary Sector Quarterly*, vol 38, no 4, pp684–700

Newell, P. (2008) 'CSR and the limits to capital', *Development and Change*, vol 39, no 6, pp1063–1078

Novellino, D. and Dressler, W. H. (2010) 'The role of "hybrid" NGOs in the conservation and development of Palawan Island, the Philippines', *Society and Natural Resources*, vol 23, pp165–180

Nugroho, Y. (2010) 'NGOs, the internet and sustainable rural development: The case of Indonesia', *Information, Communication and Society*, vol 13, no 1, pp88–120

O'Garra, T. (2009) 'Bequest values for marine resources: How important for indigenous communities in less-developed economies', *Environmental & Resource Economics*, vol 44, pp179–202

Porter, M. E. and Kramer, M. R. (2002) 'The competitive advantage of corporate philanthropy', *Harvard Business Review*, December, pp56–68

Ramutsindela, M. (2004) 'Glocalisation and nature conservation strategies in 21st-century southern Africa', *Tijdschrift voor Economische en Sociale Geografie*, vol 95, no 1, pp61–72

Ramutsindela, M. (2009) 'The interconnections between environmental philanthropy and business: Insights from the Southern African Nature Foundation', *Transformation*, vol 70, pp54–69

Rangarajan, M. (2003) 'Parks, politics and history: Conservation dilemmas in Africa', *Conservation and Society*, vol 1, no 1, pp77–98

Roué, M. (2003) 'US environmental NGOs and the Cree. An unnatural alliance for the preservation of nature?', *International Social Science Journal*, vol 178, pp619–628

Saidel, J. R. (1991) 'Resource interdependence: The relationship between state agencies and nonprofit organizations', *Public Administration Review*, vol 51, pp543–553

Saunders, C. (1996) 'Conservation covenants in New Zealand', *Land Use Policy*, vol 13, pp325–329

Sawaya, F. (2008) 'Capitalism and philanthropy in the (new) gilded age', *American Quarterly*, vol 60, no 1, pp201–213

Schramm, C. J. (2006) 'Law outside the market: The social utility of the private foundation', *Harvard Journal of Law and Public Policy*, vol 30, no 1, pp355–415

Shukla, R. and Sinclair, A. J. (2010) 'Strategies for self-organization: Learning from a village-level community-based conservation initiative in India', *Human Ecology*, vol 38, pp205–215

Simmel, G. (1965) [1908] '*The poor*', translated by Claire Jacobson, *Social Problems*, vol 13, no 2, pp118–140

Simpson, G. and Clifton, J. (2010) 'Funding and facilitation: Implications of changing government policy for the future of voluntary landcare groups in Western Australia', *Australian Geographer*, vol 41, no 1, pp403–423

Spierenburg, M. and Wels, H. (2006) '"Securing space". Mapping and fencing in transfrontier conservation in southern Africa', *Space and Culture*, vol 9, no 3, pp294–312

Spierenberg, M. and Wels, H. (2010) 'Conservative philanthropists, royalty and business elites in nature conservation in southern Africa', *Antipode*, vol 42, no 3, pp647–670

Spierenburg, M., Steenkamp, C. and Wels, H. (2008) 'Enclosing the local for the global commons: Community land rights in the Great Limpopo Transfrontier Conservation Area', *Conservation and Society*, vol 6, no 1, pp87–97

Sulek, M. (2010) 'On the modern meaning of philanthropy', *Non-Profit and Voluntary Sector Quarterly*, vol 39, no 2, pp193–212

Timmer, V. and Juma, C. (2005) 'Biodiversity conservation and poverty reduction come together in the tropics: Lessons learned from the Equator Initiative', *Environment*, vol 47, no 4, pp24–44

Warhurst, J. (1994) 'The Australian Conservation Foundation: The development of a modern environmental interest group', *Environmental Politics*, vol 3, no 1, pp68–90

Young, M. (2008) 'From conservation to environment: The Sierra Club and the organizational politics of change', *Studies in American Political Development*, vol 22, pp183–203

Index

ACF (Australian Conservation
    Foundation) 163–164
Africa 121–139
    and China 81
    colonial history 123–127
    conservation 73, 122, 128–133
    EI 146
    GEF-SGP 113
    institutionalized private philanthropy 6
    post-independence 133–139
    pre-colonial history 124
    Southern 49, 74, 93
    as special place 121, 122, 124, 125
    training 35
    wilderness 122, 123, 127
    see also Mozambique; South Africa
African National Congress (ANC) 56–57,
    58–59
African Wildlife College 35
African Wildlife Foundation (AWF) 72,
    136, 139
Africa region, GEF-SGP 113
agricultural sector 166–168
alarmist discourses 89
altruism 1
Americas 73
    see also Latin America; US
ANC (African National Congress) 56–57,
    58–59
Anderson, D. 127
anti-communism 45, 49, 56–57, 60, 62
anti-poaching 54–55, 60
Arab states 113–114
ASEAN (Association of South East Asia
    Nations) 150

Asia 6, 73, 150, 151, 183–184
Asia and Pacific region 115, 147
Association of South East Asia Nations
    (ASEAN) 150
Australia 162–172
Australian Conservation Foundation
    (ACF) 163–164
AWF (African Wildlife Foundation) 72,
    136, 139

Baartman, S. 92
Baripada Forest Reserve Initiative 149
benevolence 5
Benthota, P. 152
bequests 3, 5, 32
Bernhard, Prince 47, 48, 50, 60, 137
Bilderberg conferences 47
biodiversity 33, 109, 145, 179
biophysical environment 27
biospheres, transboundary 33
Bishop, M. 2
black rhinoceros 93
Bourdieu, P. 10
bourgeoisie 9–10
Brazil 81
BRIC (Brazil, Russia, India and China)
    countries 81
Brockington, D. 138
Brown, J. C. 124, 126
Brown, M. M. 144
brown environment 25, 26
Brundtland Commission 73
business sector see corporate sector
Buthelezi, M. 58, 59, 60
Buxton, E. N. 128, 129, 130, 131–132

California, US 70–71, 76
capital, exchange of 10
capitalism 12–14, 67, 78
carbon sequestration 82
Caribbean *see* Latin America and the Caribbean
Caring for our Country 169, 172
Carnegie, A. 2, 37
catastrophic threat 99
CBD (Convention on Biological Diversity), COP 10 Meeting 179, 185
CBNRM (community-based natural resource management) 73–74
CBOs (community-based organizations) 72–73
　connections 67
　conservation 144–149, 150, 152, 161
　funding 74
　GEF-SGP 115, 118
CCLI (Conserving California Landscape Initiative) 75–77
charity 1, 5, 6, 7, 31
chemical pollutants *see* POPs
Chen, S. M. 183
China 81, 183
Chronicle of Philanthropy 31–32
CIS (Commonwealth of Independent States) 115
CITES (Convention on International Trade in Endangered Species of Wild Fauna and Flora) 95
citizenship 14–15
class, formation 9–11
Cleaves, R. 60, 98
climate change 20, 96, 111, 184–185
Club Alpin Français 134
code of conduct 178
Cold War 45
collaborative management *see* co-management
Colombia 179
Colombo Plan 46
colonial history 123–127
colonial philanthropy 11–12
colonial present 12
co-management 151

Committee for People's Rights 152–153
Commonwealth of Independent States (CIS) 115
communal land 35
communism 56, 57
　see also anti-communism
communities, local 72–74, 79, 111, 138, 139
community-based conservation 143–157
　EI 144–149
　Indonesia 153–157
　Sri Lanka 150–153
　state-sponsored 161–163, 167–172
　see also grassroots activism
community-based natural resource management (CBNRM) 73–74
community-based organizations *see* CBOs
conduct, code of 178
Conference of the Parties (COP) of the Convention on Biological Diversity (CBD) Tenth Meeting (COP 10 Meeting) 179, 185
conflict resolution 109
connectivity, habitats 28
Conrad, J. 123
consequences, harmful 3
conservation
　Africa as special place 121, 122, 124
　capitalism 67, 78
　commodifying 77
　contemporary strategies 28
　definition 29
　elites 27, 50–51, 136
　environmental philanthropy 25–26, 30
　'fortress' 133, 135, 138
　green environment 25, 26
　local communities 73
　origins 27
　threat discourses 99
　transfrontier 33, 34–35, 75, 139
　triggers 149, 153
　western outlook 184
　see also community-based conservation
conservation easements (covenants) 33–34
Conservation Foundation 70

conservation groups 30
Conservation International 78
conservation NGOs 29, 30
conservative religious philanthropic foundations 13
Conserving California Landscape Initiative (CCLI) 75–77
conspiracy theories 48–52
Consultative Commission for the International Protection of Nature 132
Convention on Biological Diversity (CBD), COP 10 Meeting 179, 185
Convention on International Trade in Endangered Species of Wild Fauna and Flora (CITES) 95
Convention for the Preservation of Animals, Birds and Fish in Africa 129–130, 132, 133
cooperation, horizontal philanthropy 6
COP 10 Meeting (Conference of the Parties (COP) of the Convention on Biological Diversity (CBD) Tenth Meeting) 179, 185
corporate sector 67, 78, 139
corporate social responsibility (CSR) 12, 13, 79–82
corridors, ecological 28, 139
Costa Rica 179
crisis narrative 97
CSR (corporate social responsibility) 12, 13, 79–82
cultural capital 10
cultural ecosystem services 182
Cuvier, G. 91, 92

Damon, W. 2, 4
Deane, N. 54
definitions
  conservation 29
  CSR 80
  environmental philanthropy 15–16, 26
  philanthropy 6–7
  wilderness 97–98
deforestation 112, 126, 127
degradation, land 112

Delfin, F. 70–71
deregulation, agriculture 166
desertification 97, 112
development, sustainable 73, 78, 79, 107
development NGOs 30
dialogue, EI 145
donations *see* giving
dream topography 90
Dürer, A. 91

easements, conservation 33–34
Eastern Europe 115
ecological corridors 28, 139
  see also transfrontier conservation
econometric measures 5
economic capital 10
economy, global 20, 81, 181, 186
ecosystem services, cultural 182
education, environmental 35–36
Edwards, M. 2, 3
Egypt 113–114
EI (Equator Initiative) 144–149
elephants 95, 138
  see also ivory
Eliot, Sir C. 123
elite environmentalism 27
elite pacting 50–51, 52
elites
  Australia 163, 164
  class formation 10
  conservation 27, 122, 136
  elite theory 46–47, 68–69
  networking 45–52, 53, 180
elite theory 46–47, 68–69
ENGOs (environmental NGOs)
  Africa 122, 138–139
  community-based conservation 152
  connections 67, 164
  funding 78, 107
  local communities 74
  terminology 29
environment, debate on 25–26
environmental agreements, global 15
Environmental Defence Fund 78
environmental education 35–36
environmental establishment 70

Environmental Foundation Ltd 152
environmental giving 27
environmental movement 125
environmental NGOs *see* ENGOs
environmental organizations 68–72, 74, 79
environmental philanthropy 25–39
   context 180–182
   debate on environment 25–26
   definitions 15–16, 26
   future 20, 182–186
   perspectives on 177
   philanthropic priorities 37–39
   as philanthropy 178–180
   practical 31–36
   religion 9
   results of 4
   study of 178
   and wildlands philanthropy 27–31
environmental threats 89–99
equatorial region 145
Equator Initiative (EI) 144–149
Equator Prize 145, 146–148, 149, 156
Europe
   class formation 9–10
   colonial history 123–127
   conservation 73, 122
   Eastern 115
   history 91–93
   nature, concept of 184
   and US 9
Europe and CIS, GEF-SGP 115–116
exchange of capital 10
exclusion, class formation 10–11
extinction discourse 90
extinctions 89, 90, 94–97, 129

First Nation populations 73
food 164–165
'fortress' conservation 133, 135, 138
foundations 39, 46–47, 70, 71–72, 75
Friends of the Earth 70
funding 68–69
   biodiversity 179
   CBOs 74
   community-based conservation 149

diversity 72
ENGOs 78, 107
foundations 70, 71–72
patterns of 70–71, 181
see also GEF

Game Rangers Association (GRA) 54–55
game reserves 129
GEF (Global Environment Facility) 105–118
   funding mechanisms 107
   history 106–110
   SGP 106, 111–118
GEF-SGP (Global Environment Facility Small Grants Programme) 106, 111–118
general public 137, 185
gifts *see* giving
Gissibl, B. 132
giving
   Carnegie on 2
   corporate 67
   environmental 27
   general public 137, 185
   influences on 99
   patterns of 37
   pluralist perspective 69
   qualities of 98, 99
   reasons for 68
   terminology 5
   see also funding
global economic crisis 20, 181, 186
global environmental agreements 15
Global Environment Facility *see* GEF
global warming 96
   see also climate change
Gore, A. 96
Gospel of Wealth 2
governance 11–12
government *see* state
GRA (Game Rangers Association) 54–55
grants *see* funding
grassroots activism 69
   see also community-based conservation
grassroots NGOs 27

green developmentalism 26
green environment 25, 26
Greenpeace 70
green revolution 154
Grieg, I. 57–58
Grove, R. 124, 125, 127
Grzimek, B. 135
Grzimek, M. 135

habitats 28, 97
harms 2, 3
Hawke, R. 169, 170
heartlands 33
Hitchins, P. 54
hope, message of 98, 99
horizontal philanthropy 6
hotspots 33
Howard, J. 170, 171
human/non-human world 25–26
human well-being 182
hunting 126, 127, 128
Huxley, J. 134, 137

ICFP (International Conservation Financing Programme) 107–108
iconic species 96
identity formation 93
IFP (Inkatha Freedom Party) 58, 59, 60
independent sector 5
India 81, 183, 184
indigenous peoples 155
individual harms 3
Indonesia 153–157
Inkatha Freedom Party (IFP) 58, 59, 60
institutional harms 3
institutionalized private philanthropy 6
International Conservation Financing Programme (ICFP) 107–108
International Office for the Protection of Nature 133
International Union for Conservation of Nature (IUCN) 30, 78, 98, 134
International Union for the Protection of Nature (IUPN) 134
international waters 111, 115
International Year of Biodiversity 179

IUCN (International Union for Conservation of Nature) 30, 78, 98, 134
IUCN Red List of Threatened Species 94–95
IUPN (International Union for the Protection of Nature) 134
ivory 51, 72, 95, 137, 138

Japan 31
Johnston, Sir H. 124

Kazakhstan 116
Keating, P. 169
Kenya 113
knowledge, EI 145
Kumbleben commission 51

Lagnado, L. 185–186
land 32–33, 35, 112
landcare 162–163, 167–172
landscape 75–77, 125–126
land trusts 32–33
Lässig, S. 10
Latin America 6, 73
Latin America and the Caribbean, GEF-SGP/EI 116, 148
liberal capitalism 13
liberalism 14
liberation movements 57–58
liberty 3
Lippe-Biesterfeld, I. van 98
local communities 72–74, 79, 111, 138, 139
Lore Lindu Biosphere Reserve and National Park 155
lower classes 11

Madagascar 82
Mali 113
Mandela, N. 50, 51, 52
Marshall, B. 1
McCloy, J. 47
Mekong River, Asia 115
Mendes, C. 96
Meyers, N. 96

military 51, 52
Millennium Ecosystem Assessment 182
missionaries 124
'moving beyond the fences' 73
Mozambique 179
multifocal projects 113

Nash, R. F. 28
National Farmers' Federation (NFF) 163, 164–167
nationalism 125
National Landcare Programme (NLP) 162–163, 167–172
national parks 33, 134
Natural Heritage Trust (NHT) 170–172
natural resource management 35, 56
nature
  concept of 180, 182–184
  neo-liberalized 67, 77
  passion for 26, 31
  sponsoring 4, 26, 31
Nature Conservancy, The 70, 78
nature conservation *see* conservation
nature reserves 33, 128, 133
neo-liberalism 13, 16, 67, 77, 168
networking, elites 45–52, 53, 180
new philanthropy 75
NFF (National Farmers' Federation) 163, 164–167
Ngata Tora, Indonesia 155–156
NGOs (non-governmental organizations) 69–72
  capitalism 13
  categorization 29, 30
  conservation 149, 150, 151, 152, 154, 161
  development 74
  GEF-SGP 115, 118
  grassroots 27
  terminology 5
  see also ENGOs
NHT (Natural Heritage Trust) 170–172
Niger 113
NLP (National Landcare Programme) 162–163, 167–172
Noma, A. 153

non-governmental organization *see* NGOs
non-profit organizations 5, 69–70
North America *see* US
Nyerere, J. 135

off-setting 82
Operation Rhino 53
orthodox philanthropy 5–6
Ostrom, E. 182
'Our Common Future' (Brundtland Report) 73
outreach programmes 36

pacts *see* elite pacting
parks, national 33, 134
partnerships 73, 75–76
passion for nature 26, 31
peace parks 33
Peace Parks Foundation (PPF) 48, 50, 51–52
persistent organic pollutants (POPs) 112, 113
philanthrocapitalism 2, 3
philanthro-capitalists 185
philanthropic foundations *see* foundations
philanthropists
  advocacy role 185
  ENGOs 164
  giving patterns 37
  intentions 7
  personal solidarity 186
  understanding of 180
philanthropy 1–16
  capitalism 12–14
  channels of 62, 105
  citizenship 14–15
  class formation 9–11
  contexts 7–15, 178
  critiques of 7
  definitions 6–7
  governance 11–12
  motives for 68
  orthodox 5–6
  properties of 1–4
  religion 8–9
  strategic 75, 77

study of 4, 178
terminology 5
wildlands 27–31
see also environmental philanthropy; philanthropists
Philanthropy Roundtable 3–4
Philip, Prince 163, 164
Player, I. 53, 56, 60, 98
pluralist perspective 69
poaching 51, 54, 55
politics 169–170
pollutants 112, 113
poor 6, 13
see also poverty alleviation
POPs (persistent organic pollutants) 112, 113
post-colonial contexts 12
poverty alleviation 7, 145, 162
power 10, 46, 75
power relations 177–186
PPF (Peace Parks Foundation) 48, 50, 51–52
private sector 78
professionals, training 35, 36
protected areas 33, 68, 73, 77, 121, 137
protectionist discourse 127
public spending 11, 12

reciprocity, horizontal philanthropy 6
Reich, R. 3
religion 8–9
reserves *see* game reserves; nature reserves
resource-dependency theory 69
Resources Law Group 76
rhinoceros 51, 53, 91–94
Rhino Management Group (RMG) 53
rich *see* elites; wealth
Rio Tinto Mining 82
Rockerfeller, J. D., Jr. 8
Rupert, A. 47, 48, 50, 60, 137
Rush and Reed Conservation and Diversification Programme 152–153
Russia 81

SACP (South African Communist Party) 56

SADF (South African Defence Force) 51
SAFF (Southern African Freedom Foundation) 57
Sarasin, P. 132, 133
scale, contexts of 161–162, 172
scaling up 145, 162
Scholfield, K. 138
Scotland 124–125
self-organizing efforts *see* community-based conservation
Selous Scouts 61
Sierra Club 29–30
social capital 10
social democracy 14
Society for the Preservation of the Wild Fauna of the Empire 129, 130–131, 132
soil erosion 126, 127
South Africa 48, 50–52, 125–126, 185
South African Communist Party (SACP) 56
South African Defence Force (SADF) 51
South Asia 150
Southeast Asia 150, 151
Southern Africa 49, 74, 93
Southern African Freedom Foundation (SAFF) 57
Southey, S. 144
South–North connections 45–62
elite networking 48–52
reality of 105
Steele case study 53–62
world systems theories 45–48
species 94–95, 96, 97
sponsoring nature 4, 26, 31
sport hunting 126, 128
Sri Lanka 150–153
state 11–12, 105, 121
state-sponsored community conservation 161–163, 167–172
Steele, N. 53, 55, 56, 59, 60
strategic philanthropy 75, 77
subsistence hunting 126
Suharto regime, Indonesia 154
Sulawesi, Indonesia 155–156
sustainable development 73, 78, 79, 107

Sweatman, M. 108
systems theories, world 45–48

Tang, S. 70–71
Taoism 183
teak wood 149
territorialization 6
TFCAs (Transfrontier Conservation Areas) 33, 34–35, 75
Thailand 115
The Nature Conservancy 70, 78
third sector 5
threats, environmental 89–99
Touring Club de France 134
traditional peoples 155
Train, R. E. 136
training, professionals 35, 36
transboundary biospheres 33
transboundary natural resource management areas 33
transfrontier conservation 33, 34–35, 75, 139
   see also ecological corridors
Transfrontier Conservation Areas (TFCAs) 33, 34–35, 75
transnational capitalist class 78–79
triggers, conservation 149, 153
tsetse flies 131

UN (United Nations) 134
   Convention on Biological Diversity (CBD), COP 10 Meeting 179, 185
   International Year of Biodiversity 179
UNDP (United Nations Development Programme) 108, 144
UNEP (United Nations Environment Programme) 108
UNESCO (United Nations Educational, Scientific and Cultural Organization) 134
UNFCCC (United Nations Framework Convention on Climate Change) 111
unintended consequences 3
United Nations *see* UN
United States *see* US
urgency 99

US (United States)
   conservation easements 34
   conservative religious philanthropic foundations 13
   and Europe 9
   First Nation populations 73
   Sierra Club 29–30
   wildlands philanthropy 27–28

venture philanthropy 75
ventures, EI 145
Victoria, Australia 164–165
voluntarism 14
voluntary sector 5

Waterlow, Sir S. 13–14
waters, international 111, 115
WCED (World Commission on Environment and Development) 106–107
wealth 2–3, 5, 10
welfare state 12
well-being, human 182
white rhinoceros 93
wilderness 27, 28, 97–98, 122, 123, 127
Wilderness Conservancy (WILDCON) 60–61
Wilderness Leadership School 53
Wild Foundation 97, 108
wildlands philanthropy 27–31
wildlife, decline in 126–127, 129
Wildlife Conservation Society 139
wildlife management 138
Wilpattu National Park, Sri Lanka 151
Wirth, T. 144
World Bank 108, 109
World Commission on Environment and Development (WCED) 106–107
world economy 81
world systems theories 45–48
World Wilderness Congresses 53, 97, 98
WRI (World Resources Institute) 107
WWF (World Wide Fund for Nature)
   Africa 139
   elites 136
   environmental education 36

environmental establishment 70
formation 134, 135
funding 72, 78
ivory 138
mission 30
South–North connections 51

WWF International 47

Yemen 114

Zimbabwe 13
Zi Ran 183